CONTENTS

CONTENTS

CONTENTS

CONTENTS

CONTENTS

EXECUTIVE SUMMARY

EXECUTIVE SUMMARY

This fieldbook is designed to accompany The Global Trends Report. While The Global Trends Report outlines the major trends that are reshaping the world and their implications for organizations, the fieldbook focuses on the critical step of moving from data to insights to taking actions today to prepare organizations for the future. As such it provides practical suggestions for senior executives responsible for preparing their organizations for the future, based on examples of how other organizations have tackled these challenges.

We will not repeat the analyses shared in The Global Trends Report, providing only the summary implications. Rather our focus is on what these trends and other emerging game changers mean for different types of organizations and communities: businesses, governments, NGOs, and societies, and what they can practically do today to prepare for what will be an increasingly uncertain, ambiguous, and volatile future.

Chapter 1 provides an overview of the Global Trends framework, which focuses on trends in terms of how the world is changing and develops tools and ideas for understanding the implications of these trends. These trends will be highlighted in Chapters 1 and 2 of this fieldbook, with Chapter 2 providing analysis to supplement The Global Trends Report on key topics. The challenge of turning this understanding into insights and actions will be developed in Chapters 3 to 8, drawing on framework and insights developed in the book Ready? The 3Rs of preparing your organization for the future[1]. The framework reflects the experiences of 156 CEOs and senior leaders around the world in preparing their organizations for the future: what are the key trends and implications impacting the organization; how have these driven rethinking the playing field; how has the organization redefined their ambition (vision, purpose, targets, measures) as a result; what are the options they considered in building an agenda for action; how have they reshaped how they worked; and what is the ongoing process of learn-act-learn-adjust?

A critical insight from this work is the need to have a point of view on the future. As Harish Manwani, COO of Unilever puts it: "I think there is an increasing reality everywhere in the world that the only constant [now] is change," he told us. "The pace of change is getting faster and is often unpredictable. The days of long-term planning and predicting the future simply on the basis of the past are gone. The most important challenge for businesses is to create a point of view about the future and, at the same time, manage the short term more dynamically than ever before."

These two imperatives, to manage business today while creating a point of view on the future and moving the business towards that future mean bridging the gap between short- and long-term thinking, something which many organizations and leaders struggle with today. In Chapter 3 we take on Manwani's challenge, exploring the need to think differently to bridge this gap. Holding on to old ways of doing things and expecting approaches that have worked in the past to drive success in future will not work. The only way for an organization to stay ahead is to change faster than the pace of change in its environment.

This requires applying the 8 principles of thinking differently as follows:

1. Embrace ambiguity: don't just think outside the box, throw away the boxes
2. Think first from the outside-in, then inside-out
3. Identify and address root causes, not symptoms
4. Practice two-directional thinking
5. Manage in relationships/networks versus transactions
6. Focus on co-creation
7. Align purpose and profit
8. Embed continual challenge, avoid complacent compliance

[1] Thomas W. Malnight, Tracey S. Keys, and Kees van der Graaf, 2013

EXECUTIVE SUMMARY

Chapters 4 to 7 focus on how different types of organizations – businesses, governments, NGOs, and societies and communities – are translating macro implications of global trends into specific insights and actions to prepare for the future. These chapters are designed to allow executives to better focus on the opportunities and challenges facing a relevant peer group and to learn from the case studies and examples.

Within each chapter the first subsection provides some context, looking at the key trends that are impacting the landscape within which each type of organization is operating. The second subsection focuses on detailed case studies, offering insights into how the different types of organizations are approaching the challenges of preparing their countries, economies, and societies for the future. Each detailed case study explores the organization's thinking and actions using the lens of the 3Rs framework.

Beyond the case studies, the third subsection provides some "in brief" examples of how other organizations are preparing for the future in specific areas, e.g. tackling the challenges of generational shifts. The fourth subsection highlights food for thought examples, which are designed to provoke thinking on some of the key challenges facing organizations in the future, which many are grappling with, e.g. avoiding the pitfalls of disruptive technologies, and embracing responsible capitalism. Finally, in subsection five, we draw together some insights to take away from these examples using the 8 principles introduced in Chapter 3.

Chapter 4 focuses on businesses and includes case studies of BMW, DSM, and Tencent along with brief examples and food for thought about companies and topics including Amazon, Infosys, SABMiller, and Nokia, responsible capitalism, and winning in BRICS and beyond BRICS markets. In looking at the key insights from these organizations, it is clear that many, if not all, accept cross-industry competition as a way of life, and look outside the boundaries of their industry and markets to deeply understand consumer needs and potentially revolutionary market changes. These are being applied by rethinking products, services, and experiences, for example in the form of BMW's revolutionary i3 and i8 cars which combine intelligence, new energy solutions, and customer experience to reshape personal transportation. These companies go beyond the obvious symptoms of change and build capabilities to underpin their ability to shape future markets, staying ahead of change through partnerships and open platform approaches that allow them to innovate, learn, and experiment continuously. "Not invented here" is alien to these companies, and daily, incremental challenges to the status quo are embraced, including in the areas of sustainability and responsibility, which are becoming increasingly embedded in the businesses.

Government organizations discussed in **Chapter 5** range from case studies on Singapore, Ireland, and Denmark, to examples and food for thought on China, the African powerhouses of South Africa and Nigeria, South Korea, Vietnam, the UK, and the U.S. While national boxes are hard to throw away, it is clear that these nations are aware of, and in many cases, embracing the blurring of boundaries and responsibilities between the public and private sector. Public-private partnerships are strongly in evidence, driving new ways of working and new business models. Increasingly the focus of these governments and their agencies is strategic, focused on building the capabilities required to drive sustainable economies and societies, which can move up the value ladder and improve competitiveness on a global scale. Global focus is evident as some nations are building hubs of knowledge, talent, and technology that can serve not only domestic needs, but also can compete regionally and globally. One of the most important foundations for delivering on these ambitions is world-class education systems, which are a clear focus of attention.

A new type of NGO is emerging for the 21st century, along with many types of hybrid organizations that embrace non-profit goals, but may have for-profit elements. **Chapter 6** offers case studies on Realdania, the World Wildlife Fund (WWF), and Synergos, supplemented by examples and food for thought across both the developed and developing world, including philanthrocapitalism, the Granny Cloud, Watsi, Pencils of Promise, Causes, iGive, and Waste Concern. Significant innovation is happening in many areas of the sector, as cross-sector relationships are pursued to pool and partner on knowledge and resources. New business and operational models are emerging, redefining what "return" means in a much broader societal as well as financial sense, and tapping into under-utilized resources. Such partnerships require the ability to recognize the

EXECUTIVE SUMMARY

different perspectives of other stakeholders in order to build mutually beneficial solutions, with leading organizations acting as catalysts for change.

Such catalysts actively engage others in the change process, building broad and deep networks that leverage digital technologies to harness the power of the crowd – balancing this input with clear focus on priority areas where the organization and its partners and supporters can have greatest impact.

Societies and communities are changing rapidly as the case studies and examples in **Chapter 7** demonstrate. These include case studies on the reinvention of Medellín, Colombia, the rise of the crowd and the emerging sharing economy, complemented by examples and food for thought on the maker movement, the impact of resource colonization in Africa, the untapped potential of diasporas, crowdfunding Bogotá, German bioenergy villages, DoSomething.org's youth volunteers, and Creative Currency's innovative business model. Choice on an unprecedented scale is giving individuals and communities influence over their lives, even as they search for meaning, identity, and inclusion. This is leading to a hotbed of innovation in societies and communities that offer the potential to disrupt today's supply and demand paradigms and the notions of value and ownership. These innovations include new business models that harness the power of connectivity and choice, are built on the foundations of multi-stakeholder partnerships, and/or deliver both societal and business benefits. While the myriad of innovations underway may not be consciously coordinated, together the collective behavioral changes that these entail in terms of consumption, use of resources (or not), knowledge sharing, the ability to customize for local and individual needs, and relationship building have the potential to drive disruption in many industries and markets. In this networked world, trust is the critical currency. However, many institutions and businesses not only lack popular trust, but also are not keeping up with the pace of societal and economic change, which may hamper their ability to provide the regulatory and institutional context required for the fundamental societal shifts that are happening.

Finally, **Chapter 8** offers a special focus on how education is changing – and needs to change further – to prepare future generations for success. Education has been a focus in preparing all the different types of organizations investigated in this report. Education is a critical enabler of economic and social development. Yet there is increasing criticism of many education systems and institutions across the globe, as youth unemployment reaches critical levels in many countries and businesses protest that the next generations entering the workforce do not have the right skills. In fact, some leaders suggest that whole swathes of young people are unemployable.

It's nothing as simple as poor education, at least in the traditional sense, as each new generation is entering the workforce better qualified than the one before it. The problem is an emerging split between unemployable workers – those who do not have the specific knowledge or skills needed in the future – and the in-demand workers, who have these things in abundance. This mismatch is confronting societies and businesses around the world. The only way to close the gap is to make sure that workers are prepared to fill the jobs of the future, which means that governments, educators, and businesses need to rethink education and training, including who delivers it.

Preparing an organization for the future is not an easy task. It is one that requires leaders and their organizations to confront the short-term/long-term gap and think in both dimensions simultaneously. It means thinking differently and crafting an agenda that delivers today while positioning an organization for success in the future. None of the leaders and organizations we spoke with or analyzed have all the answers. However, many are making positive steps towards meeting the challenge and we hope that the case studies and examples in this fieldbook will offer valuable insights for yourselves and your own organizations.

It's time to have a point of view on the future – and to start taking action today to prepare!

1. GETTING STARTED

1. GETTING STARTED

1.1 WHAT IS THIS FIELDBOOK AND WHO IS IT FOR?

This fieldbook is designed to accompany The Global Trends Report. While The Global Trends Report outlines the major trends that are reshaping the world and their implications for organizations, the fieldbook focuses on the critical step of moving from data to insights to taking actions today to prepare organizations for the future. As such it provides practical suggestions for senior executives responsible for preparing their organizations for the future, based on examples of how other organizations have tackled these challenges.

We will not repeat the analyses shared in The Global Trends Report, providing only the summary implications. Rather our focus is on what these trends and other emerging game changers mean for different types of organizations and communities: businesses, governments, NGOs, and societies, and what they can practically do today to prepare for what will be an increasingly uncertain, ambiguous, and volatile future.

To do this, we also draw on the frameworks and examples found in *Ready? The 3Rs of preparing your organization for the future*[2], as well as our experience in working with senior executives and organizations around the world on these challenges. This book is based on interviews with 156 CEOs and senior leaders globally to understand how these leaders see the opportunities and challenges facing their organizations and themselves five or more years in the future, and what steps they are taking today to prepare for this future.

1.2 WHY ACT TODAY: FACING THE GAP

Business today operates in two time frames: the immediate, and the very long-term. In the first, businesses – and their leaders – are judged on the short-term financial results that have come to define success today. The second acknowledges that markets, consumers, and societies are changing so significantly that organizations that want to thrive in the future must start preparing for it now, even if results may not be seen for some time. We refer to the challenge of uniting the often-conflicting demands of these two time frames, and the mindset associated with each, into one coherent agenda as the "gap."

Three exploding pressures are driving businesses to focus on short-term results, even at the cost of preparing for the future. The first is strong financial market pressures, particularly for public companies, that demand consistent, predictable growing financial results, even in an era of uncertainty and volatility. While these pressures may be partly attributed to short-term speculators and financial analysts with static financial models, they are real and impact the behaviors of business leaders. A key challenge for leaders is highlighted in a quote by Warren Buffet when comparing himself to private equity and other short-term investors: "They invest to exit, I invest to own." The challenge for leaders is, first, what is the case they are making for investors to own, not exit their shares and for owning their shares for the long-term, and, second, how are they attracting these longer-term owners.

A second short-term pressure comes from increasing stress on budgets: commoditization, slowing economic growth rates, the rapid dissemination of knowledge, and the entrance of new low cost or non-traditional competitors are all having a strong impact on short-term budgets and results at many organizations. The challenge for leaders here is, rather than focusing on reacting to the symptoms of these short-term pressures, to identify, understand, and address the root causes of these growing competitive stresses, including confronting uncomfortable truths about the state of the organization today. Many organizations seem to prefer to respond reactively as problems arise. Face a problem, launch an initiative. Face another problem, launch another initiative. The alternative is to take the time and effort to understand the underlying root causes of the challenges being faced in order to develop longer-term solutions, not quick fixes.

[2] Thomas W. Malnight, Tracey S. Keys, and Kees van der Graaf, 2013

1.   GETTING STARTED

The third short-term pressure, and likely the most important one, is associated with the comfort zone of many executives, who have long worked and succeeded based on a set of known, proven tools and experiences in addressing issues. As one CEO told us: "You can't inspire an organization by restructuring Belgium yet again." But this does not stop many leaders from repeating the same activities over and over again, hoping for a new outcome. The challenge for leaders and organizations today is whether yesterday's approaches and answers can solve tomorrow's problems. If not, how do leaders and organizations step out of their comfort zone and be open to adopting new approaches and ideas to prepare their organizations for the future?

Not addressing the gap is not an option, at least for leaders concerned about the long-term success of the institutions they lead. At the same time as organizations face short-term pressures they also live in a rapidly changing world with many trends impacting the environment in which they must succeed in the future. These growing long-term challenges (and opportunities) do not call for incremental or minor changes from what has worked in the past, but often involve more fundamental changes, which take time to define and implement. How long does it take to build a new capability or business model? How long does it take to change a culture or mindset? Organizations that put off understanding and addressing these long-term trends face a significant threat to their long-term sustainable success.

Overall, the challenge facing leaders today is how to both perform and deliver in the short term while preparing their organizations, and themselves, for the future. One danger here is falling into the short-term trap: the combination of mindset and external pressures that leads executives to believe that short-term results are the most, or only, important thing on which they should focus. Very often the people caught in the short-term trap are those who already have a tendency to hold on to the past rather than preparing for and adapting to the future. But an equal threat is to focus only on the future without delivering results today.

It's time to have a point of view on the future: we have not yet met a leader with a crystal ball for predicting the future. But does this excuse a leader from being responsible for preparing for the future? We suggest that a starting point for any leader, and leadership team, is to take the time to look at the trends impacting the world in which they operate and draw on their insights and collective experiences to develop an informed point of view on the future. There is plenty of data on how the world is changing – in fact, many leaders are overloaded with it. The issue is how to move from data overload to building an understanding of the impact of these trends, then to use this understanding to create a "point of view" on the future. Whether it be right or wrong, having a point of view, based on the most informed insights about how the world is changing, is vital to enable proactive action today, to enable leaders to build options and new capabilities required for future success. Preparing for the future is not a one-time effort or initiative, it is a continual process. But the starting point is to develop, and continually challenge, this viewpoint on the future in line with the frequently cited quote: "Plans are nothing, planning is everything."

Can any organization afford not to start today? Addressing the gap, based on having a point of view on the future to balance intense short-term pressures, is a vital starting point.

1.3   FROM DATA TO UNDERSTANDING TO INSIGHTS TO ACTIONS

The framework and tools used in this report draw, as we described earlier, from two sources. The Global Trends Report focuses on trends in terms of how the world is changing and develops tools and ideas for understanding the implications of these trends. These trends will be highlighted in Chapters 1 and 2 of this fieldbook. The challenge of turning this understanding into insights and actions will be developed in Chapters 3 to 7; drawing on tools and insights developed in the book *Ready? The 3Rs of preparing your organization for the future*[3].

---

[1] Thomas W. Malnight, Tracey S. Keys, and Kees van der Graaf, 2013

1. GETTING STARTED

GT FIELDBOOK CHAPTERS 1 TO 2

DATA

OVERLOADED
WITH DATA?

GT FIELDBOOK CHAPTERS 3 TO 7

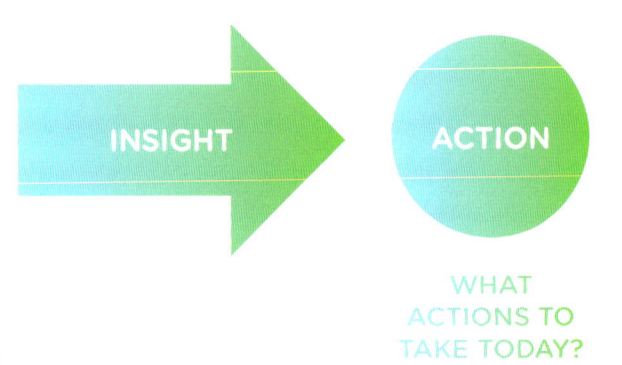

WHAT
ACTIONS TO
TAKE TODAY?

GT REPORT

Understanding the major trends shaping the future
- Resources: from abundance to scarcity
- Organizations & Communities: rapidly falling boundaries
- Shapers & Influencers: multipolar Influence

Implications for business and society
- Distributed access and control of scarce resources
- Distributed power shaping the rules of engagement
- Emerging values for a distributed world
- Distributed value creation and capture in a networked world

See "Ready? The 3Rs of preparing your organization for the future" by Thomas W. Malnight, Tracey S. Keys, and Kees van der Graff, 2013

3RS FOR ACTION TODAY

RETHINK your playing field
- Your competitors are not who you think they are
- Your consumers (and their behavior) are not who you think they are
- Your employees (and their expectations and ways of working) are not what you thought they were
- Your growth markets (and battles) are not where you think they are
- The expectations on you as a business are not what you thought they were

REDEFINE your agenda
- Your purpose of why you exist and why others want to work with you
- Your vision of where and how you will fit in based on your perspective of the future
- Your ambition defining what is success and what are the requirements of success
- Redefine your agenda for preparing your organization for the future

RESHAPE how you work
- Move from transactions to relationships with key stakeholders
- Accelerate short-term fixes to leave time and resources for long-term transformations
- Move from a culture of complacent compliance to constructive continous challenge
- Reshape how you shape everyday activities through rethinking how you create budgets, plans, and strategies

1.   GETTING STARTED

Trends reshaping the world today: Our starting point is the trends and the Global Trends Framework outlined in The Global Trends Report. This framework is built around three areas or spheres of long-term, significant change occurring in the world in which we live and operate:

1. RESOURCES:

We think about resources in a number of different categories: financial, physical, human, and societal/organizational among others. These resources may be available to individuals, societies, or organizations and may include both tangible and intangible assets. The key resources we focus on in this framework are: people, labor, knowledge, natural resources, the environment, technology, and capital. In addition, we discuss time as a resource, given the ongoing changes in the way we use and view time – or too often the lack of it.

2. ORGANIZATIONS & COMMUNITIES:

A second dimension in which change is occurring is in the organizations and communities in which we live and operate. The world is becoming small and interdependent. New communities are arising every day that impact how people think, work, and live their daily lives. Here we identify several types of communities/organizations which serve as the "umbrella" for and impact how we live and operate: geographic markets, industries, business organizations, intergovernmental organizations, political organizations, social organizations, belief-based organizations, the military, and finally also criminal organizations.

3. SHAPERS & INFLUENCERS:

"We are not alone" or so says the well-worn phrase when thinking about extra-terrestrial life. Closer to home, the phrase could be accurately applied to the myriad of people and organizations which shape and influence our lives and work. The numbers of these shapers and influencers is growing along with the channels they use to reach us, for example via the internet or mobile communications. Some of the key shapers and influencers that impact the world today include: business leaders, financial power brokers, non-governmental organizations, governments, religious leaders, the media, social networks, and academic institutions. Finally, you will notice the addition of consumers/individuals, since the power of personal choice and the ability to bring individuals together has been amplified hugely by the information technology advances of the last two decades. This is a voice that will continue to grow.

RESOURCES

What are critical resources?

What trends are impacting their availability and use?

ORGANIZATIONS & COMMUNITIES

How is the world in which we live and operate organized?

SHAPERS & INFLUENCERS

Which individuals and groups influence and shape the world in which we live and operate?

Resources	Organizations & Communities	Shapers & Influencers
People	Geographic Markets	Business Leaders
Labor	"Industry" Communities	Financial Power Brokers
Knowledge	Business Organizations	Non-governmental Organizations
Natural Resources	Intergovernmental Organizations	Governments
Environment	Political Organizations	Religious Leaders
Technology	Social Organizations	Media
Capital	Belief-based Organizations	Social Networks
Time	Military	Academic Institutions
	Criminal Organizations	Consumers/Individuals

1. GETTING STARTED

The interactions between the changes in these spheres lead to a set of dynamics, which we highlight in terms of four growing areas of competition:

- **Fight for control & access:** focuses on the growing importance and competition between organizations for control or access to key resources

- **Fight for rules of engagement:** focuses on who defines and impacts the rules of engagement between and among organizations and communities as they interact, work and live

- **Fight for value creation & capture:** explores how different organizations define "value," which are creating real value and at what point in the economic or business system, and where value is being captured

- **Fight for values & beliefs:** explores how values and beliefs shape the motivations of individuals and organizations, impact how individuals live their lives, and how organizations provide guidance about acceptable and unacceptable behaviors

VALUE CREATION & CAPTURE

RESOURCES

What are critical resources?

What trends are impacting their availability and use?

CONTROL & ACCESS

ORGANIZATIONS & COMMUNITIES

How is the world in which we live and operate organized?

RULES OF ENGAGEMENT

SHAPERS & INFLUENCERS

Which individuals and groups influence and shape the world in which we live and operate?

VALUES & BELIEFS

1.   GETTING STARTED

The 3Rs of preparing for the future The 3Rs process, based on rethinking, redefining, and reshaping, is a constant loop of learning and adjustment, which allows organizations both to identify options and to develop priorities for action over time. It can be summarized as:

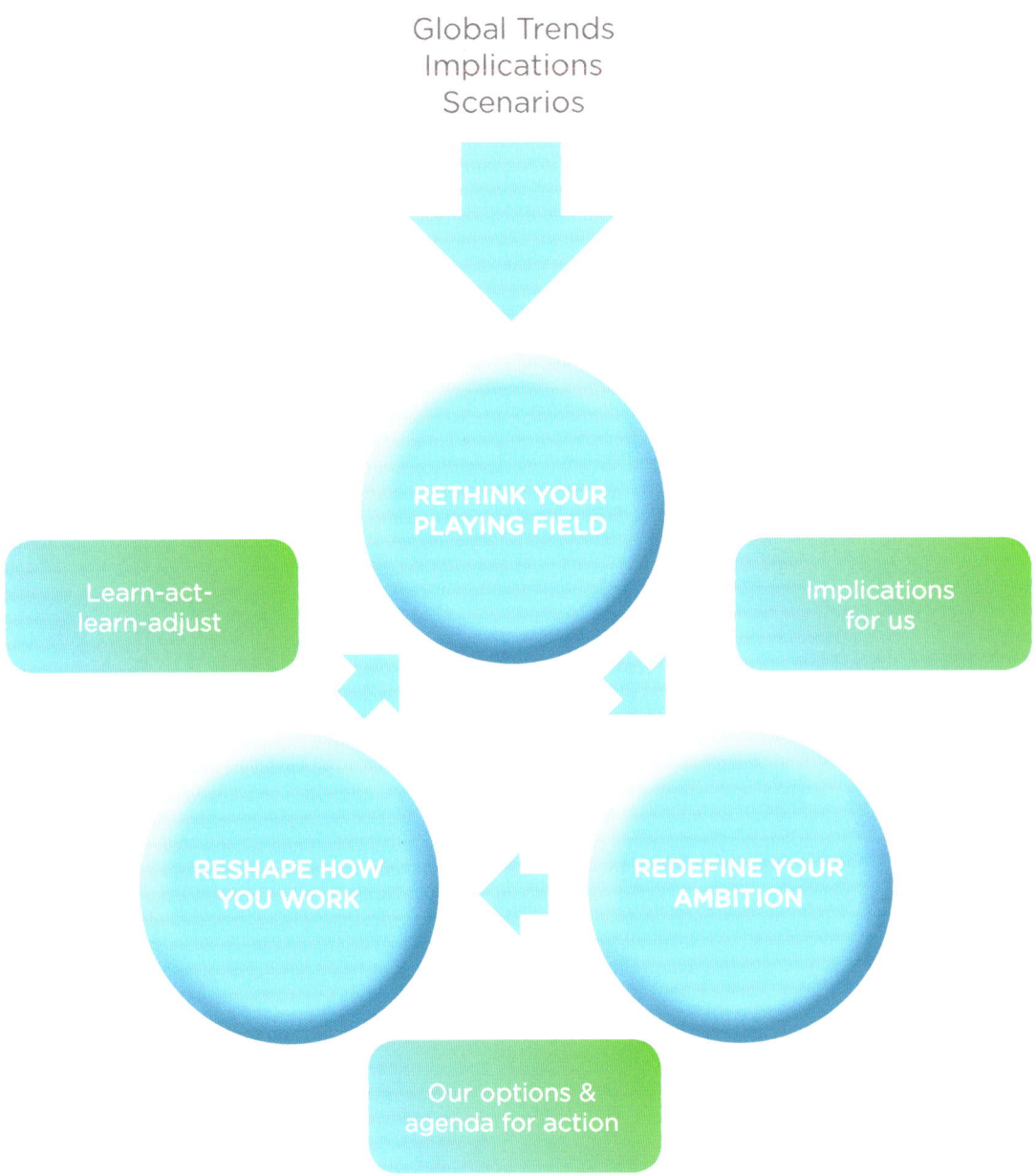

Global Trends
Implications
Scenarios

RETHINK YOUR PLAYING FIELD

Learn-act-learn-adjust

Implications for us

RESHAPE HOW YOU WORK

REDEFINE YOUR AMBITION

Our options & agenda for action

Through this fieldbook, we develop both examples of how different types of organizations have applied — whether explicitly or implicitly — this process, to provide insights for executives in putting the process into action in their own organizations.

1. GETTING STARTED

1.4 WHY PREPARING YOUR ORGANIZATION FOR THE FUTURE MATTERS: CEO PERSPECTIVES

Anticipating change is important, but knowledge is not, by itself, enough. Most leaders have all the data they could possibly want about how the world is changing – if not more. The challenge for individual leaders is not letting this data overwhelm them, but instead finding a way to use it to move from information to understanding, and then to develop insights about what these changes mean for them and their organizations.

It requires adopting a mindset of owning the future as opposed to holding on to the past, which is easier said than done given the intense pressures facing leaders and their businesses today. However, when asked, "why bother preparing for the future today," many leaders demonstrated a keen sense of the reasons why this was one of, if not the, most important aspects of their jobs, from providing the legacy for the next generations to building an organization which can realize its potential for all stakeholders in the future. Below are some of their thoughts:[1]

Pat Davies "What we're doing today was born out of a vision developed 10 years ago," the former CEO of Sasol told us as he prepared to retire. "We are just witnessing the realization of it now. And if we didn't have that vision 10 years ago, I'm quite sure we wouldn't have been as successful as we are today. So it's creating a common purpose around a vision of the future that is key for us today. This is essential. Whoever takes my place is going to have to do this again if he or she wants to take the organization into the next phase.

"We've grown rapidly but I believe we have the means to grow even more rapidly in the future. Growth is not a one-off job. It's about continually making sure you've got everyone on board and aligned and focused on the future."

Clara Gaymard The president and CEO of GE France argues that forging partnerships across sectors can help businesses shape how new playing fields develop, and can help companies to carve out roles for themselves within them.

"One thing that is very important for us is all the emerging new technologies – electric vehicles, wind energy, biomass, and so on. Often we can bring the technology and the products, but the overall shape of these industries is not yet fixed and the business model still needs to be built.

"In many of these cases the business model will be built in a public-private partnership. We have seen that in wind. We have seen that in solar. Unless you are at the table as these industries are being built, you will never be a major player in them in the future. You will at best be a commodity supplier of components.

"As a company, we must of course bring our part of the solutions, but we also have to be a key actor in the way the new business model will be developed and built."

Harish Manwani "The opportunity is truly a generational one," Unilever's COO, who is also the chairman of Hindustan Lever, told us. "The entire population growth and most economic growth is going to come from the developing world. It's a fact that developing markets, and specifically Asia, will shape the economic future of the world.

"Until five years ago, people said China manufactured for the world, and the U.S. consumed to keep the world economy going. There is now a convergence between the consuming world and the supplying world. Increasingly, consumption is shifting to the developing markets. China is already the world's largest market for luxury goods, automobiles, mobile phones, and many other products, and this shift is only just beginning."

Paul Polman "The importance of the role of business in society has always been there, but I think the [financial] crisis has made it come alive even more," the CEO of Unilever told us. "The real issue is how to get permission to be successful. "It's very clear that the parameters here are rapidly changing. I believe that it is essential for any business that is going to grow and be successful over the long term to always think carefully about how to get permission from society to grow and be successful."

[1] Quotes from *"Ready? The 3Rs of preparing your organization for the future"* by Thomas W. Malnight, Tracey S. Keys, and Kees van der Graaf, 2013

1. GETTING STARTED

Mike Brown "What worries me every day as a leader is what I am doing to make sure that I leave behind an organization that is sustainably better than the one I inherited," said the Nedbank CEO. "To me, that's the measure of success. So what worries me is not just delivery of this year's targets – we have lots of plans to make sure we do this. But the issues for me are what are we doing around building the new businesses and new products that will make us money in the years ahead?"

Feike Sijbesma The chairman and CEO of DSM's personal purpose came into focus when he thought about the world that his two sons and all other children will inherit; he said that was his responsibility too, he decided, to improve it.

"I feel a little bit like, 'Hey, we run a company here. We are in a society here. We are a part of society, and we need to take care of the next generations, those who will live here after us,'" he told us. "I cannot say to my two boys, 'Well, we had a good life, but the problems we created are all yours.'"

This insight into what mattered to him as an individual has helped him to shape not just the decisions that he makes as a leader – for example, around repositioning the former chemical company now as a life sciences and materials sciences business that can help solve social and environmental issues – but how he leads. He has seen that the next generations think and act differently from those that went before them, and that anyone who hopes to lead them will need to adapt accordingly.

Peggy Dulany "It is important that you explore the periphery of your network," the chairman of the Synergos Institute suggests. "It is important that you try to understand why something's not working, and explore why. This is the source of important new insight."

1.5   HOW TO USE THIS FIELDBOOK

The fieldbook is organized into eight chapters. After this first introduction chapter, Chapter 2 provides a recap of the key implications for organizations of the major trends reshaping the world, as well as summaries of some well-known and important scenarios. In addition, we expand on some of the game changers, which are important to bear in mind throughout the process. These are all critical inputs to allow executives to challenge their thinking as they move through the process.

Chapter 3 moves us from understanding and implications towards insights and action, offering some overall principles of preparing for the future, which are important for leaders and their teams to keep in mind as they pursue this process with their organizations.

Armed with these inputs, Chapters 4 to 7 focus on how different types of organizations – businesses, governments, NGOs, and societies – are translating macro implications into specific insights and actions to prepare for the future. The aim is to allow executives to better focus on the opportunities and challenges facing a relevant peer group and to learn from relevant case studies and examples.

Within each chapter we first provide the context facing each type of organization, including the key trends and implications that are particularly relevant to each type of organization. Then we focus on case studies and examples of how organizations have gone about preparing for the future, allowing us to draw lessons about preparing for the future that are relevant for these types of organizations. Finally, we offer some food for thought on the changes ahead for each type of organization.

The last chapter, Chapter 8, offers a special focus on how education is changing – and needs to change further – to prepare future generations for success, as education has been a focus in preparing all the different types of organizations investigated in this report.

2. WHAT'S CHANGING: BUILDING A POINT OF VIEW ON THE FUTURE

2. WHAT'S CHANGING: BUILDING A POINT OF VIEW ON THE FUTURE

2.1 BUILDING A POINT OF VIEW ON THE FUTURE

Leaders today face a changing future on many fronts simultaneously. The challenge is to develop a point of view on this future, not only in terms of what is changing but why it matters. As we highlighted in the last chapter, CEOs and senior leaders across the globe believe having such a point of view is critical to preparing their organizations for the future – not because the point of view is highly accurate. It won't be. But it does provide the insights that will allow the organization to start to take action today, because waiting for 100% accurate forecasts means a company will be so far behind as to risk its long-term success. Building new markets and capabilities, changing culture, and adopting new business models all take time. Action needs to start now, recognizing that a point of view on the future will be refined over time, and actions need to be adjusted accordingly.

Here the aim is to help leaders build their point of view on the future as we explore the key implications of the changes outlined in The Global Trends Report. These are supplemented by selected new analysis of some of the key game changers looking forward, in each of the three key areas of change identified in the Global Trends Framework: resources, organizations and communities, and shapers and influencers. Again, we note that this report should be read in conjunction with The Global Trends Report which provides greater analysis of the trends and relevant examples.

One overriding theme of The Global Trends Report 2013: Towards a Distributed Future is that we are moving towards a more distributed world, one where consumption is spread more broadly than ever before, as consumers become more mobile and the middle class expands globally. At the same time, production is also becoming more distributed, as customers and consumers increasingly co-create solutions and experiences with companies and as networks become a key organizing mechanism for innovation, production, marketing, and sales. In a distributed world, relationships and partnering become even more critical for business as delivering on rising and complex demands and addressing complex issues is more than one company can do alone. At the same time, power is also being distributed as individuals become increasingly networked, tapping into the wisdom of friends and communities – shifting relationships from one-to-one to many-to-many. Distributed consumption, production and power are becoming the norm, with important implications looking ahead.

What are the implications for your organization and your point of view on the future?

2. WHAT'S CHANGING: BUILDING A POINT OF VIEW ON THE FUTURE

2.2 WHAT ARE VALUABLE RESOURCES AND WHO CONTROLS THEM?

Resource trends highlight what is happening to a vast array of resources on which the world depends, from capital to labor to natural resources to time. The world is moving from living in a world of relative abundance to times of scarcity in terms of natural resources and many of the other resources on which the world depends. Resource crises are growing as scarcity bites, leading to intensified competition to gain/retain control of critical inputs between nations, organizations, and communities. Key implications from these trends include:

From abundance to scarcity The world has already started moving from a period of relative abundance of the resources needed to sustain and improve life, to one where increasing numbers of natural resources will be scarce and more costly to consume. Time is also becoming scarce in the age of 24/7/365 digital living and data deluge, while capital is harder to come by as the effects of austerity in the West ripple out globally. A shift in focus is needed towards how to manage in a world of constrained resources.

From fixed to mobile The world is going mobile and along with the mobile web, though still in its infancy, a whole new generation of "mobile-only" consumers are emerging. New devices, from tablets to ultrabooks, along with the mobile web are heralding the post-PC era, which will be characterized by new interfaces and consumer behaviors.

From data deluge to the democratization of knowledge Information is power – and there is no shortage of information in the digital age, particularly as the "internet of things" expands. Knowledge is becoming a source of competitive advantage between organizations, nations, and individuals. While a huge challenge is dealing with the daily data deluge, this new era is seeing knowledge become increasingly democratized – anyone with a connection can tap into the global brain, access high quality learning, and share knowledge in real-time, opening new opportunities.

From talent wars to redefining work In the not-so-distant future, smart machines will drive the job revolution, offering opportunities in terms of jobs that don't exist today and challenges such as the possible loss of knowledge jobs to machines. The key question for businesses is how to prepare themselves and the next generations of employees for this future.

From globalization to protectionism Globalization heralded the opening of markets around the world to trade, knowledge flows, and new levels of economic and social connectedness. Now the pendulum is swinging the other way, as rising protectionism starts to close market access for some goods and services, and competition between markets heats up. While it's not a return to the isolationism of the 1930s, trade flows are already being impacted with warnings of more restrictions to come, fuelled by the pressures of resource scarcity, austerity, economic slowdown, and rising nationalism. The question is how far the pendulum will swing.

From technology building blocks to game changers Nanotechnology, biotechnology, neuroscience, genomics, clean technologies, space sciences, smart materials, ubiquitous computers and sensors, artificial intelligence, geoengineering, and information technology have the potential to help address critical global issues as well as our daily lives and work in fundamental ways. Now these building block technologies are moving out of the laboratory into our lives, offering game-changing possibilities from wearable computers that constantly monitor our health, to self-healing materials that repair damage to themselves, to DNA engineered agriculture.

In the next subsections we highlight some selected new analysis of key game changers in the area of control of and access to resources.

2. WHAT'S CHANGING: BUILDING A POINT OF VIEW ON THE FUTURE

The potential for food insecurity

Data from the EIU and FAO shows that global food prices rose twice as fast as inflation in the last decade, with food prices increasing by 238% and inflation rising by 146%, impoverishing millions of people. Huge price swings for staple crops such as rice, maize, wheat, and soybeans disrupted markets and harmed both producers and consumers. Food riots in many countries during 2008 and 2011 highlight the real and serious concerns over chronic food insecurity.

Primary food commodity indices

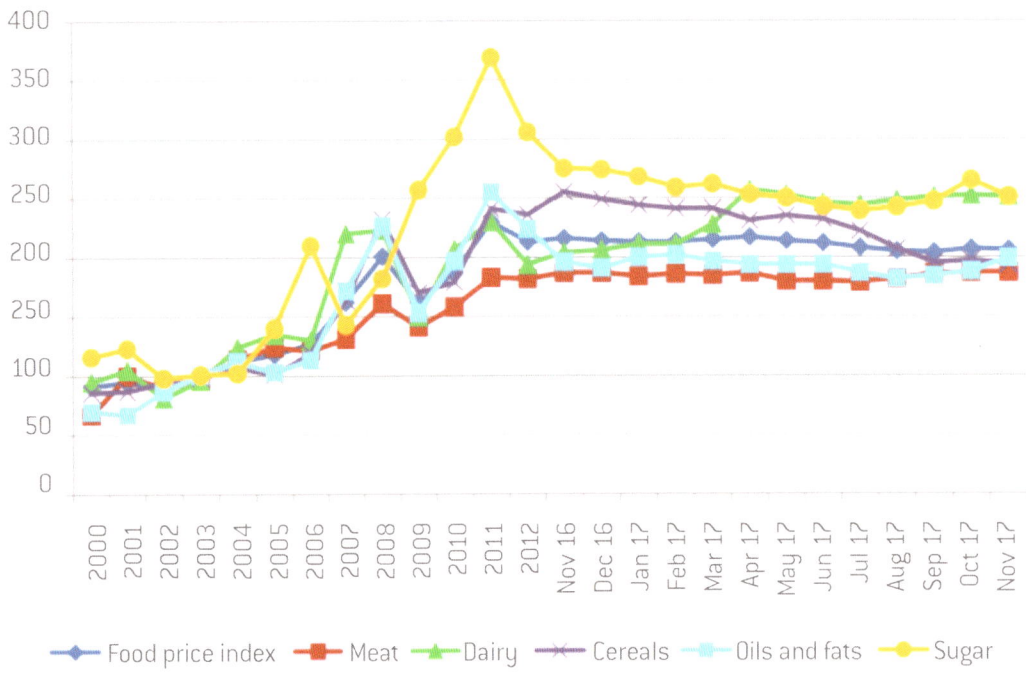

Source: FAO, "Food Price Index", December 2013

The World Bank estimates that global food price spikes in 2008 pushed 44 million people below the poverty line, most of them in poor countries. More recently, the U.S. Department of Agriculture stated that almost 15% of U.S. households were food insecure in 2011, up from 11% before the recent price jumps. Although greater food insecurity is a result, in part, of the global economic downturn, many of the longer-term pressures are not.

Looking forward, the global population is growing, while consumers in emerging markets are becoming wealthier and spending more of their income on meats and processed foods, which is driving up demand and straining supplies. Oil prices and other agricultural inputs are making production more expensive, while extreme weather increasingly threatens harvests.

The Food and Agriculture Organization (FAO) estimates that agricultural production needs to increase by 50-70% to meet global demand by 2050. (Source: The Economist, "Global Food Security Index 2012," sponsored by DuPont)

2. WHAT'S CHANGING: BUILDING A POINT OF VIEW ON THE FUTURE

Agricultural projection 2020 to 2050 (1990 = 100)

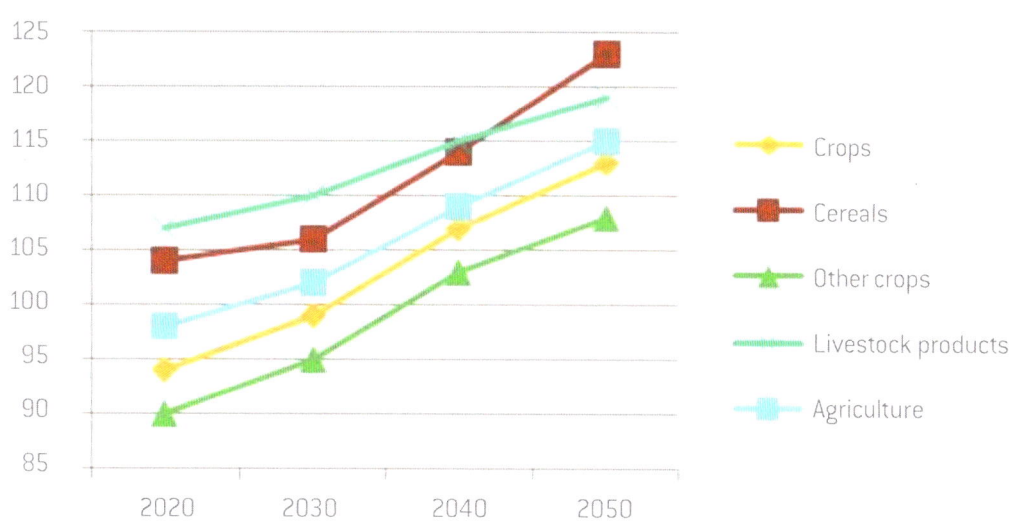

Source: FAO, "World Food and Agriculture to 2030/50"

Food insecurity is costly; ActionAid estimates that food insecurity costs developing economies around US$450 billion in lost GDP each year. It also threatens political stability. Studies show that lack of food is correlated with a substantial deterioration of democratic institutions in low-income countries, as well as a rise in communal violence, riots, human rights abuses, and civil conflict. (Source: The Economist)

In addition to necessary action on increasing production, there is a growing focus on addressing diets to reflect the dual issues of obesity and malnutrition and on reducing food waste, which is enormous worldwide. This is not just about pressuring governments and companies to take action, communities and individuals have a key role too. Tired of watching edible but unsold foods go into compost piles and landfills, farmer Nick Papadopoulos of California created CropMobster, a simple alert system for farmers and grocers in the San Francisco Bay Area. Producers and vendors post entries, e.g. tomatoes, eggs available; the information is shared via email, Twitter, and Facebook, and soon the unwanted food finds a home. CropMobster has sold or donated 100,000 pounds of produce so far. Three hundred producers and grocers have signed up to the service, with 80 to 90 using it regularly. About 5,000 people are registered for the alerts. It is a simple way to feed hungry people and reduce food waste. (Sources: Sharable, Fast Company)

2. WHAT'S CHANGING: BUILDING A POINT OF VIEW ON THE FUTURE

The potential for tensions over water

Close to 50% of the Earth's land surface area is comprised of shared river and lake basins, some 276 river basins crossing the political boundaries of two or more countries. With the prospect of a 40% gap between water supply and demand by 2030, international tensions are likely to rise over water. Even though much progress has been made, 60% of all transboundary basins still do not have any kind of cooperative management framework in place. Supply-demand imbalances are creating issues around the world, e.g. Egypt is highly dependent on the Nile river for its survival, but does not control the upstream resources. In Asia the Yangtze, Mekong, Brahmaputra (which becomes part of the Ganges), and Indus originate in the Himalayas or on the Tibetan Plateau and collectively serve 47% of the world's population, but lack cross-border agreements over use of these water resources. (Sources: SIWI, The National Bureau of Asian Research)

Examples of transboundary tensions over access to water	
Nile	Egypt and Ethiopia
Niger	Mali, Niger, Nigeria, and Guinea
Tigris and Euphrates	Iraq, Syria, and Turkey
Jordan River	Israel, Palestinian Territories, Lebanon, Syria, and Jordan
Yangtze (flows in from Tibetan Plateau)	China and Tibet
Brahmaputra River (flows in from Tibetan Plateau)	China and India
Rio Grande, Rio Bravo, Rio Conchos, and Colorado	The U.S. and northern Mexico

Sources: U.S.News, BBC

The continuing imbalance between population and water distribution is likely to continue to fuel tensions, with Asia being a potential flashpoint. In 2012 tensions rose over two proposed dams in central Asia: Kambarata-1 in Kyrgyzstan and the Rogun Dam in Tajikistan. These dams could affect water supplies in the downstream nations of Uzbekistan, Turkmenistan, and Kazakhstan. Uzbekistan's president, Islam Karimov, says the dams could cause "not just serious confrontation, but even wars." Another looming conflict could erupt between Uganda and Kenya after Kenyan Pokot herdsmen crossed the border seeking water and pasture. In October 2012, Uganda sent 5,000 soldiers to control violence among pastoralists from the two countries. (Source: Worldwater)

Water for the people

Population and water distribution don't always correspond, often leaving highly populated regions with little access to water. This is most true in Asia, which has to support 60% of the world's population with only 36% of the world's water.

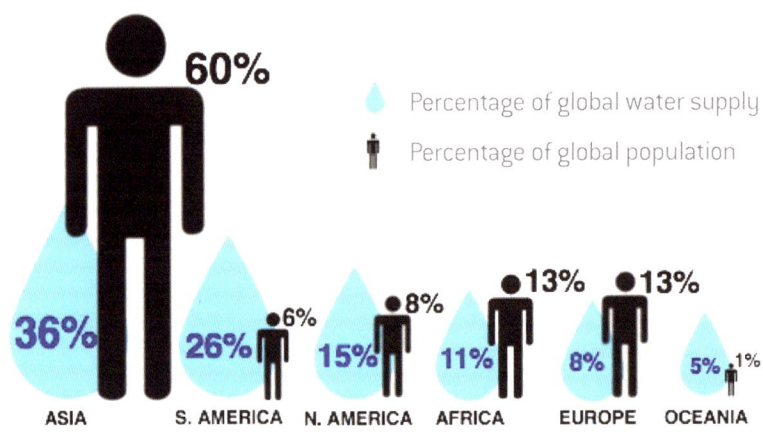

Source: Redraw from Princeton

2. WHAT'S CHANGING: BUILDING A POINT OF VIEW ON THE FUTURE

The race for the Arctic: the next emerging market

As the Arctic ice melts new opportunities arise, from shorter shipping lanes to newly accessible oil and gas reserves. According to the United States Geological Survey about 13% of undiscovered oil and 30% of undiscovered gas reserves are in the Arctic. The five countries whose territories border the Arctic – Russia, the U.S., Canada, Denmark, and Norway – all want part of the prize. They are not alone. China, Japan, and South Korea also want a share in the Arctic's resources, despite being non-Arctic states. Other non-Arctic players, e.g. India and the EU, are holding tight to the argument that Arctic is a common zone that should be accessible to every state for research, exploration, and transport purposes.

However, it is not only oil and natural gas that is of interest. The territory also contains other sought-after natural resources, including metals, fish, fresh water, and high-value minerals such as diamonds and rare earths. Plus it is home to about 4 million people from 40 ethnic groups and an economy of US$230 billion. A region ripe with opportunity, it is also one of the last true wildernesses on earth and a very challenging environment. Developing the Arctic will be a complex task and according to strategy+business, governments and businesses should start by addressing five key challenges: protection of the environment and its people, insufficient investment for infrastructure, navigation of dangerous waters, unresolved governance disagreements, and a lack of research. (Note: although this is not a complete list, it brings together current, convergent dialogues and debates about the region. Source: strategy+business)

U.S. (and others') energy independence

"We are finally poised to control our own energy future," President Barack Obama said in his February 2013 State of the Union address. It may be reliant on foreign energy sources today, but by 2030 the U.S. could be energy self-sufficient and in the near future the world's biggest oil producer. Technology advances in drilling and the recent surge in shale energy production ("tight oil" which is shale oil obtained via fracking, and shale gas) combined with greater energy efficiency could reshape the global energy landscape. (Sources: ThomasNet.com and Financial Times)

The implications of these shifts are significant, from providing the U.S. with cheap and secure energy sources to underpin a manufacturing renaissance, to redefining global geopolitical relationships. The U.S. could find its status as the world's economic superpower is prolonged as a result, although it will need to avoid complacency and innovate to stay ahead. Renewable energy initiatives could however suffer as fossil fuels increase their dominance – with negative results for climate change and pollution. One of the biggest questions is how U.S. energy independence and exports will reshape the geopolitical landscape, particularly in the Middle East and with energy-hungry Asia.

U.S. oil imports falling

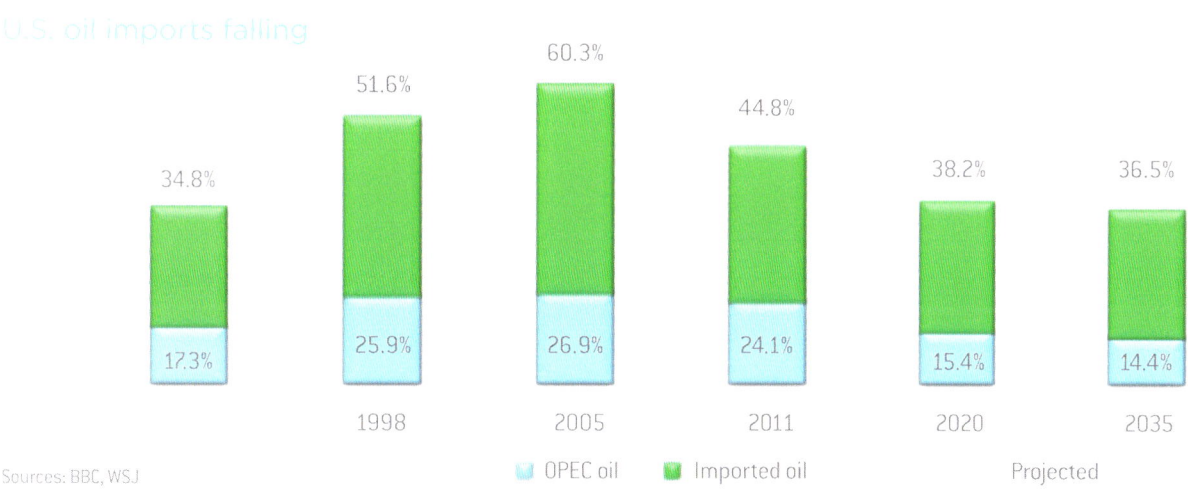

Sources: BBC, WSJ

OPEC oil · Imported oil · Projected

2. WHAT'S CHANGING: BUILDING A POINT OF VIEW ON THE FUTURE

The U.S. is not alone is seeking to reduce its reliance on foreign energy imports. Governments around the world are pursuing energy independence, or at least reduced dependence on others. In China, this has been seen in the country's focus on renewable energy sources – also important to curb the rising tide of pollution – but it may extend to seeking to access the shale oil/gas potential of the country which may be substantial. Nicaragua is also pursuing renewables; its intention is to produce 94% of the country's electricity from renewables by 2017 and reduce reliance on foreign oil from 80% to 6% within a decade, a push that has created a surge of interest in investments in the country. In Vietnam, the government has allowed a non-disclosed owner to build a refinery in order to reduce its reliance on imported crude products. Governments are not the only ones to see the potential of controlling more of a country's energy supply. Africa's richest man, Aliko Dangote, plans to double Nigeria's oil refining capacity by building a refinery with the capacity to process 450,000 barrels per day. However, he acknowledges that his plan may well be opposed as it will hurt organizations in the fuel import business.

Cutting-edge materials are impacting how things are made

According to the magazine Scientific American nothing will impact how things are made, and what they are capable of, more than the materials that manufacturers use to make those things, from cutting-edge foams to coatings, metals, and other substances. However, these new materials are the product of information, knowledge, and new technology, all of which are rapidly changing the landscape of manufacturing.

9 materials that will change the future of manufacturing (Note: some of the materials are still under development)	
Fungal foam	Biodegradable alternative to petroleum-based plastic foams used in automotive bumpers, doors, roofs, engine bays, trunk liners, dashboards, and seats. Other potential uses include tabletops, surfboards, and clothing.
Electric ink	Is easier to make than conventional electronic inks, adheres to many materials and can be printed at a lower temperature using a simple desktop device.
Waste-to-energy thermoelectric	Converting waste heat to electricity. Could be attached e.g. to vehicle tailpipes or could process the exhaust streams from glass- and brick-making factories, refineries, fossil-fuel power plants, as well as large transport ships and tankers.
NanoSHIELD Coatings	Cost far less than conventional materials such as tungsten carbide cobalt and their longer operating life improves the efficiency of the tunnel-boring process.
Designer nanocrystals	Could be useful in harvesting solar energy and delivering quantum computing.
Mega magnets	Could reduce reliance on expensive rare earth materials, access to which is largely determined by China, which produces the majority of these materials.
Cheaper, lighter carbon fiber	Important to ensure market success for cars of the future.
Ultrathin platinum	Might make it practical to reduce the amount of the metal used in fuel-cell catalysts, thereby lowering their cost significantly.
Bio-inspired plastic (Shrilk)	Could be used to make rubbish bags, packaging, and diapers that degrade quickly.

Source: Scientific American

2.   WHAT'S CHANGING: BUILDING A POINT OF VIEW ON THE FUTURE

Technology advances are reshaping the production landscape

While knowledge is increasingly driving future sources of competitive advantage, technology advances are reshaping the means of production. The ability to combine distributed knowledge, e.g. open-source software and designs, with small-scale production equipment, e.g. 3D printing, close to the point of consumption will completely change the dynamics of many industries, as well as reducing or even eliminating the need for transportation. Mass customization is increasingly taking over the world of mass production, moving towards co-creation as consumers become involved in the process of creating the exact product they crave.

Development of 3D printing from being an industrial tool to a tool for the masses

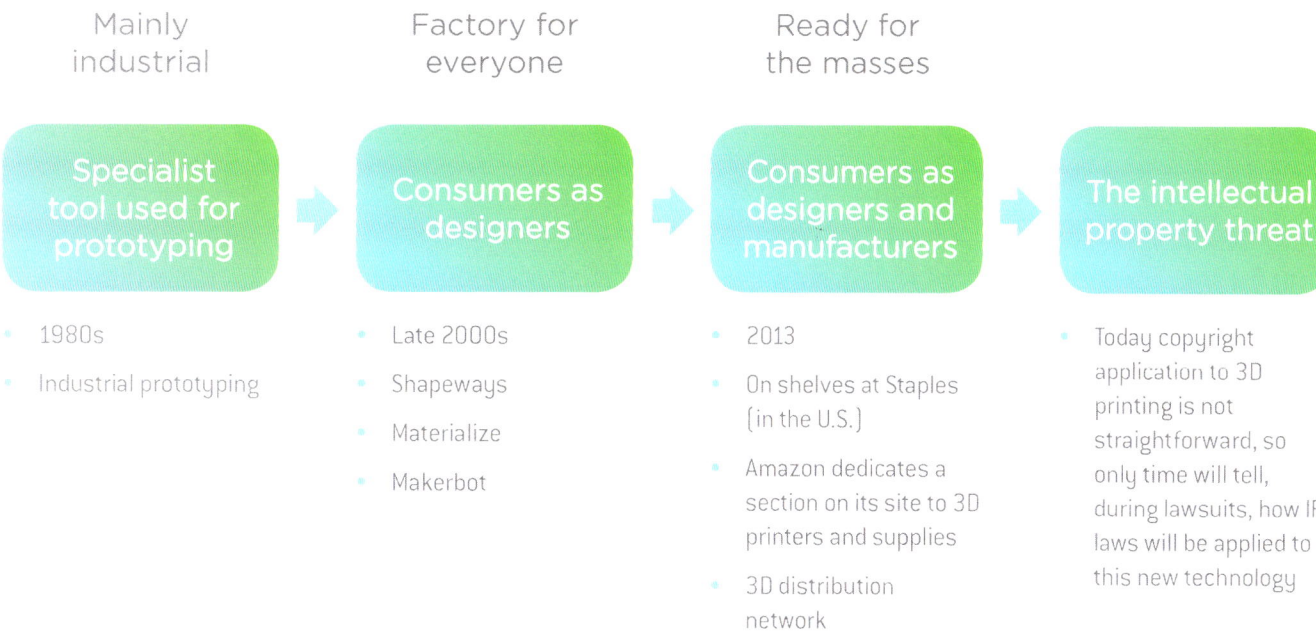

Mainly industrial	Factory for everyone	Ready for the masses	
Specialist tool used for prototyping	**Consumers as designers**	**Consumers as designers and manufacturers**	**The intellectual property threat**
• 1980s • Industrial prototyping	• Late 2000s • Shapeways • Materialize • Makerbot	• 2013 • On shelves at Staples (in the U.S.) • Amazon dedicates a section on its site to 3D printers and supplies • 3D distribution network	• Today copyright application to 3D printing is not straightforward, so only time will tell, during lawsuits, how IP laws will be applied to this new technology

Source: Strategy Dynamics Global SA analysis

According to Carl Bass, president and CEO of Autodesk, a provider of 3D design, engineering, and entertainment software, 3D printing will not replace other manufacturing technologies but rather complement them. Why? Some of the reasons include the fact that 3D printing is only one part of the accelerating software-controlled manufacturing trend which also comprises laser cutters, mills, lathes, routers, and industrial robots. This trend is getting increasingly powerful, affordable, and approachable. In addition, 3D printing remains an immature technology and everything from cost and time to amount of material increases exponentially with the volume of objects produced. He points out that, "Instead of a mass-manufacturing marketplace where everything is made the same way, I expect the "production" trajectory for 3D printing to start with low-volume, high-value objects like prosthetic devices or bespoke items like jewelry. Most 3D printing will be personal and custom, similar to the way we use our inkjet printers today." (Source: Wired)

2. WHAT'S CHANGING: BUILDING A POINT OF VIEW ON THE FUTURE

While 3D printing is getting increasingly popular, Skylar Tibbits, computer scientist and architect at Massachusetts Institute of Technology, is taking it to the next level: self-assembling 4D objects. While it's not exactly printing in four dimensions, the name "4D printing" is catchy for a concept which was inspired by the self-replication powers of Mother Nature. The process could in the future be used to install objects in hard-to-reach places such as underground water pipes and to build furniture, bikes, cars, and even buildings. (Source: BBC)

The reshaping of production through technology advances has led to a wave of reshoring — companies bringing production back from low-cost countries to advanced economies, where production is closer to end markets. This trend is not just about bringing back manufacturing jobs. It could potentially spur a more innovative and sustainable economy. Economists are increasingly building evidence to show that locating researchers and manufacturing workers in close proximity, as well as different manufacturing companies and even multiple industries, can boost innovation. In this environment, workers can exchange ideas not only at work but also outside it over a drink or at the local baseball match. Researchers from MIT have started the project "Production in the Innovation Economy" to study the subject. So far the anecdotal evidence from about 200 companies in the U.S. has proved striking, with company after company detailing the advantages of keeping makers and thinkers together. (Source: New York Times)

The human race with and against the machine

Paro is a therapeutic robot seal that was developed in Japan. The robot seal is used to provide psychological benefits, such as amusement and comfort, particularly for elderly people and children.

(This file is licensed under the Creative Commons Attribution-Share Alike 2.0 Generic license. Source: Flickr. Author: Aaron Biggs, Flickr user ehjayb)

Robots are often perceived as a threat that could displace the human worker. However, technology advances may be starting to improve the reputation of robots. In Japan, the Hybrid Assistive Limb — a battery-powered suit that functions as an exoskeleton, sensing and amplifying the wearer's muscle action — can be used by care workers for picking patients up off a bed, or it can be worn by patients to help them move around and do things independently. In the U.S. research has been done on the impact of using robots to help to reduce the pain and distress that children experience while receiving a vaccination; 86% of the children in the study preferred having a friendly robot present during a medical procedure.

Cyborg — or bionic — technology offers the potential to enhance people's lives through everything from robotic limbs to electronic eyes. Recently a patient suffering from Parkinson's Disease underwent extensive surgeries to implant a neurostimulator in the brain. The neurostimulator is internally wired to a pacemaker in the chest. Once switched on, the device's electrical current jams the misbehaving neurons responsible for PD's physical symptoms, improving the patient's life dramatically. (Sources: Medical News Today, The Economist, Singularity Hub)

2. WHAT'S CHANGING: BUILDING A POINT OF VIEW ON THE FUTURE

Such applications of new technologies and robots to human issues will refocus the race against the machine to how the machine can work with humans to improve how we live and work.

Examples of GRIN technologies (Genetics, Robotics, Information technology, Nanotechnology)	
Genetics	Altering DNA to create new and/or better genes; from crops to babies.
Robotics	Robots in production, space travel, war zones, hospitals, and more.
Information technology	Wearable technology such as Google Glass. Fitness trackers like Nike's Fuelband, Fitbit's Flex, Jawbone's Up, Sensoria socks from Heapsylon. StickNFind for tracking lost/hiding pets or children. Geak Ring can pass contact details to friends.
Nanotechnology	Modern synthetic chemistry. Sunscreens, cosmetics, surface coatings, prolonging durability, faster healing, fuel efficiency, and more.

Sources: BBC, Singularity Hub, Science Daily, Wikipedia

Already the interactions between technology and people are being seen in the increasing application of wearable technologies, with 18% of adults now using such technologies. According to a study by Rackspace, this use of technology has resulted in significant perceived benefits to users.

How has wearable technology enhanced lives?

Improved health and fitness	67%
Made them feel more intelligent	47%
Boosted self-confidence	50%
Boosted career development	37%
Enhance love lives	32%

Source: Rackspace

However, the same study suggests that the pros of such technologies also need to be balanced by reflecting on the downsides. Privacy concerns about wearable technology (along with many other technologies as we explore later) will need to be addressed, with 50% of respondents citing privacy as a barrier to adoption of wearable technology. Google Glass is one of the technologies in the firing line, with the study suggesting that one in five think Google Glass should be banned, while almost two-thirds think Google Glass and other wearable devices should be regulated. (Source: Rackspace)

2. WHAT'S CHANGING: BUILDING A POINT OF VIEW ON THE FUTURE

2.3 HOW IS THE WORLD ORGANIZED – AND REORGANIZING ITSELF?

Looking at organizations and communities, the traditional "boxes" we use to organize markets, industries, regions, work, communities, and more, no longer hold. Growing interdependence and connectivity mean that the boundaries between them are falling rapidly. Your competitors, customers, and markets may no longer be who you think they are. The growing importance of networks and communities means that companies are no longer the central players in creating value – rather the playing fields of the future will be defined around the needs of ever more demanding consumers and customers, with the ability to collaborate – as well as to compete – a critical capability. Key implications of these trends include:

From boundaries blurring to rapidly falling boundaries Your competitors are not who you think they are. The industry boundaries that have traditionally divided companies according to what they make, what they do, and how they approach their business, are collapsing. The bigger issue is that this means that competition is increasingly taking place across industries, not within them. Any organization that focuses its efforts on competing with its direct peers is at increasingly severe risk of being blindsided by a newcomer outside its frame of reference – these newcomers are not just companies, but also your customers, your channels to market, and state bodies.

From economic power in the Triad to the BRICS and Beyond (B&B) Economic power is shifting to the BRICS plus a next tier of rapidly developing economies, due to a combination of increasing financial power, resources, knowledge base, population, and consumer affluence. These markets have already taken over from the Triad (U.S., Europe, Japan) as the world's growth engines and are set to continue to play an expanding role, although the Triad markets will still account for a large part of the world's consumption in the future. In this multipolar world, organizations are going to need to be more flexible and agile, managing several business models at the same time.

From an insular to an interconnected, multipolar world Just as markets and competition are becoming multipolar and interconnected, so too are the systems which govern our societies and economies. Gone are the days when lives were lived according to one country, community, or religion's rules, unaware of the diversity beyond. Differences in beliefs, cultures, and economic systems are more transparent than ever before, challenging assumptions about which model(s) are the most appropriate to deliver societal and economic progress. Falling trust in governments and the fragmentation of societies is leading to the rise of communities of choice, across geographic and cultural borders. The challenge is to reconcile and/or tolerate multiple perspectives.

From physical to cyber security The balance of power in the last three decades has moved beyond military might towards economic strength, resource access, and knowledge. However, as terrorist activity and geopolitical tensions increase, threats to personal, organizational, and national security are rising – and cyber warfare will be a main front in conflicts. Enemies in cyberspace include both state and non-state actors, from the unsophisticated amateur to highly trained professional hackers. The challenge will be continuing to secure industry, power installations and infrastructure, academia, government, as well as the military.

From profit to purpose Tapping into a rising consciousness among customers, employees, and other stakeholders, many businesses are stepping up to a new role to enable positive innovation and change to tackle societal and economic challenges. In many areas, corporations are seeking to build legitimacy – and the license to operate – in the eyes of demanding and discerning consumers, who care about the impact and motivations of companies from whom they buy. Corporate purpose and values are increasingly central to attracting and motivating employees, customers, and partners.

From do it all organizations to networked ecosystems In an interconnected world, it is the consumer, and their extended network that is at the center of value creation. The need to deliver seamless, integrated experiences based around a consumer need – rather than a product or service – means companies are finding it harder than ever to do everything themselves. Networks and partnerships – a value creation ecosystem – are becoming imperative.

In the next subsections we highlight some selected new analysis of key game changers in the area of organizations and communities.

2. WHAT'S CHANGING: BUILDING A POINT OF VIEW ON THE FUTURE

Economic power shifts – with different mindsets

The first decade of the 21st century saw an unprecedented generational shift in economic power – one that will continue. The U.S. government's National Intelligence Council in 2013 released the report "Global Trends 2030: Alternative Worlds" predicting: "The world of 2030 will be radically transformed from our world today. By 2030, no country – whether the U.S., China, or any other large country – will be a hegemonic power. The empowerment of individuals and diffusion of power among states and from states to informal networks will have a dramatic impact, largely reversing the historic rise of the West since 1750, restoring Asia's weight in the global economy, and ushering in a new era of 'democratization' at the international and domestic level."

It has been five years since the fall of the Lehman Brothers pulled the world into the worst recession since the 1930s; five years in which the perception of the economic balance of power has shifted from West to East. While the U.S. is still regarded as the world's economic superpower many believe China will surpass it in the not too distant future. Research from Pew shows that in 2008 47% of people believed the U.S. was the world's leading economic superpower, and 20% believed it was China. In 2013 the number naming the U.S. decreased to 41% and China increased to 34%. The perception that China is the dominant superpower is especially widespread among some of America's closest allies. In 2013, just 33% in Britain and 19% in Germany named the U.S. as the leading economy – 53% and 59% respectively named China.

Global power is not only shifting from West to East but also increasingly from North to South. The United Nations Development Programme's (UNDP) 2013 Human Development Report states that, "The rise of the South is unprecedented in its speed and scale... Never in history have the living conditions and prospects of so many people changed so dramatically and so fast." The discussion of global rebalancing and increasing prosperity is often based on rapidly increasing GDP and trade numbers in a few large countries, generally the BRICS. However, more that 40 developing countries of the South shows human development gains that significantly outpace global norms. These gains have not only far-reaching implications for people's lives, for social equality, and for democratic governance at the local level, but also highlight opportunities for greater worldwide human progress. Examples of smaller economies with substantial progress include Bangladesh, Rwanda, Chile, Ghana, Mauritius, and Uganda.

Looking ahead to 2050, Goldman Sachs expects this economic trajectory to continue with emerging and growth markets' share of global GDP rising to almost 70% from just 22% in 2000. This massive economic reshaping of the world will impact not only consumption and production, but geopolitics, financial markets, innovation, and the business landscape.

Global share of GDP by markets, forecast 2050

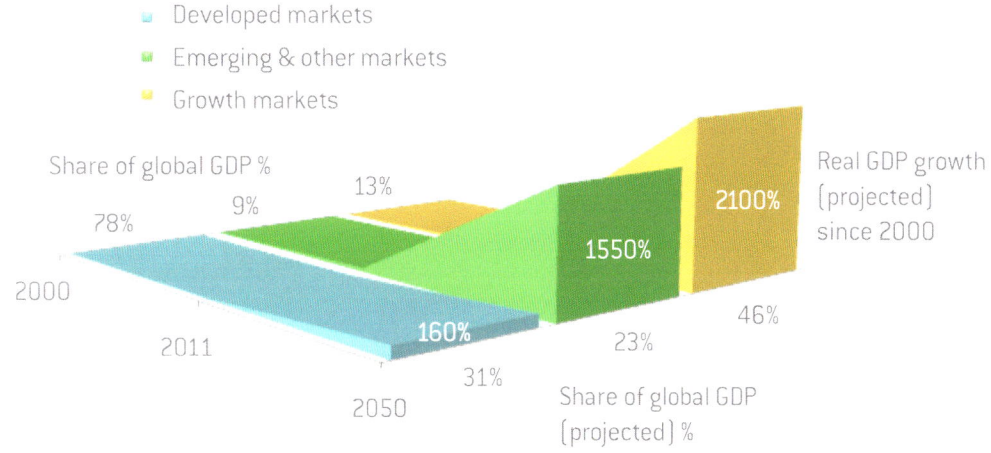

- Developed markets
- Emerging & other markets
- Growth markets

Share of global GDP %

78% · 9% · 13% — 2000

160% · 1550% · 2100% — Real GDP growth (projected) since 2000

31% · 23% · 46% — 2050 — Share of global GDP (projected) %

2011

Source: Goldman Sachs

2. WHAT'S CHANGING: BUILDING A POINT OF VIEW ON THE FUTURE

It is not just economies that are growing. Emerging markets companies are growing faster than those from developed markets even when operating in a neutral environment where none of them are based. Why? These new competitors are hungry for growth, extending their presence on the global stage, particularly into other high growth markets, leveraging strong bases in their domestic markets. The mindset of many of these players is focused on aggressive expansion and investment, in contrast to the consolidation and risk management mindsets of many traditional, developed markets' players.

Numbers from our latest report on Corporate Clout 2013: Time for Responsible Capitalism analysis highlight the rise of companies from the fastest growing economies in the world. Asian headquartered firms now make up more than 34% (172 companies) of Fortune Global 500 firms, a huge increase from 118 companies in 2001, while North American headquartered companies represent only 29% or 146 companies, down from 215 in 2001. Forbes' Global 2000 annual ranking, tells a similar story: companies in the BRICS and beyond are rapidly gaining ground on their developed world counterparts.

Revenue growth rates segmented by geographic market,* compound annual growth rate (% 1999 to 2008)

- ■ Emerging-market companies
- ■ Developed-market companies
- ■ Difference = growth-rate advantage for emerging-market companies

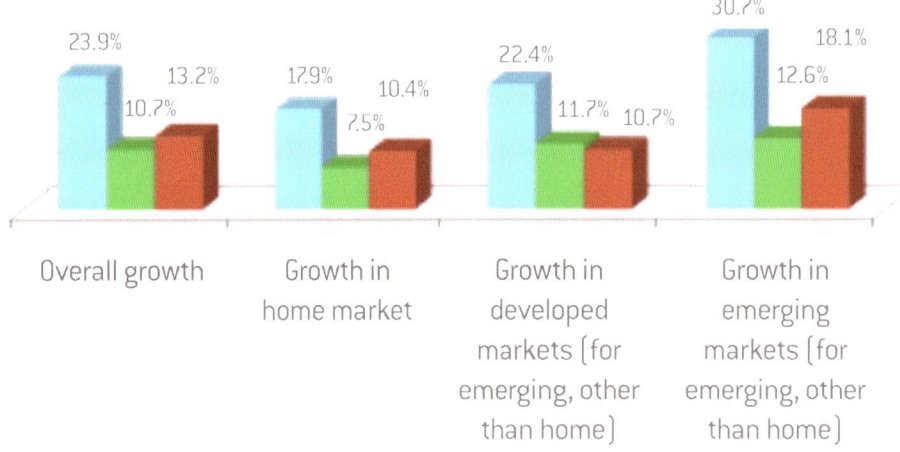

	Overall growth	Growth in home market	Growth in developed markets (for emerging, other than home)	Growth in emerging markets (for emerging, other than home)
Emerging-market	23.9%	17.9%	22.4%	30.7%
Developed-market	10.7%	7.5%	11.7%	12.6%
Difference	13.2%	10.4%	10.7%	18.1%

*Based on growth-decomposition analysis of 2,229 markets for 72 companies, spanning a number of time frames from 1999 to 2008.

Source: McKinsey & Company, "Winning the $30 trillion decathlon"

2. WHAT'S CHANGING: BUILDING A POINT OF VIEW ON THE FUTURE

Slowdown in China – the knock-on effects

Growth in emerging economies has delivered higher living standards for many millions of people in these areas while whetting their appetite for more. However, China's growth rate is slowing, falling below double-digit levels, with trade volumes down, and some investments being scaled back. At the same time the tapering of the U.S. Federal Reserve's quantitative easing (QE) policies has started. When announced in early 2013 that this would begin, investor reactions drove capital flight from the BRICS and beyond driving currencies down from India to Indonesia, although the actual implementation of tapering has seen relatively little impact on capital flight.

China's leaders have signalled that the slowdown in growth is tolerable as long as fundamentals are sound. At the G20 summit in September 2013, President Xi Jinping said: "China has realized that it has to advance structural reforms in order to solve the problems hindering its long-term economic development, even though it will mean slower growth." So what are these issues hampering growth? For the last 30 years, investment has been the principal engine of China's economy. In 2011, for the first time, consumption contributed 55.5% of China's growth and investment contributed only 48.8%, a trend that is continuing (net exports subtracted 4.3%). During the global recession China's exports fell as global demand slowed, so China propped up its high GDP growth by creating new infrastructure, housing, and factories. But you can't do that forever so its economic model needs to be refocused towards driving greater domestic demand – demand that cannot keep up the extremely high GDP growth of the 2000s. (Sources: The Economist, The Washington Post)

China is clearly not heading towards recession, with growth around 7%, but it is has slowed down dramatically since its record growth years and the knock-on effect is slowly starting to kick in. It will likely hit Southeast Asian economies, but according to the Asian Development Bank Outlook it is unlikely to lead to a steep downturn in the region's growth. On the other hand, commodity producers and countries with relatively large China trade links, mainly Australia, Canada, Brazil, Malaysia, and Korea, are likely to take a huge hit. Thailand has already been dragged into recession, Argentina could relapse into recession by 2014, and growth is slowing in Brazil and India already. (Source: various news agencies)

The IMF's October 2013 GDP growth forecasts show relative economic health among a number of the high growth countries, although in some such as India and Thailand, political issues will continue to impact economic prospects.

Country	GDP (% change)						
	2012	2013*	2014*	2015*	2016*	2017*	2018*
China	7.7	7.6	7.3	7.0	7.0	7.0	7.0
India	3.2	3.8	5.1	6.3	6.5	6.7	6.7
Russia	3.4	1.5	3.0	3.5	3.5	3.5	3.5
Brazil	0.9	2.5	2.5	3.2	3.3	3.5	3.5
South Africa	2.5	2	2.9	3.3	3.4	3.5	3.5
Thailand	6.5	3.1	5.2	5.0	4.4	4.7	4.7
Indonesia	6.2	5.3	5.5	6.0	6.0	6.0	6.0
Vietnam	5.3	5.3	5.4	5.4	5.5	5.5	5.5
Philippines	6.9	6.8	6.0	5.5	5.5	5.5	5.5
Argentina	1.9	3.5	2.8	2.8	2.8	2.8	2.8
Mexico	3.6	1.2	3.0	3.5	3.7	3.8	3.8

Sources: IMF, WEO October 2013 (data), various news sources

Environment: towards conscious/responsible capitalism

Society's expectations of business are changing. It is no longer enough for companies to avoid breaking the rules, nor to have a few, isolated corporate social responsibility (CSR) activities. They need to take an active approach to improving the world around them or risk losing the trust of customers, employees, institutions, and communities. Increasingly businesses are embracing the approaches of shared value and responsible capitalism, strengthening their businesses by creatively addressing key global and societal issues and engaging their employees to participate actively in these efforts.

Company activities supporting sustainability versus employee participation (all employed FT/PT) in these activities

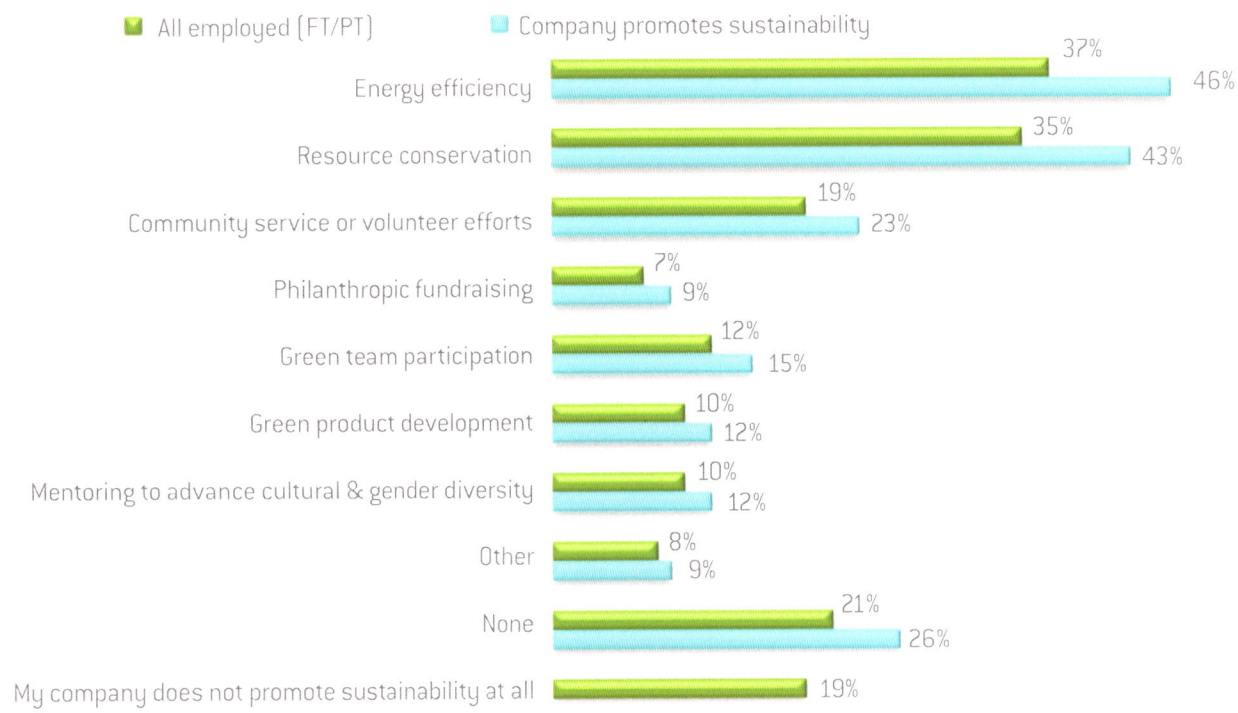

Source: Gibbs-Soell, "Sense & Sustainability Study," 2013

2. WHAT'S CHANGING: BUILDING A POINT OF VIEW ON THE FUTURE

Some businesses take these approaches even further, putting responsibility at the heart of the firm. According to B Corp founder, Andrew Kassoy, there is a generation of entrepreneurs and stakeholders who want business to be about more than just money. They want purpose. This is where B Corp comes in. For a company to become a certified B Corporation they must meet rigorous standards of social and environmental performance, accountability, and transparency. B Corp certification is to sustainable business what Fair Trade certification is to coffee, or USDA Organic certification is to milk. Today, there are more than 778 Certified B Corps from 27 countries in 60 industries. The B Corp stamp is designed to give consumers and investors alike the ability to identify companies with responsible management across the board: good companies as a whole, not just good products. (Sources: B Corp, The Guardian)

Examples of Certified B Corporations	
Ben & Jerry's Vermont, U.S.	Use high-quality ingredients including cage free eggs, fairly traded products, and milk/cream from family farmers who do not treat their cows with the synthetic hormone rBGH.
Juhudi Kilimo Nairobi, Kenya	Provides rural smallholder farmers with micro-asset financing to purchase agriculture assets such as dairy cows, poultry, greenhouses, and biogas digesters.
Volans London, UK	Future-focused consultancy and think-tank. Helps corporations focus on, implement and measure social responsibilities.
Acción Verde Bogota, Colombia	Strive to generate ecological restoration in strategic places of Colombia, prevent natural disasters while mitigating climate change.
X-runner Venture Lima, Peru	Provides waterless toilets and waste management to families that do not have standard toilets. Daily lives become more comfortable, providing a cleaner and healthier environment to live in.

Source: B Corp

Digitization is driving growth and job creation, BUT not everyone is ready – interconnected but unequal

Technology advances are creating growth and employment. But how does mass adoption of connected digital services by consumers, organizations and government really impact the world? According to the study Digitization for Economic Growth and Job Creation (April 2013) from Booz & Company, digitization boosted the world's economy by US$193 billion and created 6 million jobs in 2011. Yet growth is uneven as developed economies benefited most from digitization in terms of GDP growth, by a factor of about 25%. However, developed countries get less employment growth compared with developing countries. Another recent study from Associate Professor Diego A. Comin of Harvard Business School supports the importance of technology adaption for growth and prosperity, with his results suggesting that 70% of differences in cross-country per capita income can be explained by differences in technology adoption. (Sources: Booz & Company, HBS Working Knowledge)

2. WHAT'S CHANGING: BUILDING A POINT OF VIEW ON THE FUTURE

Digitization's impact on GDP and jobs, 2011 regional impact

Region	GDP impact (US$ billions)	Number of jobs created
Africa	8.3	618,699
Commonwealth of Independent States	11.8	340,820
East Asia and the Pacific	55.8	2,370,241
Eastern Europe	7.0	159,015
Latin America/Caribbean	27.0	636,737
Middle East and North Africa	16.5	377,772
North America	25.3	167,650
South Asia	9.4	1,117,753
Western Europe	31.5	213,578
Total	192.6	6,002,266

Source: Booz & Company, "Digitization for Economic Growth and Job Creation," April 2013

The networked readiness map highlights the new global digital divide. It is measured by using four subindexes: the environment for information and communications technologies (ICTs), the readiness of a society to use ICTs, the actual usage of all main stakeholders, and the impact that ICTs generate in the economy and in society.

The networked readiness index map

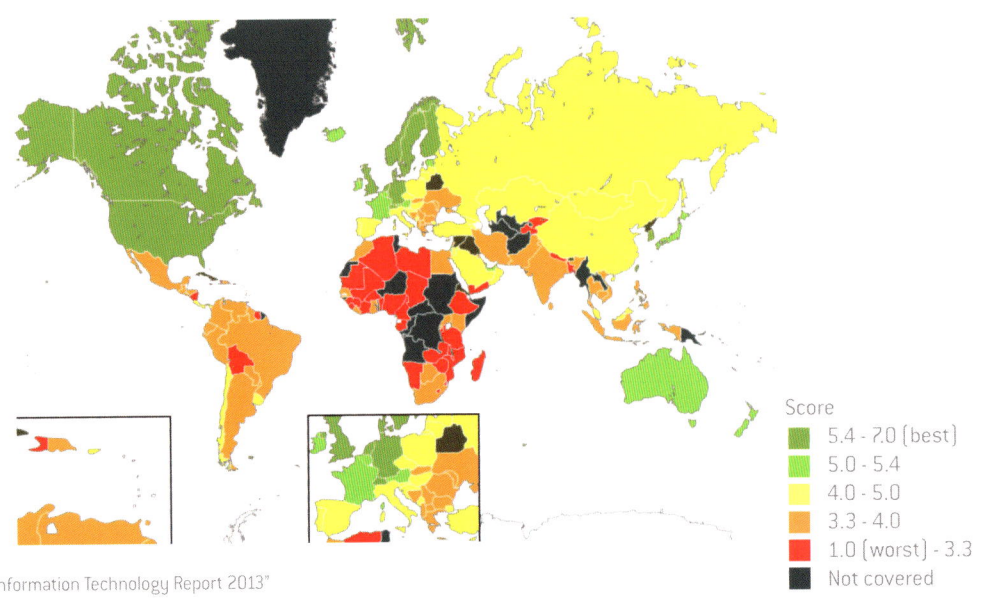

Score	
	5.4 - 7.0 (best)
	5.0 - 5.4
	4.0 - 5.0
	3.3 - 4.0
	1.0 (worst) - 3.3
	Not covered

Source: WEF, "The Global Information Technology Report 2013"

2. WHAT'S CHANGING: BUILDING A POINT OF VIEW ON THE FUTURE

The "breakdown" of the traditional shopping experience

Retailers are facing a digitally driven perfect storm. Connectivity, rising consumer influence, time scarcity, mobile payments, and the internet of things are changing where, when, and how we shop. The boundaries between physical and virtual retail spaces are blurring and retailers are increasingly being forced to question the role, function, and relevance of the traditional shopping space. The future of shops will be increasingly defined by experiential spaces offering personalized service, integrated online and offline value propositions, and pop-up stores to satisfy demands for immediacy and surprise. Today the focus for retailers must be on engaging customers and consumers through experience instead of simply trying to sell more goods and services to its customers.

Reflecting this focus, pop-up stores are becoming increasingly popular. Such stores also offer retailers (and others) the chance to experiment and obtain rapid feedback in a fast changing consumer landscape. The pop-up concept is particularly prevalent at Halloween and at Christmas but is found all year and in every industry. In 2012 the number of pop-up shops in the U.S. was 2,380 (68.1% of which were Halloween themed) up from 2,043 three years earlier. (Source: IBISWorld)

Examples of pop-up store concepts	
London's Crazy Horse	Paris's avant-garde cabaret performed at a custom-made temporary theater in South Bank in the fall of 2012.
Cube by Electrolux	A restaurant that has toured the world touching down in Brussels, Milan, and London.
Design Hotels' Papaya Playa Project	Has appeared on a beach near Tulum, Mexico, with 85 cabanas and casitas, and a restaurant.
Rapha Cycle Club	Pop-up is a combination gallery, cycling shop, and WiFi café. The club organizes events around cycling races, is a meeting hub for biking enthusiasts, and also generates revenue from foot traffic.

Sources: Wharton, Travel+Leisure, CradlePoint, Fast Company

Taking pop-up a step further, STORY, a 2000 square foot store located in Manhattan's burgeoning new retail corridor of 10th Avenue, is all about customer experience. The experimental STORY is a retail space that has the point of view of a magazine, changes like a gallery, and sells like a store. Every four to eight weeks, STORY will change all its merchandise, design, and fixtures, reinventing the store around a different story-based theme. Each of the themes is sponsored by at least one company, e.g. GE sponsored the Making Things STORY, HP and Quirky the Holiday STORY, and Nerve.com the Love STORY.

So what's next for the shopper experience? eBay has launched a new innovative hybrid shopping concept 'digital storefronts' or 'Connected Glass' technology that makes it possible to enjoy aspects of both the online and the offline world at the same time. In Westfield San Francisco Centre giant touchscreen windows allow customers to browse through retailers' products, in this case from Sony, TOMS, and Rebecca Minkoff. With a single swipe a customer can hit the 'order' button and a link will be sent to their mobile phone, allowing them to pay through PayPal or with a credit or debit card. The customer can choose to have the purchased item sent to a pick-up point or delivered to their door, mostly with free delivery, and in some cases on the same day. (Source: CNN)

2. WHAT'S CHANGING: BUILDING A POINT OF VIEW ON THE FUTURE

2.4   WHO IS SHAPING THE FUTURE?

The landscape of shapers and influencers is shifting, as the rise of empowered individuals and communities – with a growing array of choices and technologies to connect – means that power is moving away from traditional institutions, in whom trust is falling. The emerging landscape is one of multiple stakeholders and influencers – many of whom are engaged in turf wars to expand their influence and impact – who are demanding a rethink of the roles of government, society and business to meet the needs of a complex, multipolar world. Key implications of these trends include:

From institutional authority to peer and community power Trust in governments to do what is right is plummeting with government officials now the least trusted spokespeople in the world. Instead, people are turning to communities of choice to be heard and to take control of their own lives, aided by communications and social technologies.

From governments as "voices of the people" to activists Even as trust in government falls, politicians are taking a more activist role in economies and societies as the impact of the economic and financial crises continues. Countries across the world are seeing an increasing level of state activism, from stimulus packages to drive growth to trade policies to protect jobs and industries to interventions in financial markets. Will this lead to a stronger global system long-term?

From shareholders to multiple stakeholders Many trends are coming together to demand a rethink of what business will be and how it will operate in the future. From increasing global challenges that cannot be tackled by governments or NGOs alone, to the spread of social technologies that are changing relationships between companies and their customers and employees. This is a world where businesses have to shift perspective from a sole focus on delivering value to shareholders, to creating and sharing value with multiple stakeholders around mutual objectives.

From baby boomers to multiple generations For the first time four distinct generations are present in the workforce. The resulting differences in generational ambitions, attitudes, technology skills, and ethics are impacting management styles, how work is done, and the ability to attract talent – as well as how we live our daily lives. Outside the workplace the generational differences are also impacting consumption behaviors and how companies build relationships with their consumers.

From simplicity and tradition to complexity, ambiguity, and uncertainty The world is becoming more complex, ambiguous, and uncertain. Change seems to be the only constant. Global challenges, economic downturn, rising conflicts, disruptive technologies, and an always-on lifestyle are stretching our resources and ability to individually and collectively respond, even as traditional social structures fragment. Learning to live and work in this world will require new capabilities of leaders societies and communities. Are we ready to take on the challenge?

From tolerance to conflict In this world of uncertainty and ambiguity, the impact on behaviors of beliefs, cultures, and history is very powerful. As globalization and transparency about differences between belief systems and cultures increases, we are seeing increasing tensions between societies and systems plus fragmentation within them, often with history as a catalyst. Think separatist movements, tensions between religions, and the rise of extremist groups. The challenge is that intolerance is rising – and leading to increasing conflict.

In the next subsections we highlight some selected new analysis of key game changers in the area of shapers and influencers.

2. WHAT'S CHANGING: BUILDING A POINT OF VIEW ON THE FUTURE

Generational shifts

Generation Y is the first transformational generation. They have grown up in a radically different world from that of their parents, surrounded by modern technologies and a society of consumerism – and it shows in the way they live, work, use, and consume. While some of Generation Y vaguely remember a world with only limited technology, today's young teenagers, Generation Z, have never experienced a world without it. Technology is in their DNA, which is probably the single most important difference between Generations Y and Z and older generations.

Technology has been an important influence in driving a different mindset among younger generations. In the U.S., young Silicon Valley pioneers have changed the world with their technology and now they want to do the same to politics. Sean Parker, the 33 year old former Facebook president worth US$2 billion, points out that: "We feel for a long time that Silicon Valley hasn't been properly represented at a federal level. To a certain extent we are starting to come into a realization of our own power and our own capability, not just as innovators and technology pioneers but also in a political sense." (Source: Time)

However, it is not only in developed countries that younger generations want influence, change, and a different lifestyle. These needs were also a factor in the Arab Spring and other popular uprisings. Young people don't want the life of their parent or grandparent. The article "The New Globalist: Meet the Transformers" suggests that the best way to understand the newly emerging markets is to meet its young people – the Transformers. They are a part of the "I want more generation" and number in the millions around the world. They are optimistic, hyperconnected, educated, and have disposable income to spend. They are also demanding, wanting Western staples, luxuries, and the opportunity to travel.

Whether they are the children of developed or developing countries, one common denominator amongst these new generations is the desire for freedom: to choose not only products and experiences but also how to live their lives. This desire is another important influence on younger generations' mindsets and applies to work too. Research from Millennial Branding and oDesk finds freedom is the top reason for millennials quitting their jobs and that 58% of Generation Y classify themselves as entrepreneurs.

From entrepreneur as an occupation to entrepreneur as a mindset

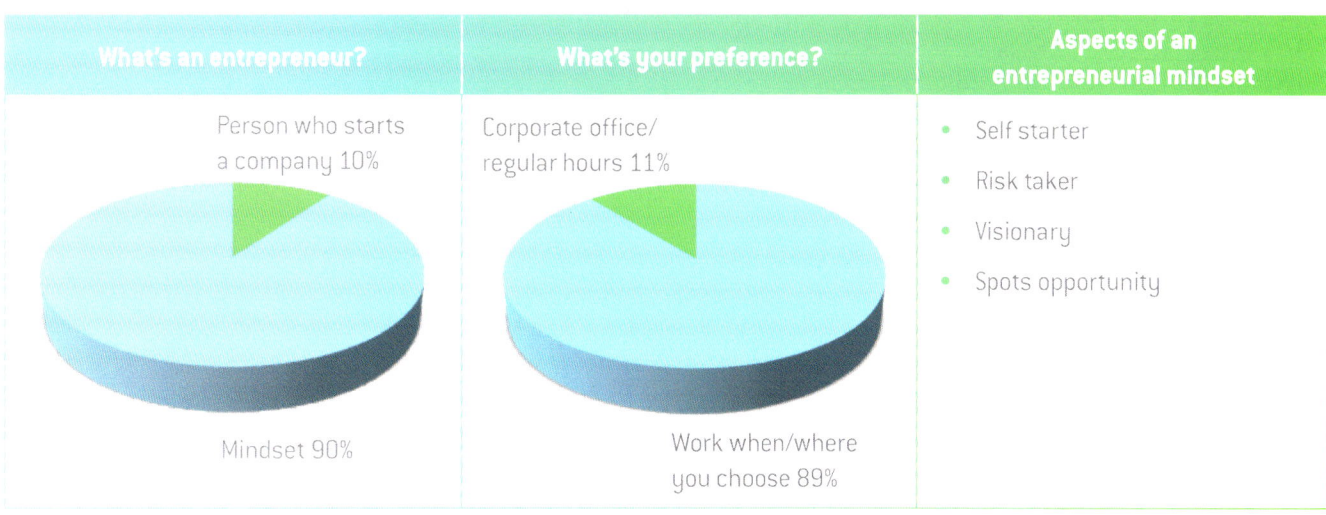

What's an entrepreneur?	What's your preference?	Aspects of an entrepreneurial mindset
Person who starts a company 10% / Mindset 90%	Corporate office/ regular hours 11% / Work when/where you choose 89%	• Self starter • Risk taker • Visionary • Spots opportunity

Source: Millennial Branding and oDesk, "Millennials and the Future of Work", 2013

2. WHAT'S CHANGING: BUILDING A POINT OF VIEW ON THE FUTURE

All organizations will need to adapt to the shift in mindsets of the next generations as employees, consumers, advocates, and activists. The first step is to start to understand their traits, desires, and styles. Managing the balance in serving and employing different generations will not be easy, but will become increasingly important.

	Born	Traits	Desires	Style
Traditionalists	1900-1945	Patriotic, loyal, conservative, have faith in institutions	Help in, or easing into, retirement	Command and control leadership, top-down communication, uncomfortable with technology, feel that it's unwise to change jobs
Baby boomers	1946-1964	Competitive, question authority, desire to put own stamp on institutions, optimistic	Robust careers, help juggling it all	"Get it done" approach to leadership, protective in communication, unsure of technology, feel that changing jobs can be a setback
Generation X	1965-1980	Eclectic, resourceful, self-reliant, skeptical of institutions, adaptive, independent	Balance and freedom	Want coaching style leadership, network approach to communication, technology is essential for work, changing jobs is necessary
Generation Y (aka millennials, net generation, digital natives, Generation Next, trophy kids)	1981-1994	Globally concerned, integrated, cyberliterate, media savvy, realistic, environmentally conscious	Meaningful work	Want partnership leadership, collaborative approach to communication, latest technology must be provided, job changing normal and frequent
Generation Z (aka Gen C, iGeneration, net generation, internet generation, digital natives)	1995-onwards	Globally focused, multicultural, technology in their DNA, always connected, socially and environmentally active, compulsive multitaskers, live in a customized world, short attention spans, ownership less important than experience	Work that constantly stimulates and engages	Desire to customize their own approach versus rigid instructions, expect flexible working and real-time communications, peer driven, collaborative approach to leadership, networked inside and outside organization, entrepreneurial, always in search of something new

2. WHAT'S CHANGING: BUILDING A POINT OF VIEW ON THE FUTURE

Power shifts from institutions to individuals/communities

The number of channels through which influence can be purveyed is exploding with continuing advances in communications technology. Ideas, norms, rules, and opinions, created by individuals and social networks as well as established shapers and influencers, can be tweeted or IM'd (instant messaged) around the world in no time.

Peer and word of mouth influence is rising, real-time feedback is increasingly expected, and the global brain is alive and active. Those organizations that do not actively listen to and act on the opinions of their stakeholders will find their work increasingly challenging. For example, research from NewVoiceMedia suggests that 31% of us will post online following poor customer service. Women are nearly twice as likely as men to take their frustrations online, and among the 16-24 age group, this was the case for more than 40%. (Source: NewVoiceMedia)

People are turning to peers and communities for direction on norms and behaviors, and for action on critical issues, accelerating a shift of power away from traditional institutions towards society.

Likelihood that U.S. social media users will make a purchase based on a friend's social media post, by demographic, January 2014

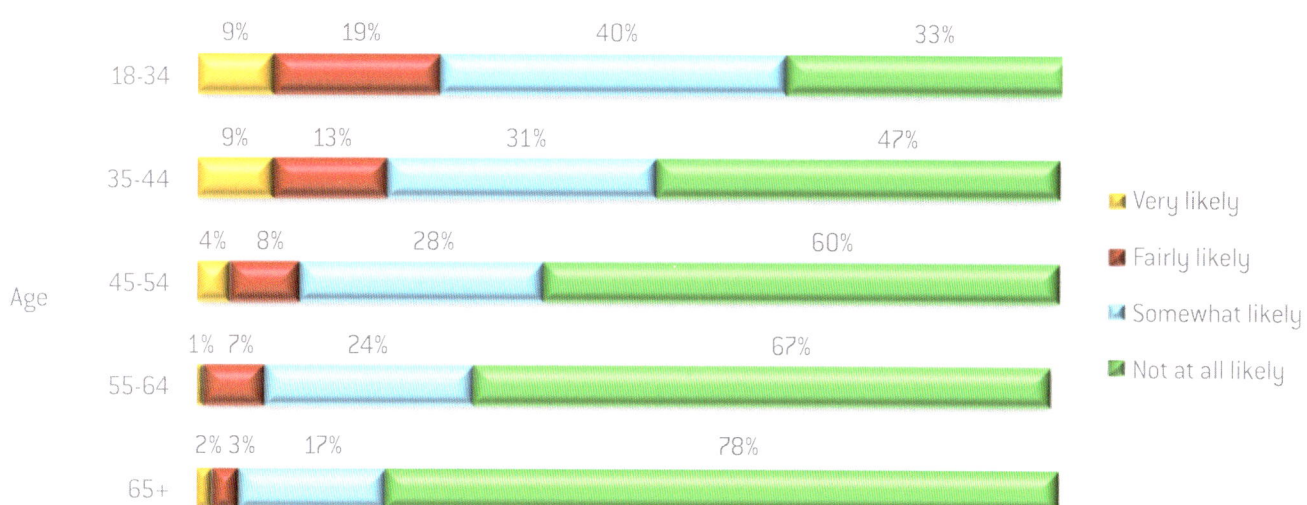

Source: eMarketer

2. WHAT'S CHANGING: BUILDING A POINT OF VIEW ON THE FUTURE

Top purchase influencer, by category and generation for each category, the top 3 are listed by top-2 box score (extremely/slightly influential) January 2014			
Apparel		**Packaged Goods**	
Millennials	**Baby Boomers**	**Millennials**	**Baby Boomers**
Word of mouth	Online shopping sites	Word of mouth	Advertising
Online shopping sites	Advertising	Advertising	Recommendation from sales reps
Search engines	Recommendation from sales reps	Search engines	Word of mouth
Financial products		**Big-ticket purchases (e.g. travel, electronic, etc.)**	
Millennials	**Baby Boomers**	**Millennials**	**Baby Boomers**
Word of mouth	Word of mouth	Word of mouth	Word of mouth
Company website	Advertising	Search engines	Company website
Search engines	Company website	Advertising	Advertising

Source: Radius Global Marketing Research

The 2014 Edelman Trust Barometer shows a stable level of trust in business and NGOs but a decrease in government and media levels. Generally the level of trust in institutions remains low. This lack of faith in traditional leaders reflects an ongoing litany of widely publicized missteps and wrongdoings. Academics and technical experts along with 'a person like yourself' are now trusted nearly twice as much as a CEO or government official. (Source: Edelman) This is reflected in a growing lack of confidence in governance mechanisms around the world, including the EU.

2. WHAT'S CHANGING: BUILDING A POINT OF VIEW ON THE FUTURE

The young are losing confidence in European project:
Among 18- to 29-year-olds – Favorable of EU (%)

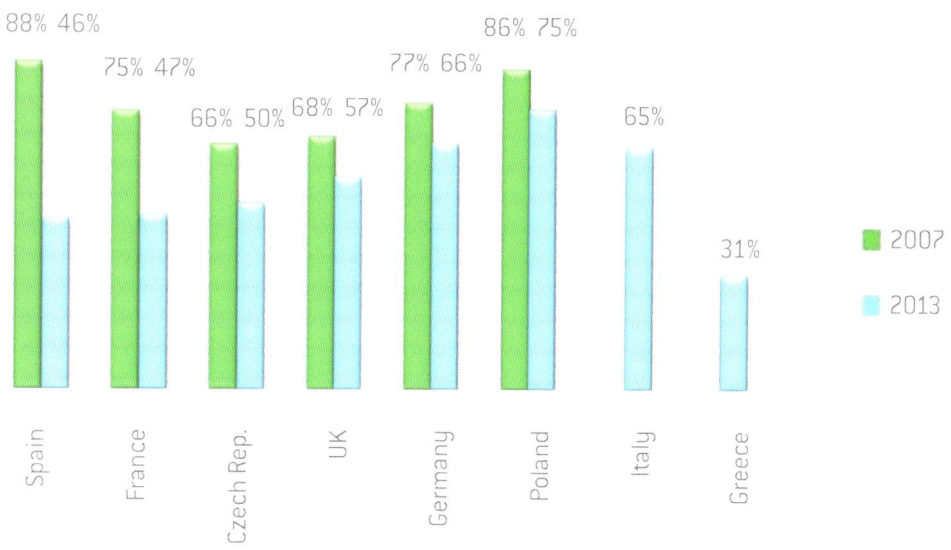

Source: Pew Research, "The New Sick Man of Europe: the European Union," May 2013

As trust becomes the currency of an interconnected world of peer-to-peer, horizontal networks of trust, it is important to take into account not only which people are communicating on behalf of an organization but also where and how they are communicating.

The privacy issue

The concept of privacy was first noted in the UK during the 16th century and was a simple matter of construction. Later, the invention of the camera motivated the "right to privacy" – also known as "the right to be left alone." Today the capability of new digital technologies has led to the collection, storage, and trading of personal data on an unprecedented scale. In the UK alone, 200 agencies are authorized to access people's personal data. China has 50,000 police officers monitoring the use of internet in the country. American company Acxiom makes over US$ 77 million every year selling data. We humans produced 1,800 billion gigabytes of data in 2011 and 68% of us globally are concerned about people or companies misusing personal data. It's hard to keep up – it would take 608 hours to read the privacy policies on the top 75 websites on the internet. (Source: The Futures Company)

In recent years, the focus on privacy (more often the lack of it) has risen significantly. Wikileaks highlighted government vulnerabilities and now the tables are turned to an extent. When whistle-blower Edward Snowden leaked details of top secret U.S. government mass surveillance programs, covering phone records on millions of Americans, and the PRISM and Tempora internet surveillance programs, many people were stunned. Others were less so. The implications of "big brother watching" have been debated by civil liberties watchdogs for years. The National Security Agency (NSA) continues to state that they are merely gathering "metadata" from phone records. Metadata, in simple terms, is everything around the conversation such as phone numbers involved, time and length of call, locations of people involved, and so on – but not the conversation itself.

2.   WHAT'S CHANGING: BUILDING A POINT OF VIEW ON THE FUTURE

At the time of writing, Edward Snowden is still in Russia on the run from U.S. government and continuing to reveal insights into government surveillance programs. Is he a hero or traitor? According to Pew Research Center, the American public is divided over the NSA leak and by extension the notion of applying the right to privacy. What is perhaps most interesting is that even though more people think Snowden has served the public interest versus harmed it, most think he should be prosecuted. [Sources: The Guardian, CNN, KPBS, Pew Research]

Divided views of Snowden's leak, support for his prosecution

Release of classified information about government phone, internet data collection program...

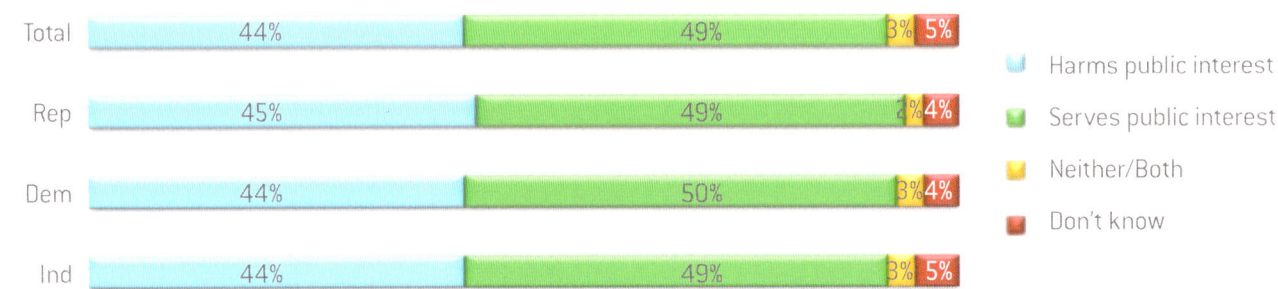

Should government pursue a criminal case against the person responsible for leaking the classified information?

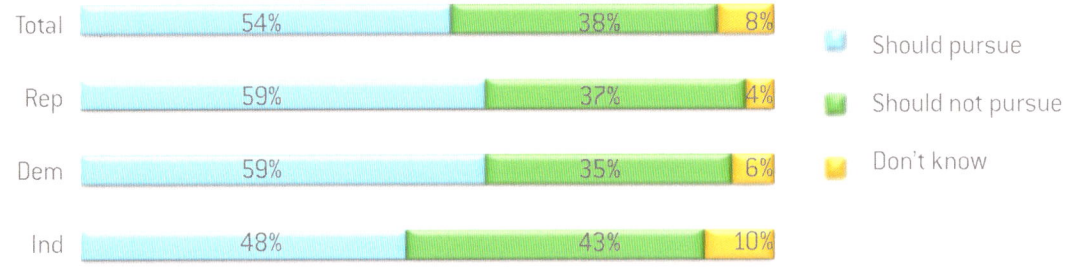

Source: Pew Research Center, "Public Split over Impact of NSA Leak," June 2013

Understandably, the public is not very happy about mass surveillance by the U.S. government; nor are foreign leaders or the tech companies whose data has been accessed. With the January 2014 revelations about potential corporate surveillance, businesses are likely to join the growing ranks of discontent. In December 2013 tech giants, including Apple, Google, Microsoft, Yahoo, LinkedIn, Facebook, Twitter, and AOL, took the unusual step of putting rivalry aside to jointly demand that Washington stops collecting vast amounts of phone and internet data, and limits powers to compel technology providers to hand over data. As the story and additional leaks continue to make the news, it seems, at the time of writing, that Barack Obama is seeking to rein in some of the spy agencies' efforts, but the genie may well be out of the bottle already.
[Sources: FT, various news sources]

2. WHAT'S CHANGING: BUILDING A POINT OF VIEW ON THE FUTURE

2.5 THE IMPLICATIONS OF A CHANGING WORLD

The fight for control & access: the evolving challenge

The world is scrambling to deal with natural resource scarcity and the explosion of digital resources. Competition is increasing at both a corporate and national level to build the capabilities that will drive long-term success, from education to R&D to new technologies and talent.

On one hand, this is driving organizations and countries to try to concentrate power and leadership in critical resources. Nationalism and protectionism over resources is increasing globally. On the other, it is driving innovation and new business models that allow greater control over resources at a regional, local, and community level to ensure long-term access and sustainability.

Driving these new approaches is a greater understanding of the cost of wasting resources along with extended value chains and a shift in the way consumers define value. Ownership is becoming less important than access through sharing and renting goods for an increasing number of people.

Yet, distributed control and access to resources is only possible due to continued technology advances – advances including nanotechnology and small-scale manufacturing technology, plus the increasing levels of connectivity which provide the means to coordinate distribution of resources.

However, some of these advances, including smart machines and robots have the potential to completely reshape the availability and value of critical resources, from labor to resource extraction.

Key drivers of the challenge 2012

- Supply-demand imbalances
- Geopolitical ambitions/ security/competition
- Conflict across business systems
- Technology advances
- Concern over global issues
- Demographic shifts
- Knowledge as a competitive advantage
- Shifting economic power – hungry giants

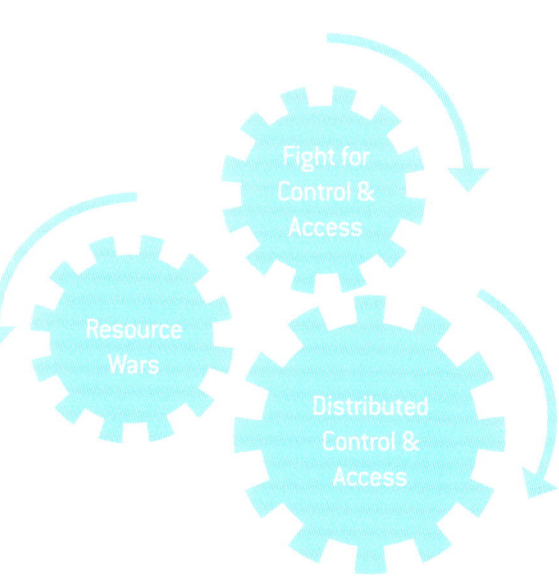

Accelerating drivers of the challenge 2013

- Technology advances: nanotechnology, small-scale manufacturing
- Connectivity/mobility – internet of things
- Focus on waste and productivity
- Increasing nationalism and protectionism
- Consumers redefining value
- Increasing power shifts towards communities and corporations
- Declining trust
- Volatility and uncertainty intensifying

2. WHAT'S CHANGING: BUILDING A POINT OF VIEW ON THE FUTURE

The implications of this evolving challenge include:

From control and ownership to shaping the network Changes in resource availability and the competitive landscape mean not only that competition will come from new directions, but also that companies will require collaborative as well as competitive strategies and tactics to succeed in the future. Firms are moving from being the central players in a physical value chain, to being nodes in open networks of value creation that span the physical and digital worlds. No single organization can meet all of its customers' needs alone. It demands a shift in mindset, from controlling the network to shaping it; and from controlling the business model to developing it with partners.

From imbalances to shifting competitive behaviors: control, conflict, and cooperation As the reality of resource imbalances – whether digital overload or scarcity of natural resources – starts to bite, nations, companies, and individuals are starting to change competitive behaviors. Three key types of competitive behavior are starting to emerge: control, where organizations and states seek to own or have significant influence over resources; conflict, which escalates from the need to control; and cooperation, where multiple stakeholders work together to address the resource challenges.

From institutional response and control to power to communities and corporations Companies are stepping up to the challenges of dealing with different types of resource challenges – partly through pressure from stakeholders, including employees who want to be proud of what their company is doing, and customers who are increasingly looking at a company's environmental and corporate responsibility credentials. Communities are also pursuing creative ways to tackle local resource challenges.

From reducing usage to rethinking usage Securing adequate natural resources to meet demand is a pressing economic as well as an environmental challenge for governments, businesses, and consumers worldwide. In the quest to free themselves from others controlling access to important natural resources, governments and business are not just trying to reduce usage – and therefore dependence – but rethinking the concept of how resources are used and what they may be replaced with. Technology advances will be critical enablers for these strategies.

From direct impact to holistic impact Food, water, and energy challenges are constantly hitting the headlines as reports from the world's leading intergovernmental organizations once again confirm the scale of world's challenges. Many businesses are now recognizing these challenges and taking them on. More and more major corporates are taking responsibility for their own impact on the environment and the societies in which they operate, and also educating consumers, who are increasingly aware of the issues themselves. The leading players are moving beyond a focus on their own direct impact to working on the impact of their entire supply chain, managing products and services from cradle to cradle.

2. WHAT'S CHANGING: BUILDING A POINT OF VIEW ON THE FUTURE

The fight for rules of engagement: the evolving challenge

More people have more choices than ever before: the impact is being felt from politics to the high street to innovation. The consequences of the democratization of everything include responsibility and accountability at an individual as well as at a collective level.

Gradually it seems that people and communities are starting to get a grip on this new found power, taking greater control of their lives from institutions which are seen as increasingly out of touch and self-absorbed, particularly in the developed world. A two-speed world is emerging with the mindset of growth driven by the BRICS and beyond, even as Europe languishes in austerity. The pressure – and need – for corporate responsibility is also increasing to fill the gaps left by institutions in society. But the work for firms is challenging as power shifts from predictable one-to-one to fluid many-to-many relationships.

While networks flourish, enabled by ever-expanding connectivity and smart machines, there is a subtle shift away from the need to just connect, to the need to be part of a community. Even as connectivity has liberated us, the associated threats to privacy and from cybercrime are driving the need for trust and control. We are slowly learning to manage the democratization of everything. The question is as power becomes more distributed, how do we continue to ensure cohesive societies – not anarchy?

Key drivers of the challenge 2012	Accelerating drivers of the challenge 2013

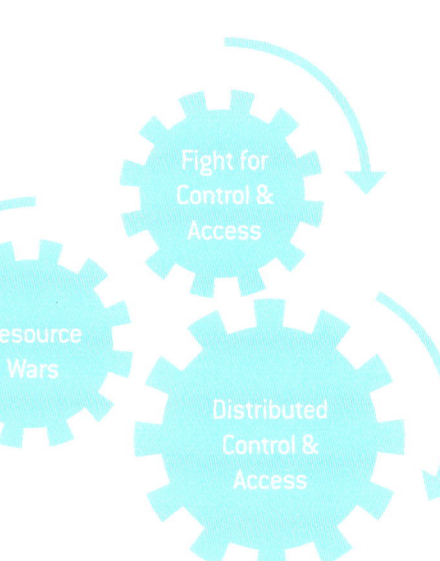

Key drivers of the challenge 2012

- The mobile time machine
- Open systems/networks
- Exploding channels of influence
- Individual choice and power rising
- Increasing interconnections
- Competition for impact
- Shifting mindsets

Accelerating drivers of the challenge 2013

- Increasing power of communities
- Connectivity/mobility – including the internet of things
- Many-to-many relationships
- Taking back control of overstressed lives
- Falling trust in institutions
- Two speed world – shifting economic power
- Beyond turf wars
- Corporate clout
- Privacy concerns/cybercrime

2. WHAT'S CHANGING: BUILDING A POINT OF VIEW ON THE FUTURE

The implications of this evolving challenge include:

From shifting economic power to competing economic and social systems Markets and competition are becoming multipolar; so too are the systems, which govern our societies and economies. Economically, the Western system of free market capitalism is being challenged by the consequences of the financial system crisis and economic recession since 2007. However, alternative political, economic, and social systems, such as those in the Middle East and China, are also under pressure from citizens wanting change. For businesses, the diversity of competitors and mindsets is exploding, from focused and hungry firms from rapidly developing economies building from their growing local markets to expand across the globe to not just for profit competitors and nimble start-ups.

From corporate and institutional clout to societal clout An increasing number of diverse shapers and influencers is competing to set the "rules of engagement" and to hold entities and individuals accountable for them. This is driving greater uncertainty and ambiguity for individuals and organizations about which rules to follow, with an ongoing and significant shift of power away from "traditional" institutions such as governments and firms towards social networks, consumers/individuals, and communities of influence.

From social networks to social everything Social needs, mobility, communities, societal impact, and connectedness are at the heart of the business environment of the future. We are moving from a world where relationships, communications, and marketing were focused on forming strong one-to-one bonds, to a world where we need to manage many-to-many relationships – at the same time as we nurture the individual, personalized relationship.

From gaining power to using power effectively People have more choices than ever before and with choices comes power and freedom: power to increasingly influence our own life whether it is personal life, work, political, religious, and social affiliations, or consumption patterns. However, it also means figuring out how to use all these choices in an effective and progressive way – the world and each of us as individuals is only at the start of this process.

From transparency to privacy and security We are spending an increasing amount of our lives living virtually as connectivity becomes an integral part of our lives. For many people being connected equals freedom, not realising that being connected also means being more exposed and vulnerable. Participating in communities of choice and social networks offers the illusion of protection and insulation, as people share ideas and opinions in their own environment, believing in many cases that the internet makes them anonymous. This is far from the case. Once data goes up on a network, the genie is out of the bottle and cannot be put back in – privacy and security as thus becoming critical issues in a networked world.

2. WHAT'S CHANGING: BUILDING A POINT OF VIEW ON THE FUTURE

The fight for value creation & capture: the evolving challenge

In a world where competition is breaking down traditional industry and firm boundaries, where the focus and basis of competition itself – or the playing field – is around customer and consumer needs, the notion of value is shifting.

Goods and services are no longer enough – experiences and solutions are required, often personalized and developed with the active participation of the customer themselves. "Pure" business benefits will not satisfy the requirement for broader positive impact on society. Even ownership is becoming less valued, particularly by younger, mobile generations for whom experiences are the status symbols that possessions used to provide. New players and needs from the growth markets of the BRICS and beyond are emerging, driving new forms of innovation and business models. New technologies, including the ability to manufacture at small scale, are reshaping where value can be created – and by whom.

This world is one where networks are required between firms to meet customer needs, and where exploding channels of influence and channels to market offer the potential to enhance or detract from the firm's value proposition. Relationships are no longer one-to-one but many-to-many as word of mouth means marketing is not only to the buyer – but also to their whole network. The question is who will control the relationship to the consumer or customer?

Key drivers of the challenge 2012

- Blurring boundaries
- The fight to own the consumer
- Increasing mobility
- Competing interdependence: collaboration & co-opetition
- Battling business models
- Disruptive innovation

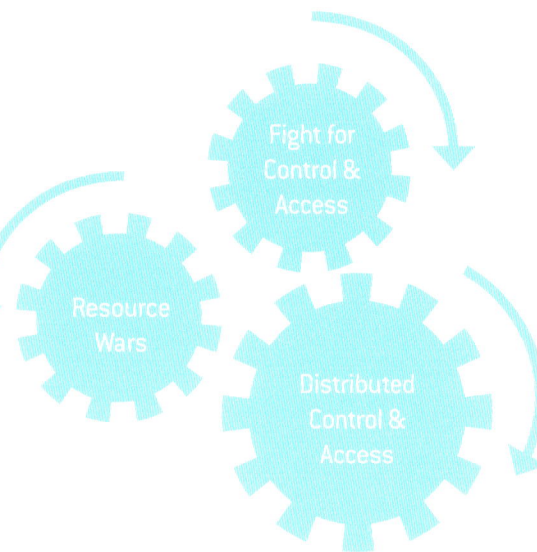

Accelerating drivers of the challenge 2013

- Co-creation is back
- Crowdsourcing/crowdfunding/ the global brain
- Consumers redefining value
- Exploding channels of influence and to market – increasing risk of losing consumer relationship
- Shared value
- Beyond scale – technology advances
- Many-to-many relationships
- Rise of BRICS & beyond
- Increasing need for security

2. WHAT'S CHANGING: BUILDING A POINT OF VIEW ON THE FUTURE

The implications of this evolving challenge include:

From concern over issues to redefining value and re-evaluating consumption In a world where competition is breaking down traditional industry and firm boundaries, where the playing field is defined around increasingly demanding customers and consumers, and where public awareness of global issues is increasing, the notion of value is shifting. Value will increasingly be determined by the customer/consumer – and their broader communities and networks – around customized experiences and solutions. There is also a shift towards defining value around the benefits delivered to all stakeholders, not just to business and the customer/consumer.

From mass (made for me) to personalized/customized (made with me) Goods and services are no longer enough – experiences and solutions are required, often personalized and developed with the active participation of the customers themselves. We are moving from a world of firm mass-customization to a world of co-creation with consumers, from a mindset of "made for me" to "made with me."

From ownership to ownerless Possessions are no longer what they once were in terms of conferring status and a feeling of personal worth, particularly for younger generations who have grown up in a world of growing affluence, but a world where their future and that of the planet are far less certain than was the case for their parents. More aware of global issues and empowered by technology to find new ways of consuming, these young people are at the forefront of an impending ownerless economy, where needed goods are rented or shared rather than owned – or simply not needed.

From one-to-one to many-to-many relationships Social needs, mobility, communities, societal impact, and connectedness are at the heart of the business environment of the future. The bottom line for business: we are moving from a world where relationships, communications, and marketing were focused on forming strong one-to-one bonds, to a world where we need to manage many-to-many relationships – at the same time as we nurture the individual, personalized relationship.

From clear channels to the fight for the interface It's not only channels of influence that are exploding, so too are channels to market. Between them, businesses and consumers need to manage a growing array of channels and intermediaries through which their information and purchase choices are filtered, aggregated, and relayed. And there are intense battles going on for control of these key interfaces. At the same time, physical channels to market are undergoing fundamental shifts as technologies drive new purchase behaviors. In this environment, the threat of losing direct consumer or customer relationships for businesses and channel operators is increasing. The challenge: how to be where your customers are and deliver value that is relevant to them where and when they want it.

From scale to distributed scale and network power In an era of mass production and consumption, scale was king. As we move into an age where knowledge dominates, technology advances will once again reshape economies and how and where production happens. At its most extreme, consumers producing their own customized goods using 3D printing in the home could make factories and some industries obsolete, while completely eliminating the need for transportation. The internet of things and intelligent materials could similarly reshape service industries, as consumers manage their own services or have sensors and computers do it for them. In this world, scale is trumped by the ability to configure flexible, agile production networks and to produce close to the location of consumption.

From winning in industries to shaping the playing fields In an interconnected world, the consumer and their extended network are at the center of value creation. The need to deliver seamless, integrated experiences based around a consumer need – rather than a product or service – is making industry definitions meaningless. Cross-industry competition is the future. Winning in industries no longer assures success; rather the challenge is to shape the playing fields of the future around consumer needs. As we said earlier, firms are moving from being the central players in a physical value chain, to being nodes in open networks of value creation that span the physical and digital worlds. Rethinking the playing fields means figuring out how to shape these networks to deliver value and realize success – in partnership with others.

2. WHAT'S CHANGING: BUILDING A POINT OF VIEW ON THE FUTURE

From leveraging growth markets to innovating from growth markets BRICS and beyond (B&B) markets are the economic growth engines of the future – and everyone wants to be there. In the past, Western companies have leveraged their portfolios and strengths, establishing positions in these markets, as well as building production and R&D bases to take advantage of cost differentials. The philosophy: adapt from the developed world. Now the philosophy is changing – driven in large part by the rapid development of the B&B markets in terms of wealth, consumption, and knowledge and the strong competitors that these regions are nurturing. Radically different perspectives on business, new business models, new innovations, and new consumer demands originating from the B&B are now challenging Western models of thinking. It is no longer "developed in Europe, assembled in China, adapted for China" but "developed in China, made in China, made for China."

The fight for values & beliefs: the evolving challenge

In a multipolar world of interconnected communities, societies, and economies, ideas are increasingly mobile, leading towards a world of multiple, sometimes conflicting, laws and regulations, codes of conduct, and traditions. There is an emerging struggle to find common values, a moral compass which will transcend boundaries and bridge divides.

As power becomes more distributed, shifts are becoming more evident, for example in terms of economic power, wealth, generations, and between institutions. Trust and collaboration have never been more important – nor more elusive. Rising nationalist sentiment is being fuelled by concerns over personal, community, and state security against a backdrop of resource challenges, economic crises, and rising inequality. Young adults are becoming disenfranchised as youth unemployment rises. Corporate values – and the ability to create value for firms and society at the same time – are becoming increasingly important, for employees, customers, and the constituencies in which business operates. The question is whether these can also positively influence societies towards common values.

The potential for a clash of civilizations is rising: a pandemic of short-term thinking is breaking out, particularly in the developed world. It will take courage and conscious leadership from individuals, communities of choice, corporations, and governments to find the common ground we need to co-exist and address shared global challenges in the long-term.

Key drivers of the challenge 2012

- Shifting cultural and generational values
- Fragmenting social fabric
- Exploding channels of influence
- Balancing consumption and frugality in an unequal world
- Tensions of globalization and fragmentation
- Falling trust and credibility

Accelerating drivers of the challenge 2013

- Values increasingly important
- Trust and collaboration critical – but lacking
- Increasing need for conscious, non-partisan leadership
- The increasing challenge of security – rising nationalism in a globalizing world
- Rising influence of the ne(x)t generations
- The legacy of crisis
- Short-term thinking
- Potential for a clash of civilizations in a multipolar world

2. WHAT'S CHANGING: BUILDING A POINT OF VIEW ON THE FUTURE

The implications of this evolving challenge include:

From single value systems to multiple, sometimes conflicting value systems In a multicultural world where mobility is increasing, people have increasing visibility on value systems other than their own. The challenge, almost daily, is to rethink and sometimes shift individual or community values to accept or integrate with those of other systems. While in some cases, this is relatively straightforward, where value systems conflict, clashes between systems are increasingly likely.

From rising quality of life to rising inequalities For several decades standards of living have generally been rising across the globe. However, inequalities too have been rising, both in the developed world and in rapidly developing economies. With greater connectivity and transparency, these divides are becoming more visible — exacerbated by the effects of global economic slowdown, they are helping to fuel social unrest.

From stable leadership and security to rising insecurity and crisis management As world leaders struggle to stabilize the global economy, there are ongoing political shifts due to elections in major economies, and increasing outcries from citizens over pressures including unemployment, austerity, and inequality. Instability and insecurity is focusing attention on short-term national issues and crisis management.

From trust in institutions to trust in communities and peers As social technologies and connectivity spread globally, we are moving from the "wisdom of crowds" to the "wisdom of friends." This shift in trust away from institutions towards our chosen communities and peers is impacting values, social behaviors, how knowledge is shared, purchasing decisions, and which organizations are favored.

From global focus to local focus The combination of the implications above with growing concerns over global environmental challenges is driving attitude and behavior changes amongst politicians, businesses, and communities. From embracing the benefits of globalization, the focus is moving much closer to home as movements to produce locally rather than offshore gather steam, along with consumers seeking to buy local both to reduce environmental impact and to sustain local communities.

From rising choices to search for meaning Growing cross-border migration, plus huge growth in global trade, tourism, social media, and information access means we have the opportunity to know more about the lifestyles, values, and beliefs of others around the world than ever before — and to choose how this influences our own values and beliefs. At the same time the world is more uncertain and insecure, with trust falling in institutions and a growing struggle to develop values and ethics for a distributed world. In this environment there is a growing search among individuals and communities to find meaning.

2. WHAT'S CHANGING: BUILDING A POINT OF VIEW ON THE FUTURE

2.6 FIVE IMPERATIVES FOR BUSINESS...

1. Rethinking the playing field: the competitive imperative

The business landscape is changing dramatically in terms of markets, industries, competitors, and consumers. There is a huge shift in power and focus to new high growth markets, not only in terms of production but also in terms of consumption and increasingly innovation. Cross-industry competition is growing as different types of players focus on serving the same or related consumer needs: your competitors are no longer just those who look, act, and think like you, doing similar activities. They now come from different backgrounds with different objectives, different business models, different value propositions, and different mindsets. New players with radical new approaches are targeting slow, cost-heavy, established players. Some may even have different purposes, not being purely commercially driven. Of course, there are also increasing numbers of partnerships, collaborations, and alliances between all the different types of players, underscoring the growing interdependence between them. What will be your playing field of the future and how can your organization today prepare to rethink not only who are your competitors, but also what is the focus and basis of this competition?

2. Rethinking the consumer: the value imperative

The value landscape – what consumers are willing to pay a premium for versus what is destined for accelerating commoditization – is rapidly changing and will continue to do so. Part of the shift is already reflected in firms moving from focusing on products to services to holistic experiences. But this is only part of the story. New consumer groups and communities are emerging, demanding with increasing desire and power to create solutions around their own needs. As such, we are moving from a world of firm mass-customization to a world of co-creation with consumers, from a mindset of "made for me" to "made with me." And possibly even "not owned by me," but "shared with me." This trend is not just impacting end consumers; the same can be said for businesses. The imperative for firms today is to understand how trends are impacting the nature of your future demand, what will be the key drivers of "value" in this new world, and what it will take for you to create and capture value. Answering these questions is critical to your creating sustainable revenue growth models for the future.

3. Rethinking how you connect: the relationship imperative

We are moving from a world of competing firms towards a world of competing business models and networks. In this shift, interactions between players are increasingly moving from being based on transactions to being built around deeper and broader relationships. The challenge for business in defining and managing ongoing relationships requires a dramatic shift from the days of optimizing self-interest at every point of time. The choices of what activities a firm undertakes – and which it does not – and how it defines and manages critical activities is moving to the forefront. Already there is an accelerating shift in emphasis from scale to agility as sources of competitive power, but this shift may go much further. What will be the critical resources of the future, who will own and control access to them, how will these resources be utilized within a firm – or accessed through a firm's extended network? These resources are not just raw materials, but also critical employees and knowledge resources. How will future business models and inter-firm networks evolve in a world of changing value propositions and playing fields?

4. Rethinking your agenda – the change imperative

The world today is increasingly divided between firms holding on to and protecting the past versus those investing in and passionate to own the future. The former often focus on incremental innovation – so as not to adversely impact past investments and short-term financial results – and rationally manage change. Theirs is a mindset of "what can we do" given our overall current position. In contrast, firms striving to own the future focus on leapfrogging investments to create new capabilities and platforms for success. They tackle innovation in every conceivable aspect of the business, rather than in products and services only. Often they have the advantage of growing home markets, e.g. domestic markets for BRICS players or high growth firms in emerging industries. These firms demonstrate a mindset shift from "what can we do" to "what must we do" across all activities to reflect whatever it will take to prepare for and own the exciting growth opportunities exploding for the future. For firms wishing to be successful, continuous change is not an option; it is a requirement for success. How prepared is your organization to compete in this environment?

5. Rethinking vision, values, and your role as a leader: the leadership imperative

Success in the future requires pro-active action, but without a clear picture of and commitment to where an organization is heading, how can a firm do anything but react? This simple reality presents a major leadership challenge of how to move vision, purpose, and values from "words on a wall," from marketing propaganda, to defining and aligning an organization around the path ahead. What is the difference between "having a vision" and "leading by vision"? Looking forward what role will future requirements – as opposed to short-term pressures and results – play in organizational and leadership mindsets and ways of working? In a world where yesterday's solutions could provide answers to future challenges, these questions may not be critical. But in our volatile, uncertain, changing world, the emphasis on leadership is changing towards leading with the future front of mind. In no way does this involve throwing away past strengths and the glue that holds together, aligns, and motivates organizations – often reflected in strong shared values. Rather it challenges leaders moving forward to think about: What will it take to be a successful leader in the future? What role will they play in the organization? What tools and approaches will they need to employ? These are all parts of the emerging leadership imperative.

2. WHAT'S CHANGING: BUILDING A POINT OF VIEW ON THE FUTURE

2.7 FIVE IMPERATIVES FOR SOCIETY...

1. Ensuring the future of the planet: the sustainability imperative

Population growth, increasing affluence, climate change, and environmental challenges will continue to strain the resources we have available to sustain basic needs and rising levels of consumption. Already we are consuming more resources than the planet can supply. This is not a sustainable situation either today or for the future generations that will inhabit this planet – and yet few nations or societies have comprehensive strategies in place to manage critical resources in the long term. However, national or regional resource strategies will not be enough. Given the substantial differences in resource endowments, population growth, and economic growth between countries and regions, global frameworks will be required to ensure long-term sustainability – and in some cases rebuilding – of critical resources. The challenge and imperative for societies will be to establish the unprecedented cooperation that this will require – at local, national, and international levels – and to shift mindsets to support sustainable resource goals, which ultimately may mean rethinking the basis of future consumption.

2. Improving the quality of life globally: the development imperative

Ensuring an acceptable and improving quality of life for the citizens of the world has many interconnected facets, from economic growth to fair distribution of wealth to education to freedom of expression to peace and security – and is the paramount goal of most societies and citizens in this world. Today we face growing challenges to continuing the progress which has been made in recent decades in improving the quality of life of people globally, including improvements in education and poverty reduction. Key aspects include rises in income inequality and poverty, falling freedoms of expression, continued gender inequality, and increasing austerity in the economically depressed developed world, plus a lack of jobs for the next generations. Looking ahead the imperative for societies will therefore be to work to address these issues to promote improvements in quality of life – which may require challenging traditional frameworks and assumptions, including models of capitalism, education, and governance. Again, international cooperation will play an important part in building quality of life in an interconnected world.

3. Bridging divides, avoiding crises: the co-existence imperative

The forces of globalization, fragmentation, and democratization are colliding to make divides within and between societies more transparent than ever, creating tensions. The World Bank estimates that 1.5 billion people live in areas affected by fragility, conflict, or large-scale, organized criminal violence, with new threats including civil unrest due to global economic shocks and terrorism. In this world, peace, security, and tolerance are becoming more critical but more difficult to find – and crises of governance are increasing. A key imperative for societies moving forward will therefore be to understand the root causes of divides and tensions, and to build the societal values, behaviors, legitimate institutions, and governance that will bridge the emerging divides and promote peaceful co-existence, today and in the future.

4. Creating legitimacy, taking action: the institutional imperative

The world is becoming more multipolar, with many different models of economic, social, and political systems and an exploding range of often competing regulations and governance systems. At the same time, trust in institutions of all types is falling, whether national government, intergovernmental, belief-based, or business organizations, tainted by scandals, vested interests, and an inability to deliver positive action on pressing global issues or even local crises. The challenge for societies globally is therefore to build institutions, both domestic and international, which are legitimate in the eyes of their constituents and citizens. But these cannot be toothless talking shops – these institutions need to be committed to building and supporting the long-term development of their nations, societies, and the interconnected global community through positive, non-partisan actions. While this will take brave choices in an uncertain and volatile world, institutional leadership is critical to the world's collective future.

5. Preparing for constant disruptive opportunities: the technology imperative

Technology advances are accelerating, impacting many areas of our lives and work, from health to resource management to knowledge creation – and they will continue to do so, often in disruptive ways. The impact will be felt not only by individual citizens or commercial players, but also in terms of the fundamental building blocks of societies including how they are organized, the demands they serve and the infrastructure they provide. Advances in areas including medicine and health, such as genetic engineering or enhanced humans, will also challenge deep moral beliefs and ethical standards. From a societal perspective one challenge is to understand the potential implications of technology advances on society. The associated challenge is to stay far enough ahead of these to be able to provide the guidance, services, and infrastructure to allow individuals, communities, and other organizations to make sense of the changes – and to support the positive deployment of beneficial advances, whether through education, new forms of governance, or investment.

2. WHAT'S CHANGING: BUILDING A POINT OF VIEW ON THE FUTURE

2.8 BUILDING A POINT OF VIEW ON THE FUTURE: THE ROLE OF SCENARIOS

The implications of a shifting world and the imperatives for business and society are big, broad, and can be difficult to translate into a point of view on the future, let alone action. The key is to find tools to help organizations to do so. One common approach is to use scenarios to construct possible and plausible future worlds within which an organization can test its point of view about how strategies and tactics may hold up in very different environments. However, scenarios are just one tool in the toolbox that organizations need to be able to use to prepare for the future – we discuss more approaches in the case studies in subsequent chapters and more information can also be found on the www.globaltrends.com website.

Given scenarios are but one tool, it is important to understand their role in building a point of view on the future. Typically scenarios have long time horizons and are constructed to present a range of different environments to highlight the fundamental changes under way. Some scenarios are designed to be complementary, as in the Shell approach, to avoid the human tendency to choose between them, given that none of the futures will develop exactly as predicted – as the National Intelligence Council's Global Trends 2030 report says, the future will likely include parts of all four scenarios they present. The point is not accuracy, but generating a different type of thinking as we outline in the next chapter.

The role of scenarios is therefore important both at the start of the process of building a point of view to open up thinking to what is possible, and to move away from short-term thinking. Scenarios are also important to test extremes, which is where much learning can be done rather than in thinking through familiar and comfortable assumptions. It can highlight issues to be explored and assumptions that need testing. As well as a starting point, scenarios can also be used at the end of the process of building a point of view on the future to test options and pathways through which an organization may move forward.

Here we offer short summaries of some of the more widely used and recent scenarios as food for thought in translating global trends into action. For more detail, consult the source documents and bear in mind that each is written with a specific point of view reflecting its sponsoring organization(s).

National Intelligence Council: Global Trends 2030, Alternative Worlds

The report "National Intelligence Council: Global Trends 2030, Alternative Worlds" is intended to stimulate thinking about the rapid and vast geopolitical changes characterizing the world today and possible global trajectories during the next 15 to 20 years. It does not seek to predict the future. Instead it seeks to provide a framework for thinking about possible futures and their implications. The tectonic shifts identified that will change how the world operates include: growth of the global middle class, wider access to lethal and disruptive technologies, economic power shifts, aging populations, urbanization, food and water scarcity, and U.S. energy independence. Based on these shifts the NIC explores how the core megatrends and game changers highlighted in the box below, and the interactions between them, could shape the world in 2030.

Megatrends	Game changers
Individual empowerment	Crisis-prone global economy
Diffusion of power	Governance gap
Demographic patterns	Potential for increased conflict
Food, water, energy nexus	Wider scope of regional instability
	Impact of new technologies
	Role of the U.S.

2. WHAT'S CHANGING: BUILDING A POINT OF VIEW ON THE FUTURE

The result is a picture of four archetypal futures that represent distinct pathways for the world out to 2030. None of these *alternative worlds* is inevitable. In reality, the future will probably include elements from all four scenarios. However, thinking through the implications of each of the scenarios creates valuable "memories of the future" that can help policy makers and corporate leaders as they grapple with the long-term consequences of today's decisions.

Four scenarios representing distinct pathways for the world out to 2030	
1.	The worst case scenario is "**Stalled engines**" in which the risk of interstate conflict rises due to a new "great game" in Asia, global growth slows, and the U.S. and Europe turn inwards, no longer interested in sustaining global leadership. The Eurozone unravels quickly, causing Europe to be mired in recession. The U.S. energy revolution fails to materialize, dimming prospects for an economic recovery.
2.	"**Fusion**" is the best-case scenario where a collaborative, interconnected West and East work together to address and solve the world's major challenges, emerging economies continue to grow fast, and growth picks up in advanced economies. Technological innovation – rooted in expanded exchanges and joint international efforts – is critical to the world staying ahead of the rising financial and resource constraints that would accompany a rapid boost in prosperity.
3.	"**Gini out-of-the-bottle**" is the scenario of extremes where inequality dominates in many countries leading to social and political tensions. Major powers are at odds; the potential for conflict rises, as some countries become big winners and others fail. The world will be reasonably wealthy but less secure. Without completely disengaging, the U.S. is no longer the "global policeman." Economic performance in emerging and advanced economies leads to less than stellar global growth, far below that in the Fusion scenario, but not as bad as in Stalled engines. The lack of societal cohesion domestically is mirrored at the international level.
4.	Driven by technology the "**Nonstate world**" actors such as NGOs, multinational businesses, academic institutions, and wealthy individuals – as well as subnational units (megacities, for example) flourish and take the lead in confronting global challenges. Security threats pose an increasing challenge as access to lethal and disruptive technologies expands, enabling individuals and small groups to perpetuate violence and disruption on a large scale. Economically, global growth does slightly better than in the Gini out-of-the-bottle scenario because more cooperation occurs on major global challenges in this world, which is also more stable and socially cohesive.

Source: National Intelligence Council, U.S.

2. WHAT'S CHANGING: BUILDING A POINT OF VIEW ON THE FUTURE

Shell: New Lens Scenarios – A shift in perspective for a world in transition

In the report "New lens scenarios – A shift in perspective for a world in transition" Shell has developed two long-term global scenarios on the possible paths for global economic development and has explored their implications for the global energy system, as well as greenhouse gas emissions.

In a volatile and uncertain world Shell suggests that it is unrealistic to view the future world through one single lens. Rather it seeks to take a range of perspectives ("lenses") on core global trends, from networks of power and the pace of change to the policy agenda and resource landscape, to shape views on how the world will look tomorrow. According to Shell, given that the world's population is steadily increasing and millions of people are climbing out of poverty, this is a world where global energy demand could potentially increase by as much as 80% by 2050.

The aim of Shell's scenarios is to bring into sharper focus the possible outcomes of today's choices made by governments, businesses, and individuals worldwide. While what is in the pipeline 30 or even 70 years from now is unknown, Shell's two scenarios offer food for thought and context for important organizational and policy choices.

Mountain	Ocean
In **Mountain** the world is full of self-perpetuating oligarchies controlling growth and information both in advanced and emerging markets. It is a place that favors the "already privileged," although from time to time young people stand up for themselves by protesting for freedom of information and social justice. It is a world of status quo, locked in by entities and people who have existing influence, resulting in system rigidities that dampen economic growth and stifle social mobility.	**Ocean** is a more prosperous and uncertain world. The global population is growing and economic growth is strong. It is a world of compromises and accommodated interests. Economic activity surges due to a huge wave of new reforms that pushes up energy demand, even as social and political tensions are rife.
Security concerns are high and the ruling elite understands that international co-operation is necessary to deal with these challenges. A slowdown in economic growth takes the pace off the energy demand. New policies unlock plentiful natural gas resources – making it the largest global energy source by the 2030s.	Market forces and society shape the global energy system much more than government policies and as power is more distributed, it takes longer for governments to agree on major decisions. It takes about 30 years longer to become carbon neutral in the *Ocean* scenario versus the *Mountain* scenario, as oil and coal remain central to the energy mix.
By the end of the century, cars and trucks are mainly running on electricity and hydrogen, while accelerated carbon capture and storage technology supports a cleaner energy system. Greenhouse gas emissions begin to fall after 2030. Carbon capture and storage receives major investments. By 2060 electricity production is carbon neutral, yet temperatures rise by 2°C globally.	However, high energy prices encourage efficiency improvements, with solar power becoming the world's largest primary source of energy by the 2060s.

Source: Shell

2. WHAT'S CHANGING: BUILDING A POINT OF VIEW ON THE FUTURE

Deutsche Post DHL: Delivering tomorrow – Logistics 2050

The study "Delivering tomorrow: Logistics 2050" released by Deutsche Post DHL in 2013 is based on the expectations and projections of 42 experts with different professional backgrounds. With eyes firmly towards the future, they explore the future of trade, business, and society as well as the implications for the logistics industry. The outcome is five different scenarios of how life could unfold in 2050: *Untamed economy-impending collapse* describes an economy propelled by unsustainable lifestyles and the uncontrolled exploitation of natural resources; *Megaefficiency in megacities* puts forward the notion of megacities becoming the world's power centers and drivers of "green" growth in the future; *Customized lifestyles* describes a world where consumers are empowered to create, design, and make their own products leading to a rise in regional trade flows; *Paralyzing protectionism* focuses on a world mired in economic hardship, excessive nationalism, and protectionist barriers as well as lagging in technological developments; *Global resilience – local adaption* assumes that the world's high consumption and accelerating climate changes lead to frequent catastrophes resulting in repeated supply failures. (Source: Deutsche Post DHL)

Industrial Research Institute: Four future scenarios and implications for research and management

The Industrial Research Institute has explored four diverse scenarios and their implications for the development of business processes, regulations, and other spheres that will impact the art and science of research and technology management over the next 25 years. The first scenario, *Africa leapfrogs developed countries*, assumes that the developed world is struggling with an inability to build new productive capacity due to increasing environmental regulations, allowing Africa to jump ahead of the developed world because it has a lower installed asset base and a better ability to leverage its natural resources. *Death of distance versus megacities* describes a world where smart cities become the powerhouses of development as resource constraints force a political and economic restructuring of the world. The third scenario, *Three roads to innovation*, reflects on how virtual work and prize-driven motivation create three roads towards innovation in society. *Everything in beta* focuses on how the collapse of the complex global manufacturing ecosystem leads to a bifurcated economy underpinned by local manufacturing. The scenarios can also be watched as short YouTube videos. (Source: Industrial Research Institute)

However, as we said earlier, scenarios alone are not enough. Data and analysis needs to be converted into insights, implications, and ultimately decisions and actions to prepare organizations effectively for the future. Organizations will require a broad range of tools as they prepare for a future which may – or may not – resemble the various possible worlds outlined in this section.

3. THINKING DIFFERENTLY – 8 PRINCIPLES FOR PREPARING YOUR ORGANIZATION, AND YOURSELF, FOR THE FUTURE

3. THINKING DIFFERENTLY – 8 PRINCIPLES FOR PREPARING YOUR ORGANIZATION, AND YOURSELF, FOR THE FUTURE

Reliable crystal balls are in short supply – which is a problem as leaders and executives need to cope with an increasing amount of change coupled with uncertainty and volatility in the environment and their markets looking forward. "If you are not able to manage ambiguity, and you need to understand everything before you start doing anything, you narrow everything and reduce your options and possibilities," Clara Gaymard, the president and CEO of GE France, told us.[5] "This will not work in the future."

Preparing an organization for the future – translating data and trends into insights and actions today – requires thinking differently. The playing field in which companies operate is changing. So too are the players, their roles, and even the game itself. Leaders who continue to act as if the old rules apply will find themselves and their organizations sidelined or left behind. Old mindsets will need to be abandoned and replaced with a fresh approach based on what the world is becoming, not what it used to be.

Easily said, but most organizations, and the executives leading them, are very busy. Most are grappling with an ever-expanding array of initiatives brought in to address a variety of short-term challenges. Many feel they barely have time to stay afloat, much less spend time on thinking differently to prepare their organizations for the long-term changes ahead. However, not taking the time to prepare for the future is a choice. A bad one. Companies such as Kodak, and more recently Nokia, failed to keep up with technological and consumer behavior changes that they themselves once led and shaped – resulting in the former case in bankruptcy and the latter in selling off the "crown jewels."

This chapter offers 8 principles for thinking differently, recognizing that the value is in the thinking and readiness for the future that this brings rather than in detailed planning as plans will need to evolve over time.

3.1 EMBRACE AMBIGUITY: DON'T JUST THINK OUTSIDE THE BOX, THROW AWAY THE BOXES

Business executives divide the world into boxes – industry boxes, geographic boxes, institutional boxes, functional boxes, and the list goes on. Why? Because boxes provide a basis for simplifying and structuring our world. They help us to break down complex problems into manageable tasks, and they help us to define the knowledge and skills required to succeed within each box. Yet in aiming to maintain simplicity through viewing the world in distinct boxes, business leaders are in fact creating a paradox, one that challenges the future of the organizations themselves as the world around them changes.

What happens when these boxes no longer reflect reality because the world we operate in no longer fits nicely into them? How do leaders and organizations need to change if what happens between the boxes becomes just as important, or perhaps more important, than what happens inside them?

The reality today is that traditional boxes no longer adequately reflect the world in which we live and operate, a world increasingly without boundaries and with growing connections and interdependence. As these connections grow at an unprecedented rate in terms of number, speed, and type, they are changing the world in which business operates. The challenge is how to prepare businesses and leaders to compete in a connected future where it is no longer enough to think outside the box, but requires throwing the boxes away.

Industries are one area where businesses have been divided into simple boxes. We have traditionally divided them based on groups of companies that look and act the same, produce the same products or conduct the same types of activities. This view

[5] *"Ready? The 3Rs of preparing your organization for the future"* by Thomas W. Malnight, Tracey S. Keys, and Kees van der Graaf, 2013

3. THINKING DIFFERENTLY – 8 PRINCIPLES FOR PREPARING YOUR ORGANIZATION, AND YOURSELF, FOR THE FUTURE

simplifies our jobs – we compete against businesses that look, act, and think like we do. Industry analysis has been a core strategy tool for many years. But for most industries today, the interesting competition is taking place across industries, not within them, and it is this cross-industry competition that is shaping the future.

If we look at the *geographic markets*, businesses generally look at the world as a set of independent countries, and ask individual leaders, or country heads, to focus on managing activities and delivering results in their market. However, it is well known that countries, not just companies compete and the connections between countries are constantly growing.

Institutional sectors include, among others, businesses, NGOs, social organizations, and governments. Traditionally each has its own role and mission – businesses make money, NGOs protect specific areas of interest, and governments provide public services, protect the interests of the population, and regulate and define laws. But again these classifications do not reflect the current emerging reality and organizations will be held back if their leaders remain within the confines of these boxes. Relationships between businesses and other institutions are evolving and becoming much more fluid and interconnected in many regards.

We traditionally look at *companies* or *firms* as independent entities, interacting with the rest of the world through a set of transactions. How does our company interact with other companies when purchasing raw materials and supplies (getting the lowest prices possible), selling products and services to customers (getting the highest prices possible), hiring employees and providing results and financial returns to shareholders? In this view, the firm is an independent entity or box with self-interest – or its own results – as its prime focus. However, in today's reality it is very difficult for any single firm to possess all of the resources or skills necessary to optimize its activities. No individual firm can own and manage all of the critical assets or supply all the products and services required to provide consumer experiences.

Finally, if we look inside organizations today, the concept of silos and their impact on reducing the effectiveness and capacity of firms is well known. These silos simplify the tasks of individual units, but this focus is once again often at the cost of the collective effectiveness of the entire organization.

The current reality is that many firms are stuck in their boxes or silos for the sake of simplicity, but the primary opportunities are associated with the interconnections and interdependencies between them. Firms and their leaders must find a way to create an environment where their organizations are not bound by silos or boxes.

What does this mean today for leaders today? First, there is a clear need to recognize that we are moving from an environment where it was useful – and often necessary – to divide the world and think in boxes to a future where the connections between the boxes offer the greatest challenges and prospects for success in the future. This does not mean that our ability and skills to manage within boxes is not important; it means that they are not sufficient and – if blindly applied – can serve as a major barrier holding back our businesses and our leaders.

Rather than seeking simplicity through traditional divides, the challenge facing leaders is to embrace the ambiguity of the growing importance of relationships and interdependence between industries, countries, companies, organizations, and functions. Increasingly opportunities and challenges can be found through these interconnections between traditional boxes, rather than focusing on optimizing performance within them. The task of leadership, rather than optimizing performance in an individual function, country, or product area, requires viewing activities as elements of an organization's network of operations and focusing on identifying and leveraging the interconnections and interdependencies within this network. This shift focuses on enhancing collective output, as opposed to individual activity output.

3. THINKING DIFFERENTLY – 8 PRINCIPLES FOR PREPARING YOUR ORGANIZATION, AND YOURSELF, FOR THE FUTURE

3.2 THINK FIRST FROM THE OUTSIDE-IN, THEN INSIDE-OUT

The comfort zone of most leaders and organizations today is to center and define the world around them based on their current activities. Most look at the world through the lens of the products or services they provide today, and think about what opportunities and challenges exist for these products or services. They look at changes in consumers or markets based on how they impact current activities. Most planning activities are based on seeking incremental improvements in current activities, thus most undertake product planning or market planning based on how they can strengthen positions and incrementally improve performance. This approach locks thinking and activities based on past decisions and choices, as opposed to openly understanding where the world is heading and how the organization can best fit into it.

The only way to understand the new reality being formed around us is by observing and analyzing it on its own terms. Preparing for the future requires moving beyond emphasizing consistency and predictability around current activities to looking at the implications of changes from the outside-in – that is, with an unbiased and open perspective on what is happening in the environment and then what it means for us – rather than focusing on optimising today's products, markets and functions. It demands an attitude of what *must* we do in the future to succeed as opposed to what *can* we do to incrementally improve results today. Doing this requires leaders to take a fresh, clear-eyed look at the world around them. This should allow them to spot the trends shaping the future so that they can work out what they need to do to claim a place in it.

This sounds simple, but it's not. Fresh eyes, and objectively looking at the world around us from the perspectives of others, as opposed to our own current reality, is difficult, if not impossible in many organizations with a strong emphasis on optimizing current performance. Most companies that define the world by what they do now – from the inside-out – find it incredibly hard to put those definitions aside to take a genuinely open-minded look at what is changing and where the world is heading. Looking from the outside-in means making your starting point for the future not what you do now, but what people will need and others will do in that future, and then understanding how your organization will need to change to meet those needs and new roles.

"We focus on what the client needs, not what we can provide," Marcelo Odebrecht, the group chairman of the large Brazilian conglomerate that bears his name, told us.[6] "If the client needs something that we have traditionally not done, our issue is to learn and deliver, therefore, dreaming the client's dream. The government of a country in Africa or Latin America, for example, may not need someone to provide only infrastructure. They may need someone that can build and operate enterprises from supermarkets to hospitals and schools."

Outside-in thinking can be generated in many ways, but the key is to take the perspective of another stakeholder in the markets in which you hope to operate in the future. This can be done through "market dives" where executives explore through primary experience (i.e., visiting and discussing issues and opportunities with leaders from other companies or institutions) and secondary research into how companies in their own and other industries/markets develop best practices and leadership in areas of interest. Another lens can be provided by experts and other stakeholders that influence the markets of interest, e.g. regulators, technology providers, NGOs, and more. Online, social, and mobile technology can offer further perspectives by allowing executives to tap into the wisdom of crowds or the "global brain" through crowdsourcing, open source movements, and open innovation. Organizations and individuals are turning more and more to these collaborative networks to find, create, and leverage knowledge and expertise, faster and at lower cost than in old "closed loop" models controlled within a company. Whichever routes are chosen, the key is to embrace the perspective of others to challenge today's assumptions, business models, value propositions, and ways of working, and to build a view of what it will take to succeed in a very different future. Again, thinking from the outside-in means that the starting point for the future is not what you do now, but what people will need and others will do in that future.

[6] "Ready? The 3Rs of preparing your organization for the future" by Thomas W. Malnight, Tracey S. Keys, and Kees van der Graaf, 2013

3. THINKING DIFFERENTLY – 8 PRINCIPLES FOR PREPARING YOUR ORGANIZATION, AND YOURSELF, FOR THE FUTURE

3.3 IDENTIFY AND ADDRESS ROOT CAUSES, NOT SYMPTOMS

Many organizations are facing a growing set of challenges that impact their short-term performance. These trends include the commoditization of products and services, slowing economic growth rates, new non-traditional competitors, more demanding consumers, and customers expecting, but not willing to pay for additional features, and the rapid dissemination of knowledge and know-how, among many others. These trends often have a direct impact on immediate performance and budgets. Given the strong emphasis on short-term results, these threats to current budgets and performance typically attract a high degree of attention and focus within organizations. While there is often not time to discuss how to prepare an organization for the future, organizations make plenty of time to address threats to current performance.

As a result of this focus on short-term performance, many organizations seek to address the current threats, launching initiatives to address immediate performance issues, as opposed to taking the time to understanding the underlying causes of these threats. In doing so, organizations typically pay more attention to the current symptoms of challenges they face, rather than diving deeply into understanding root causes.

While many leaders and organizations are extremely busy addressing short-term challenges, such firefighting based on the current symptoms of more fundamental longer-term challenges will only get you so far. At some point, leaders must start thinking about why the fires keep starting, and what they can do to prevent them. They need to step away from symptom management so that they can identify, and then remedy, the underlying cause of the problem.

A key challenge here is to ask if old ways of working, or past formulae for success, are adequate to solve future problems and pursue future opportunities. Leaders in many organizations are in their comfort zone addressing short-term challenges with tried and trusted approaches that have worked in the past. But as Einstein is often quoted as saying, "Insanity is trying the same things over and over and expecting a different result." Firefighting symptoms of today's issues often holds back organizations seeking to prepare for the future.

If this seems obvious, well, yes, it is. Why isn't addressing the root causes happening? For much the same reason that many leaders emphasize short-term performance and results at the cost of the long-term: they know how to fight fires. They're good at it. They win praise for it. They are proud of their ability to pull a team together at short notice and address and overcome immediate threats that others consider unquenchable.

Fire prevention, or identifying and addressing today's underlying root causes of issues and opportunities, is a lot less exciting than dealing with the immediate challenges of today. But the result is often exhausted organizations repeating the same activities over and over, hoping for different results.

Leaders need to think about how they take the time, and reward people, not just simply for putting out fires, but for spotting risky areas ahead of time and avoiding them entirely. While addressing root causes may take more time and effort, the solutions are much more likely to last longer. One CEO recommended "zero basing" as a way of identifying and remedying the real problems underlying business difficulties. "If we are confronted with a major issue we go back to zero," he told us. "We zero base everything and start from scratch with our thinking."

Zero basing means recognizing that if one approach has not worked, tinkering with it is unlikely to improve things. Instead, stop what's not working, look at the problem with fresh eyes, and find an approach that will. It means always having your eyes on winning the future, not on protecting sunk costs and past decisions.

3. THINKING DIFFERENTLY – 8 PRINCIPLES FOR PREPARING YOUR ORGANIZATION, AND YOURSELF, FOR THE FUTURE

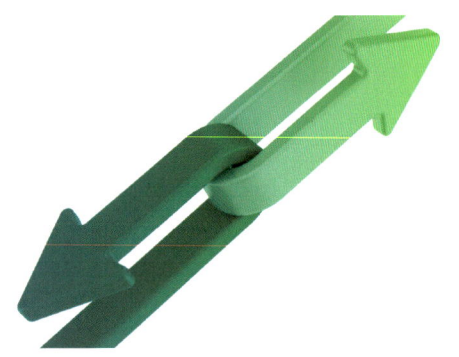

3.4 PRACTICE TWO-DIRECTIONAL THINKING

The challenge facing leaders today isn't just building perspectives from the outside-in, but also finding the right way to use these to drive action today. In addition to a strong internal focus bias, many organizations also tend to focus their thinking in the past, emphasizing historical data, results, and choices even as they are tasked with thinking about future opportunities and challenges. The only real option to challenge this approach is two-directional thinking.

The first direction is the usual one: thinking from where you are in the present towards where you want to be in the future. Thinking in this direction ensures that short-term demands are taken into account, because they can be seen on the path ahead. It helps to identify what can be achieved with the business as it is. The aim here is to focus and accelerate ongoing initiatives to ensure the foundation is in place for the business to grow – the challenge to leaders is to ask how fast this can be done rather than taking a "business as usual" approach.

Using two-directional thinking to identify sprints and marathons

3. THINKING DIFFERENTLY – 8 PRINCIPLES FOR PREPARING YOUR ORGANIZATION, AND YOURSELF, FOR THE FUTURE

Thinking from the second direction – something which must happen at the same time – means taking a view on what you think the future will hold, then identifying and choosing the direction in which to lead the organization in the future, reflecting both its ambition for success and what the leadership team collectively believes it will take to be successful in the future, irrespective of the organization's position today. From there it is a matter of looking back towards the present so that you can see what fundamental steps you need to take to get there, given the changes you've identified happening around you along the way. The aim here is to identify necessary and often fundamental changes to enable the organization to move towards its ambition, which can be used to shape and drive choices. These actions are essential to starting to prepare the organization for the future, today.

Using two-directional thinking allows leaders to identify sprints and marathons. Sprints accelerate immediate actions and priorities, while marathons shape and drive transformational change that take time to develop and implement in an organization. They also often address issues where the objectives are long term in nature and focus on learning and creating options for the future, as opposed to sprints which focus on more direct immediate results. Together, they form the foundation for continuous reshaping of the organization to prepare for the future.

One clear way to fail in most marathons is to treat and measure and manage them in the same way as one manages sprints. In other words, a clear way to kill a long-term initiative is to manage it in the same manner as short-term initiatives, as they vary in objective, focus, and timeframe.

Søren Skou, the CEO of Maersk Line, offers a good example of this in action[7]. When he took over in 2012, the company was losing millions of dollars a day and had not delivered value to its shareholders for a long time. Skou and his leadership team identified that the company had to improve its immediate profitability in the short term while making long-term changes that would stop the cycle of volatility. His response was a three-stage agenda with overlapping phases: the first restored profitability within a year ("back to black"), the second is clarifying what the company needs to be successful in the future ("finish the foundation"), and the third is considering the fundamental nature of the company and its place in the world ("defining the agenda for long-term value creation").

Having this dual perspective helps to overcome executives' tendency to discount all long-term planning on the basis that the future is too uncertain to predict, and can help to prevent leaders from making ambiguity an excuse for inaction.

[7] Example from "Bridging the Gap: How can business leaders balance short- and long-term pressures?" by Professor Thomas W. Malnight, Tracey S. Keys, and Kees van der Graaf, IMD Tomorrow's Challenge, 2013

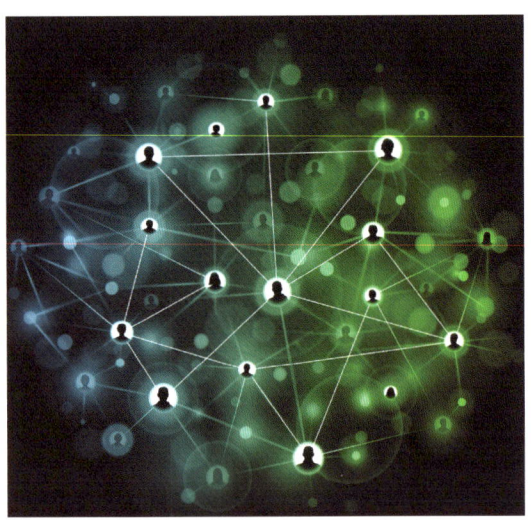

3.5 MANAGE IN RELATIONSHIPS/ NETWORKS VERSUS TRANSACTIONS

Relationships will be central to success in the future. In a world defined by networks and connections it is no longer possible to rely on one-off transactions to define what we do and how we do it.

Businesses are no longer at the center of value creation, consumers are. Organizations that move from transactions to relationships will be more flexible and better able to make the most of changes such as the rise of connected communities while managing the implications of, for example, changing social expectations of business. Companies that insist on sticking to the old ways of doing things will not be prepared for the future.

Connections and relationships are starting to play a larger role in addressing global challenges. Climate change, food shortages, inequality, and other serious issues facing the world are driving an increasing number of partnerships between businesses, NGOs, governments, and other stakeholders. In some cases these partnerships are fostering pre-competitive cooperation between competitors, for example to address the usage of critical resources to ensure their sustainability.

In other cases, emerging industries are better created through partnerships between business and government. Take electric cars as an example. Customers won't buy electric vehicles unless they can charge them easily and battery costs fall. Investing in the necessary infrastructure and in research and development is expensive and could encourage car makers to keep focusing on petroleum-driven cars instead. This means that it may be necessary for the government to provide subsidies or other support during the early stages so that electric cars can compete with their fossil-fuel ancestors. But it's in their long-term interests – and those of the planet – to help reduce our dependence on gas and oil.

Making the most of new technologies, electric cars included, will take more from business than an analysis of costs, demands, and markets. It also means developing regulations, defining industry standards, even defining industries. This will be done by representatives from a variety of sectors and industries; if you are not part of these discussions, you will not be able to shape policy – and your own organization's business model – in a way that will allow you to be a major player for those industries. You are either at the table shaping the future, or you are outside waiting to play catch-up.

No one individual or organization has all the insights, knowledge, resources, or capabilities needed to succeed in the future. To that end, leaders must engage with stakeholders inside and outside their organization if they are to identify and shape the opportunities and challenges ahead. This requires rethinking relationships from a learning perspective and finding new ways of working together. When business is about connections, how those connections are made and maintained matters.

As one CEO described it: "We are building relationships that result in enduring benefits not only for us, but also for those we interact with every day. If I do something where I win and you lose, you're not going to come back. Getting this right means creating a sustainable relationship where we both win."

3. THINKING DIFFERENTLY – 8 PRINCIPLES FOR PREPARING YOUR ORGANIZATION, AND YOURSELF, FOR THE FUTURE

3.6 FOCUS ON CO-CREATION

The connected consumer and customer increasingly define value. Gone are the days of the passive consumer, with more and more consumer power being exerted in not only demanding "what I want" and "where I want it," but also "how I want it." The focus of transactions and consumption is shifting from emphasizing products, to related services, to the overall consumption experience.

Today there is a strong trend toward commoditization of many products and services, while, simultaneously, large premiums are being paid for other products, services, and experiences. A key challenge looking forward is for organizations to focus on two factors, what consumers and customers are willing to pay premiums for and what they are looking for in the companies they associate with. For both of these factors, co-creation with consumers and customers plays a major role.

Experience deals not only with the products or services provided, but also the reputation, legitimacy, and attractiveness of the providing organization itself. Consumers and customers are increasingly evaluating whether they want to be associated with an institution as part of the transaction process. In this regard to succeed in the future, executives need to also shape and influence their business' extended networks and the exploding number of channels to the consumer to build reputation, trust, loyalty, and ultimately their license to compete. Consumers not only want to be engaged, they care about whom they are engaging with.

End-user customization may ultimately consign mass consumption to the past as more people decide that they want to choose the color and trim on their sneakers, as Nike allows, or select which parts of a digital newspaper they want on their tablet. Co-creation, which takes customization several steps further, is on the rise as more consumers demonstrate the awareness, interest, and ability to provide input throughout the design process.

Consumer involvement in business does not have to stop with product design. Business models, too, are being reshaped by consumers. Take crowdfunding where consumers invest in a business or product so that it can be created and they can buy it. This and other crowd-led approaches can create organizations that blur the line between consumption and business.

The movement toward co-creation reflects a major change in the business model and mindset of many organizations. From a world of mass production (efficiently producing standard products) there have been shifts toward mass commoditization (efficiently producing standardized components that can be combined in expanding the variety of offers) toward customization (with the producer producing products of services based on the specific requests of individual consumers or customers). Co-creation goes a step further involving individuals, or communities of individuals, in the process of innovation and product or consumption experience design.

3. THINKING DIFFERENTLY – 8 PRINCIPLES FOR PREPARING YOUR ORGANIZATION, AND YOURSELF, FOR THE FUTURE

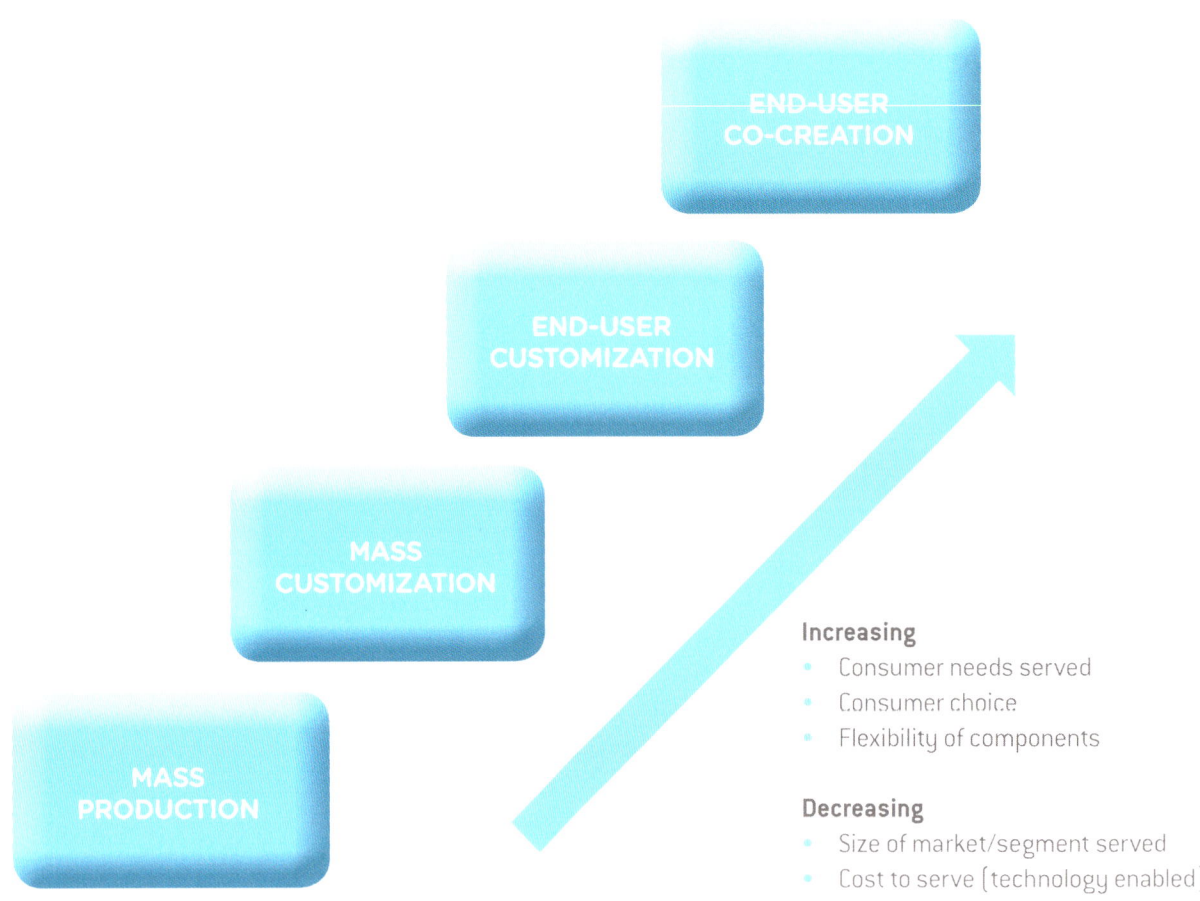

Increasing
- Consumer needs served
- Consumer choice
- Flexibility of components

Decreasing
- Size of market/segment served
- Cost to serve (technology enabled)

Benefits to companies of moving towards co-creation include not only the potential for expanded sales, but also significant opportunities for deeper consumer insights and understanding which can support innovation and other internal processes. At the same time, co-creation fundamentally changes the relationship between suppliers and buyers. As this relationship becomes more connected and interdependent, the potential benefits to both the supplier and consumer expand. Applying old formulas to new situations will not work; instead leaders need to manage the co-creation of new answers. The challenge is to identify both what will be needed to succeed and applying these new approaches and solutions. For this, leaders need a mindset that prizes curiosity, continuous exploration, and creativity.

3. THINKING DIFFERENTLY – 8 PRINCIPLES FOR PREPARING YOUR ORGANIZATION, AND YOURSELF, FOR THE FUTURE

3.7   ALIGN PURPOSE AND PROFIT

Traditional operational rigor and discipline will obviously remain critical and necessary for success in years to come but they will increasingly not be sufficient for success in the future; leaders must also address people's need for meaning and purpose, societal expectations, and demands on organizations. Paul Polman, CEO of Unilever, highlights the importance of purpose in his call for responsible capitalism as an enabler of future success.[8] "There is a huge opportunity for businesses that embrace this new model of responsible capitalism, but it does require a different approach. This goes well beyond CSR. It's about moving to a licence to lead."

In discussions at one large investment bank, one senior executive commented, "Investment banking – although this sounds terribly arrogant – relies on the fact that it gets the best brains. Probably per square inch, there is a greater brainpower in this building than you could find in most any other building anywhere. We attract these individuals because we pay them through the nose. And we retain them because we continue to pay them through the nose." Contrast this approach with a view espoused by Anand Mahindra, the chairman of the Mahindra & Mahindra Group, "We will challenge conventional thinking and innovatively use all our resources to drive positive change in the lives of our stakeholders and communities across the world, to enable them to rise."

The interesting factor in this comparison is that Mahindra, with its purpose driven approach, has been far more successful, with its stock price rising over 20 times since it introduced its approach (compared with six times for the Indian stock exchange). Mahindra explained how this approach worked inside the company, "We follow three basic tenets: accepting no limits, thinking alternatively, and driving positive change in everything we do. These pillars guide all our actions and business decisions from deciding whether or not to enter a new field or planning a portfolio of services."

Finally Mahindra continued, "The biggest malaise of the 21st century is a lack of meaning in people's lives. You have to tell people to work toward a transcending goal, toward something more than achieving the next quarter's earnings."

The role of purpose is in clarifying why an organization exists, what is its reason for being and why should others, employees and other stakeholders, wish to interact with the organization. Is this association just another job or transaction, or is there a deeper motivation associated with the relationship? In an increasingly interdependent world, and also one that is searching for meaning, the role of purpose is playing a bigger and bigger role is shaping successful organizations for the future.

Talking about purpose does not mean talking about charity, but rather viewing it as a primary driver for developing and engaging motivated employees, and identifying and focusing on market opportunities and needs where there is significant potential for shared value creation. The logic is that operational discipline and rigor is necessary but not sufficient for success; purpose is an additional requirement for success in the future.

So why does your organization exist and why would any stakeholder want to associate with, or trust, you in a world of growing choice and consumer and societal power?

[8] Foreword to "Ready? The 3Rs of preparing your organization for the future" by Thomas W. Malnight, Tracey S. Keys, and Kees van der Graaf, 2013

3. THINKING DIFFERENTLY – 8 PRINCIPLES FOR PREPARING YOUR ORGANIZATION, AND YOURSELF, FOR THE FUTURE

3.8 EMBED CONTINUAL CHALLENGE, AVOID COMPLACENT COMPLIANCE

Throughout this report we highlight changes that are taking place in, and fundamentally altering, the environment in which organizations will operate in the future. Yet even in a rapidly changing world, strong resistance to change can be found in many organizations. Often leaders do not resist the notion of the need for change, they just resist when it comes to their changing. In the face of change many leaders, and individuals, find reasons to hold onto old ways of working. However, whenever the pace of change in the outside world is faster than the pace of change inside, the organization is essentially falling behind.

Some individuals suggest that there needs to be a burning platform in order to drive change. Unfortunately often this burning platform is associated with immediate operating or financial crises. When operating in such a pressured situation, the major challenge is that there is a significant reduction in options available, as the driver for change is often addressing the crisis, not preparing an organization for the future. An alternative to waiting for a burning platform internally is to recognize that the need for change is driven by the need to stay ahead of the changes occurring in the organization's environment, essentially continually preparing the organization for the future rather than being driven by what we described earlier as the short-term trap. It means moving from a reactive view of change, resisting change until forced to do so, and then focusing the change on the immediate crisis or challenge, to a proactive view of change, focusing on staying ahead on a continual basis.

However, an important barrier to moving from a reactive to a proactive view of change is organizational complacency, which can come in many shapes and forms. Most leaders will be familiar with people who insist that they are doing everything that they can given the limits of their job, or who promise that they have initiatives underway to address a particular issue, meaning that there is no need to give it further consideration – even if those initiatives are adding no real value. Clear indications of complacency can be seen in a pervading mindset of "We are a big successful company and will remain so," or "Don't worry, we have time." What all forms of complacency share is an underlying preference for holding on to the past and sticking with the old ways of doing things. Tackling this issue requires leaders to build the courage, capacity, and commitment of individuals right across the organization so that they are all willing and able to challenge the status quo. Courage, in this scenario, is the understanding that stepping beyond traditional boundaries in every day work is accepted, and indeed expected. Courage is about building a drive to stay ahead, and not just keep up with changes taking place around an organization. It is about having leaders put as much commitment into ensuring sustainable success as they do into meeting short-term financial and operating metrics and targets.

Capacity requires having the tools and support needed to provide an effective challenge to traditional ways of working. It means developing a leader's and an organization's capacity to continually listen, learn, and understand what is happening in the environment, with all stakeholders, as opposed to being driven by internally focused, backward looking financial and operating metrics. Capacity involves developing the capability to move from data on what is changing, to understanding and developing insights on the implications of the changes for the organization, as a basis for developing a proactive action agenda to stay ahead.

Commitment is a personal and organizational passion to contribute to the long-term success of the organization. Commitment is driven by a belief in the purpose of the organization, including the benefits for its multiple stakeholders. It involves developing shared, aligned, and focused ownership of the agenda to keep the organization ahead of the changes taking place in the emerging future environment. Addressing complacency requires leaders to foster a workplace that provides the space for innovation and challenge, where people take ownership of the future direction of the firm. It's not about engaging in disruptive exchanges and internal battles and competition. Rather, the aim is to create an environment where employees are encouraged – expected, even – to constantly challenge the way the organization works in order to continually improve and strengthen its operations.

4. PREPARING BUSINESS FOR THE FUTURE

4. PREPARING BUSINESS FOR THE FUTURE

Chapter four is the first of four chapters that focus on how different types of organizations – business, governments, NGOs, and society – are translating macro implications into specific insights and actions to prepare for the future. These chapters are designed to allow executives to better focus on the opportunities and challenges facing a relevant peer group and to learn from the case studies and examples.

Within each chapter the first subsection provides some context, looking the key trends that are impacting the landscape within which each type of organizations is operating. The second subsection focuses on detailed case studies, offering insights into how different types of organizations – in this chapter, businesses – are approaching the challenges of preparing their countries, economies, and societies for the future. Each detailed case study explores the organization's thinking and actions using the lens of the 3Rs model below: what are the key trends and implications impacting the organization; how did these drive rethinking the playing field; how did the organization redefine their ambition (vision, purpose, targets, measures) as a result; what were the options they considered in building an agenda for action; how did they reshape how they worked; and what is the ongoing process of learn-act-learn-adjust.

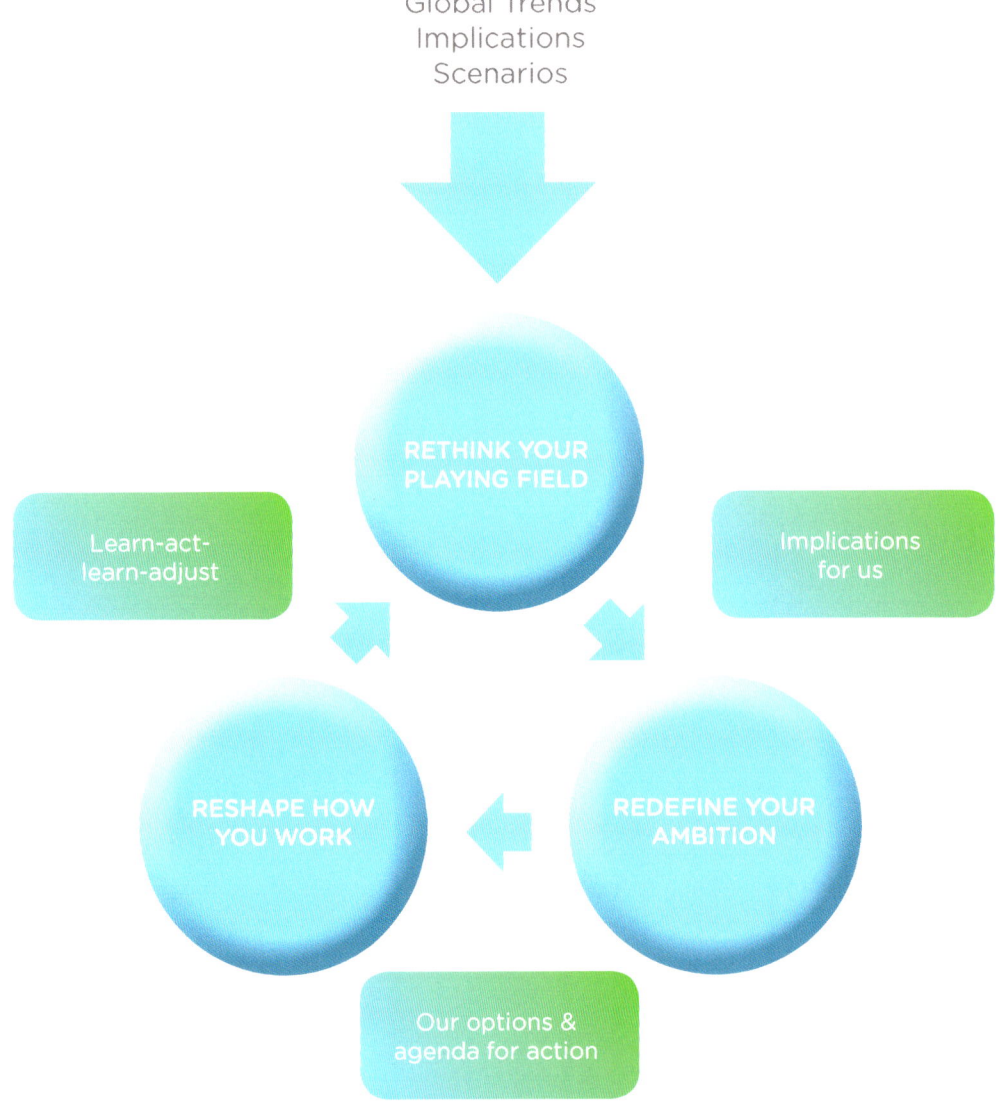

Global Trends
Implications
Scenarios

RETHINK YOUR PLAYING FIELD

Learn-act-learn-adjust

Implications for us

RESHAPE HOW YOU WORK

REDEFINE YOUR AMBITION

Our options & agenda for action

4. PREPARING BUSINESS FOR THE FUTURE

Beyond the case studies, the third subsection provides some "in brief" examples of how other organizations are preparing for the future in specific areas, e.g. tackling the challenge of generational shifts. The fourth subsection highlights food for thought examples, which are designed to provoke thinking on some of the key challenges facing organizations in the future, which many businesses are grappling with, e.g. avoiding the pitfalls of disruptive technologies, and embracing responsible capitalism. Finally, in subsection five, we draw together some insights to take away from these examples using the 8 principles introduced in Chapter 3.

4.1 RETHINKING THE BUSINESS LANDSCAPE

Today competition is increasingly taking place across industry boundaries, and there are clear differences in mindsets, business models, and focus between developed market companies and those from high growth markets. In addition, virtual/digital and physical worlds are becoming ever more intertwined and the pressure on businesses to step up to a greater role in society is increasing. Let's briefly explore what this means for the business landscape looking forward.

Competition is changing. That does not simply mean that it's becoming tougher, although it is, or that businesses in developed markets need to prepare for vigorous competition from those in high-growth economies, although they must. What it means is something much more fundamental: the very nature of competition is changing. In the future, the greatest threats to established businesses will not come from traditional competitors but from those in apparently unrelated fields. A bank might be pushed aside by a mobile phone company, say, or a record business by a computer manufacturer.

This change has come about because cross-industry competition is intensifying as the industry boundaries that have traditionally divided companies collapse. Business leaders who continue to focus on competing with their organization's direct peers are at severe risk of being blindsided by newcomers outside their frame of reference.

The music industry is a prime example of this. In the past, competition happened between record labels, which owned the content that artists created, and controlled how consumers could access it. Today, they are barely part of the picture. Competition is
coming from tech companies like Apple, which enable consumers to experience music wherever and whenever they want, alongside the various other mobile apps they offer. Their focus is not music per se, but owning consumers' mobile devices – or rather, their pockets.

Competition is also coming from social media channels such as YouTube, which offer another perspective: Why just buy and listen to music when you could make and upload your own music or share and discuss it with your friends? Again, music is just one part of a much bigger connected lifestyle and community.

The products, services and value propositions of each of these players vary dramatically, as does how each makes money. But from a consumer's perspective, this is the competition around music. Who will win – and who would you invest in: record labels, mobile device companies, or social networks? And by the way, the question is not about winning in an "industry" any more – it's about winning the battle to deliver on consumer needs, expectations, and relevance.

This change is not unique to music. Senior executives across multiple industries and geographies are facing similar challenges. However, not all have grasped what this implies: rethinking competition means focusing on what consumers want, not what your industry has historically done. Take pharmaceuticals: many leaders of these companies define their competitors as other pharmaceutical businesses, because this is what they have always done. What happens if you start thinking from the perspective of the consumer who is a person living a full life in which their illness is just one component; patients are people who are healthy and who want to stay that way.

4. PREPARING BUSINESS FOR THE FUTURE

So who are this company's competitors, if we accept that staying healthy and well is the overriding consumer need? They would include Nestlé, known for food and drink, but redefining itself as a nutrition, health, and wellness company; WebMD, an internet medical information provider; and Nike, which promotes a healthy life through sports. You can also add IBM, which is working on managing personal healthcare information, and L'Oréal, with its "cosmeceutical" products marketed as things that can help people to look and feel good.

This does not mean that anyone producing any product is a potential competitor. What it means is that business leaders need to assess their playing field by starting with what consumers/customers want, not the products and services that their organization currently provides. Rethinking the competitive playing field in this way raises an important challenge for many players used to going it alone. Few, if any, companies possess all of the resources, knowledge, or offerings required to deliver on complex consumer needs without the involvement of others. Companies are therefore likely to require a mix of collaborative and competitive strategies to succeed, building, and leveraging connections across many types of organizations.

Dealing with cross-industry competitors is only one challenge for business. As noted earlier competition across geographic markets is also shifting the business landscape. High growth developing markets are home to a whole new generation of companies taking to the global stage, for example Tata and Mahindra in India, Lenovo and Haier in China, and Cemex in Mexico. In the IT services industry firms like Infosys, Tata consulting services, and WIPRO have pioneered the concept of a "global delivery model" challenging IBM and Accenture to redefine their business models. Brazil's Embraer is giving Canada's Bombardier a run for its money in regional jets. China's Huawei is challenging global telecommunications companies including Siemens, Ericsson, Alcatel-Lucent, and Cisco. They all started as local companies in rapidly developing markets before going global. Now they offer competition to multinational corporations, not just in emerging markets but also in developed markets. (Source: HBR Blog Network) Look out for these companies to drive trends and innovations for the future, including new business models that will reshape the basis of business in many markets.

These may not however be physical markets. Virtual and physical worlds are increasingly intertwined, demanding that business interact with customers and consumers across an increasing array of connected channels. The consumer can no longer be regarded solely as an individual, self-determining entity. They are connected, for better or worse, and that means that the business-consumer relationship extends beyond the "target" of the relationship, i.e. the consumer, out to the extended networks and communities of which that individual is a part. This is a world where word of mouth and, increasingly, word of mouse dominate. There is nothing new about using our friends as source of best advice. What is relatively new is the way more and more people do it, moving consumers away from "wisdom of crowds" to the "wisdom of friends." Trust is the currency of the connected world.

On the other side of the equation firms are increasingly becoming part of open networks of value creation, collaborating as well as competing with others to deliver experiences and solutions for customers and consumers. The bottom line: we are moving from a world where relationships, communications, and marketing were focused on forming strong one-to-one bonds to a world where we need to manage many-to-many relationships – at the same time as we nurture the individual, personalized relationship.

A further driver reshaping the business landscape is societal needs. With some multinational corporations the size of not small, but medium-sized economies, they are often richer and more powerful than the nations that seek to control them. Rapid corporate and financial market deregulation and globalization since the 1980s has allowed such firms to build broader and deeper international networks of markets and operations. Today, these companies have significant impact globally, including on: consumption, raw materials, economic growth, employment, capital flows, trade, politics, the environment, and even popular culture.

Yet many of these companies seem to be decoupled from the economies and societies in which they operate and sell their products and services – the primary focus of end of the twentieth century capitalism was maximizing returns to shareholders. Waves of corporate scandals, accusations of human rights abuses, environmental degradation, and more have damaged consumer and societal trust in companies. NGOs along with the increasing power of consumers, social networks, and media have highlighted many of these transgressions. This has translated into huge pressures on corporations – whether or not good citizens – to actively

4.   PREPARING BUSINESS FOR THE FUTURE

address the needs of all their stakeholders and to become involved in the key challenges facing society, including climate change, poverty, health, and resource management.

Quite simply these challenges are too big for single organization or institution to address alone, and business has a role to play. The last ten years have seen a growing momentum among companies to focus on corporate social responsibility – although many companies are still wrestling with what really is "good citizenship" and "responsibility"? Businesses have also been partnering with governments, international organizations, and civil society, for example through the UN's Global Compact, a strategic policy initiative for businesses that are committed to aligning their operations and strategies with ten universally accepted principles in the areas of human rights, labor, environment, and anti-corruption.

Companies at the forefront of addressing the needs of business and society simultaneously have also been successful in creating win-win partnerships. As more companies embrace the new reality, their influence, and that of their leaders, will increase relative to other shapers and influencers. Some of the leading businesses have embraced this reality and made an impact, with many of the others either active on societal challenges or actively reaching out to global society, e.g. Mahindra & Mahindra and Unilever.[9]

Given these trends, how are businesses preparing for the future? Rather than looking at examples by industry, an increasingly outdated framework, let's explore them using the framework below, which looks at companies based on their primary country of origin/headquarters, and whether the products and services that they provide are primarily physical or virtual/digital in nature. We also include a B2B and B2C lens:

High growth markets	Leveraging growth to own the future B2B: Cemex (betting on collaborative innovation) B2C: Mahindra (combining purpose and profit), SABMiller (integrating sustainable development)	Leveraging population size to own the game: leapfrogging B2B: Infosys (collaborating for the future), Alibaba (poised to go public) B2C: Tencent (taking on the world)
Developed markets	Redefining businesses, reinventing industries B2B: DSM (reinventing mature industries), GE (embracing innovation and the maker movement) B2C: BMW (reinventing personal transportation for a connected world), Nestlé (moving from food to nutrition to health and wellness)	Building and owning the platform/fighting to own the interface B2B: IBM (keeping on transitioning), Disney (engaging with the internet) B2C: Amazon (owning the consumer), Facebook (fighting for the interface)
	Physical	Virtual/digital

In the following case studies and in brief examples we explore how these companies are preparing for the future.

See "The Global Trends Report 2013" for more information on how these two companies are taking action

4.   PREPARING BUSINESS FOR THE FUTURE

4.2   PREPARING BUSINESS FOR THE FUTURE: CASE STUDIES

BMW: redefining personal transportation

Implications of global trends Like many other industries, the financial crisis wreaked havoc within the automotive sector, changing it irrevocably. Some might argue this was a good thing – but whatever your point of view, vast structural changes were rapidly accelerated. During the 2008-2009 crisis, two of the three big automakers in the U.S. – General Motors and Chrysler – sought and secured government bailouts. Meanwhile, sales in 2009 slumped to their lowest levels in 27 years.

Even as the crisis was starting to play out in 2007/2008, the industry was facing other challenges. The traditional days of manufacturing and selling vehicles that fulfilled consumers' needs for transport and aspirations for status are a thing of the past. Today's landscape is one where the central role of the vehicle itself is less important. "Tell me what car you drive and I will tell you who you are" is increasingly nuanced. In some regions of the world and particularly amongst younger generations, the car is no longer a "status" symbol.

Personal transportation is increasingly focused on service and experience – enabled by technological advances and peer-to-peer networks. Demand for vehicles with reduced environmental footprints continues to grow and even the behemoths of the industry are playing in this space – or planning to do so. Peer-to-peer solutions mean new options for consumers not necessarily based on private ownership. Furthermore, the automotive industry may be heading the same way as software: instead of "software as a service" (SaaS) think "transport as a service" or "TaaS."

A growing global middle class means change for the markets of the future as both population and affluence grows. China now surpasses the U.S. in total car sales and is officially the world's largest automotive market. The ability to connect anywhere, anytime, including from a vehicle is redefining the way we want to spend our driving time – at the wheel or connecting? These phenomena have attracted new players into the market, including the likes of Google and Tata Motors and venture capital investments in new entrants RelayRides and Wheelz. (Source: The Energy Collective)

Even as high growth markets offer the potential for increased sales, other factors including traffic congestion and rising urbanization are depressing demand and fuelling the rise of alternative transportation solutions such as car-sharing. An ageing population along with heightened awareness of environmental issues are also having a negative effect on the demand for high performance cars as well as driving innovation, including the next generations of electric vehicles.

Looking ahead, consumer needs will likely reshape of the future automotive market – and the players competing in it – around the following value proposition: "smarter, greener, cheaper, safer personal transportation."

4. PREPARING BUSINESS FOR THE FUTURE

The emerging automotive landscape

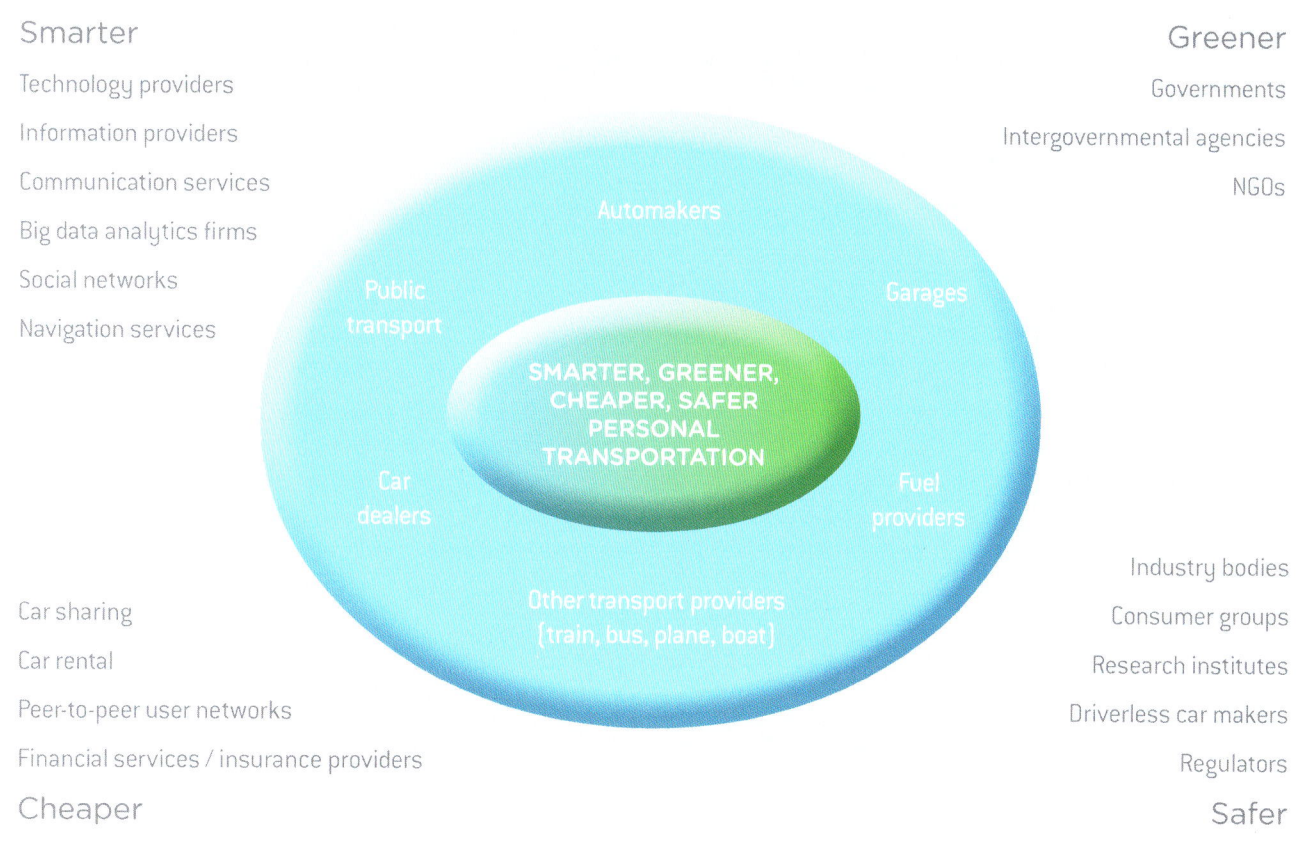

Smarter

Technology providers

Information providers

Communication services

Big data analytics firms

Social networks

Navigation services

Car sharing

Car rental

Peer-to-peer user networks

Financial services / insurance providers

Cheaper

Greener

Governments

Intergovernmental agencies

NGOs

Industry bodies

Consumer groups

Research institutes

Driverless car makers

Regulators

Safer

Rethinking your playing field BMW has long been renowned for its advanced research and innovation – the car has always been the center of focus. However, when Norbert Reithofer, a manufacturing specialist, was appointed as CEO in 2007, BMW faced challenges that technological innovations would not solve. Manufacturing costs were going up at the same time as automakers had to invest large sums to meet emissions standards, while demand for high performance cars was slipping. BMW's survival as an independent company was under threat.

Reithofer launched a project to understand the threats to the company and what was impacting its profitability, identifying some 200 economic, technological, and social trends that would help shape the company's future. While the project was controversial, because many could not understand why the company that had been so successful, needed to change, Reithofer explained: "It became obvious that our competitive position was at stake. We couldn't carry on as before." (Source: Fortune)

4. PREPARING BUSINESS FOR THE FUTURE

Redefining your ambition The project led to BMW revising its mission and strategy, aspiring to become the "world's leading provider of premium products and premium services for individual mobility." Strategy No. 1 which came out of the project set a date of 2020 for this ambition. While the new direction recognized BMW's belief that the luxury car market would continue to thrive, it also highlighted two needs that its buyers were showing increasing interest in: sustainability and interconnectedness. "There is no doubt," Reithofer told Fortune, "that sustainable thinking and action is an essential condition for long-term growth, higher profitability, and the development of new customer segments and pioneering technologies."

The next question was how to redefine personal transportation for the 21st century in order to realize the company's ambition. Reithofer brought together some of the company's most innovative thinkers in spring 2008, challenging them to do just this. Over nine months, the team travelled globally, visiting cities, drivers, and urban planners, to explore their options. The result was two parallel paths of action: the first was evolutionary and centered on the traditional business, where the activities would focus on efficient combustion engines and the associated technologies. The second path was revolutionary, focusing on electric powertrains, recyclable materials, and software-driven mobility services.

Creating options The key initiative from the latter path was "project i" which stood for intelligent, innovative, and international. From 2009 the project has seen a series of innovations, from the experimental Mini E which offered BMW the opportunity to learn about batteries and owner usage, to the concept i3 car introduced at the Frankfurt Auto Show in 2011, which highlighted the company's moves into completely new areas. The i3 boasted a carbon fiber body, lithium-ion batteries which would provide power for 100 miles and were rechargeable to 80% in 30 minutes, an electric engine, and a lower frame of aluminum. While two large pivot doors were perhaps the most obvious physical innovation, the intelligent part of the "i" was perhaps most striking: networked software would allow drivers to find charging locations (including summoning a mobile charging truck), swap to a fuel-powered car for longer trips, operate the navigation system, and connect the driver to other devices, including smartphone apps to facilitate mobility.

All these innovations have opened the door for BMW to create new options for growth and preparing for a more connected, sustainable future. However, to finance and underpin this focus, it also maintains a very strong focus on delivering today. Strong growth in China and the U.S. boosted the company ahead of its 2012 financial targets and may bring its goal of selling 2 million cars by 2020 four years forward.

Reshaping how you work Moving into new areas has required BMW not just to embrace network thinking for its customers, but also for itself as an organization. The i3's carbon fiber body was the result of a joint venture with U.S. based SGL Automotive Carbon Fibers with which it built a US$100 million manufacturing facility in Washington State. A unique feature of the plant is that it uses hydropower from a nearby dam – embedding the aspiration for sustainability further into the company's operations, beyond the design of the car itself.

To keep ahead of mobility services and improve features for customers the company has also gone way beyond its manufacturing roots to set up a US$100 million venture capital operation in New York to invest in these services. Investments include services to find and book parking spaces, and charging stations for electric cars. In another joint venture with Sixt, BMW now offers its own premium car sharing service, DriveNow in Munich, Berlin, Düsseldorf, and San Francisco – featuring electric and petrol-powered BMW cars. However, one thing has not changed at BMW: the need for profitability. The i investments have already been recouped and Reithofer told Fortune: "If everything goes according to plan, we will earn a reasonable margin per vehicle and make money on every car. We don't build vehicles that are not profitable."

Learn-act-learn-adjust BMW is continually raising its standards and refining its offerings to create premium driving experiences as well as practical, sustainable, intelligent cars such as the concept i3. The learning from its new areas of focus are be continuously applied to new models, such as the i8 grand tourer, a performance car due in 2014, which offers combined gas and electric motors. Expect it to also offer some new and interesting services for the driver of the future.

Sources: "BMW gets plugged in" by Alex Taylor III, Fortune, April 1, 2013; www.bmw.com; "You want a car with what? Redefining the automotive playing field" a Global Trends Industry Brief, March 2012; www.us.drive-now.com; www.de.drive-now.com

4. PREPARING BUSINESS FOR THE FUTURE

DSM: reinventing mature industries

Implications of global trends Royal DSM, the materials and life sciences company, began life 110 years ago as a coal mining business. Since then it has transformed itself a number of times in response to changing trends and demands. Key areas of change that the company is focusing on include global shifts, climate change and energy, and health and wellness. Specific trends within these areas include: an ageing population, population growth, resource constraints, healthcare costs, urbanization, energy security, food security, wealth, and sustainability. In its Company Factbook 2013, DSM highlights some of these challenges, many of which are due to population growth, with an expected 9 billion people on the planet in 2050 versus just over 7 billion in 2013. This population is not only ageing, it is also becoming increasingly urban and wealthy. The key trends they identify include:

- *Global shifts:* urbanization and economic prosperity are promoting dietary changes and increased spending on housing, transport, lifestyle, and energy. Increased demand around the world is also driving a higher use of natural resources, underlining the need for further efficiency improvements.

- *Climate and energy:* climate change is a reality and future energy is a central challenge for society both in terms of how to create it and how to get more out of it. In this context, customers are seeking sustainable value chains with higher yields, reduced waste, lower energy use, and fewer greenhouse-gas emissions. At the same time there is a growing focus on renewable energy sources.

- *Health and wellness:* the drive to improve well-being and the increasing life span among the growing middle classes of high growth economies contrasts with the continuing struggle to effectively feed populations in less well-off parts of the world. There is an increasing need to address core health issues, whether through nutrition, medicines, or lifestyle improvements.

Rethinking your playing field DSM's goal is to find ways that it can solve some of the challenges that these changes pose. It aims for innovative solutions in the areas of health, nutrition, and materials.

"We focus on life sciences and materials sciences," Feike Sijbesma, the company's chairman and CEO, said. "That's about improving health and food where we can, but it's also about things like making cars lighter, which helps with the energy and climate change problem."

Redefining your ambition In the company's long history, it has moved from coal to fertilizers, to petrochemicals and plastics, to life sciences and materials sciences. DSM's mission and vision today is described in two sentences: "Our purpose is to create brighter lives for people today and generations to come" and "We connect our unique competences in life sciences and materials sciences to create solutions that nourish, protect, and improve performance." Its logo summarizes this in the words "Bright science. Brighter living."

When Sijbesma spoke about his vision, he said: "We look at the issues facing the world. Based on these we developed a strategy, a direction. And we hold firmly to that: staying the course. Our values are key in the way we implement our strategy. And since in our case this resulted in a transformation of our company we needed not only to adjust our portfolio but also our culture and leadership style." Taking this into account, he continued: "We are much more than a chemical, or nowadays a life sciences and materials sciences company. We transformed the company, but a key part of that transformation is improving things for the people on this planet and the planet itself, not just the business alone."

"If you look at success as a pure economist, then you may well conclude that profit is the highest value," Sijbesma opines. "From a purely economic point of view, that might be true. But companies are also a part of society, and you cannot measure the success of one without reference to the success of the others. We need to learn that we have to create value on three dimensions simultaneously, all balanced equally: societal, environmental, and economic. I call that People, Planet, and Profit."

4. PREPARING BUSINESS FOR THE FUTURE

Creating options When shifting the company's portfolio to create options and opportunities for the future, Sijbesma noted in an interview with the Financial Times that this is not easy, for example the company's move away from petrochemicals in the late 1990s and early 2000s. Timing is important he said, if value is to be realized and reinvested: this means making the shift while a business is still contributing a substantial amount of profit, even though this may be difficult.

Creating options for the future also requires substantial investment in innovation – including establishing clear metrics for success. In its Factbook, the company sets out its goals for innovation to 2015: by 2015, DSM wants innovative products and solutions to account for 20% of its total sales. Innovation sales, defined as sales created by new products and applications introduced in the last five years, accounted for 18% of total sales in 2012.

Innovation is not only driven within the company, but through open innovation partnerships across the world. DSM also has venturing activities, which allow it to invest at arm's length in innovative start-ups in health, nutrition, and materials areas, while providing these companies with access to knowledge, resources, and networks. For example, it has invested in Novomer, which, according to DSM's website, is a revolutionary new materials company pioneering a family of low-cost, high-performance, sustainable plastics, polymers, and other chemicals. Novomer's technology allows carbon dioxide and other renewable feedstocks to be cost-effectively transformed into polymers, plastics, and other chemicals for a wide variety of industrial markets.

Reshaping how you work Redefining the company's mission and the areas in which it operates has required changes in attitudes, capabilities, skills, and personnel. Sijbesma told the Financial Times that senior executives tend to be good at leading a company's existing portfolio. However, that does not mean that they will work well in the new portfolio. As the company transitioned out of petrochemicals a number of senior executives needed to be eased out.

Along with reshaping the company, Sijbesma is also reshaping his role as the head of a large company. A strong advocate of moving all manufacturing to being 100% renewable, and of international standards for assessing companies' impacts on the environment and society, he recognizes the responsibility of business to help address environmental and social issues globally – rather than depending on governments to act. Not content to wait until retirement, he wants to have a hand in shaping how the world responds to these issues while he is still running a company which aims to make a difference in these areas.

Learn-act-learn-adjust Looking forward, in addition to constant innovation, Sijbesma also sees a need to address the changes being driven by the next generations of employees who grew up assuming that team working, collaboration, and (virtual) social connections are a normal part of life – attitudes that will have an impact on organizational structures as well as work habits, according to Sijbesma.

"They have completely different ways of using information and working, and I see that as a challenge, perhaps not in five to ten years but maybe in 10 to 15 years," he said. "We will need to organize ourselves differently into a much more networked style of organization, which is different than the way we are structured now with one guy on the top.

"While we would not do that today, because the organization works well, we can't postpone the change for ten years. We are already experimenting around this today, but I think in 10 to 15 years, we're going to have to address the real issue, because then those guys are not 15 years old anymore. They will be 30 and getting into more senior positions here.

"This change to a next generation which is much more used to working in flat networks provides many opportunities to deal better with the increasingly fast, complex, and global nature of businesses."

Sources: *"Ready? The 3Rs of preparing your organization for the future"* by Thomas W. Malnight, Tracey S. Keys, and Kees van der Graaf, 2013; www.dsm.com; Company Presentation 2013 and Company Factbook (from company website); interview with Feike Sijbesma, Financial Times, August 18, 2013 by Matt Steinglass

4. PREPARING BUSINESS FOR THE FUTURE

Tencent takes on the world

Tencent is the largest internet company in China measured by value (approximately US$50 billion) but still a relatively unknown company for many people in developed markets. Founded in 1998 by Pony Ma and four college classmates, the company was initially built around what is still its core product, the QQ instant messenger service.

Implications of global trends The World Wide Web along with its continuously developing technological interfaces plays a crucial role in all aspects of our lives. It impacts and influences what consumers know, want, and how they interact with brands, products, services, and businesses. It shapes future attitudes and the behavior of businesses, individuals, and society. Social technologies are now ubiquitous, a fact of life for many people around the world. More than 2.7 billion people are connected to the internet, and more than 1.73 billion people use social networking sites. The world of social technologies may be extremely crowded, with Facebook still the king of the networks, but new and innovative players are not deterred from seeking their own space in it. In a world full of young generations constantly craving new, better, and different ways to connect there is always room for improvement and innovative thinking. "No change – no customer" is the rule for companies in the social technologies space – and for those unafraid of change, the opportunities are huge.

Rethinking your playing field Against this backdrop, Tencent has succeeded in creating a more lucrative business model than its Western peers who are all facing the issue of making good profits. In fact, it makes more money than Facebook; Tencent's revenues for the first half of 2013 were US$4.5 billion, with a gross profit of US$2.5 billion while Facebook recorded revenues of US$3.3 billion and a gross profit of US$935 million.

What makes Tencent different? Today many internet companies build a customer base by giving things away whether search results or social-networking tools, seeking to monetize their user bases through online advertising. The textbook examples of this are Facebook, Twitter, and Google, while other companies try to make money through services, e-commerce, or premium applications. Tencent is not immune to giving services away. However, rather than making most of its revenue from advertising, it attracts users by offering online games along with other services such as WeChat. Once users are hooked on a game, this opens the door for the company to provide paid-for, value-added services such as weapons, costumes, and online VIP rooms. The result: Tencent's revenue mix today is 90% from user fees, and less than 10% from advertising.

Redefining your ambition The driver for redefining its ambitions and business model was fierce competition in China, which demanded that Tencent bolster its business through new innovations. The company responded by launching its own Twitter-like micro-blogger service, WeChat, an app that is similar to the American mobile social networking app WhatsApp. WeChat combines multimedia chat with a social network and had a growth rate higher than Facebook 24 months after launch.

Unlike local Twitter-equivalent Sina Weibo and Facebook-equivalent RenRen, Tencent does not restrict its services to China. It has rebranded and upgraded its WeChat app and made it available to international users with significant success: in just four months, between May and September 2013, its overseas user base doubled from 50 million to 100 million. The growth has been attributed to a worldwide marketing campaign, featuring Argentine footballer Lionel Messi, which has expanded the product's reach across 15 different markets, and boosted its popularity among users outside China. Moreover, the introduction of WeChat has increased Tencent's brand value tremendously. In Millward Brown's 2013 BrandZ™ Top 100 most valuable global brands Tencent rose 52%, making it one of the top 10 Risers in the BrandZ™ top 100 list, moving up from 37th to 21st place.

Creating options To create new options for future growth, the company has partnered with leading domestic and foreign brands, including Vinagame in Vietnam and LevelUp in Singapore, as well as Epic Games, Activation Blizzard, and Zynga in the U.S. In addition, Tencent has diversified its business into social networks, web portals, e-commerce, and multiplayer online games. With its sharpened focus on mobile internet experiences and aggressive investments in products, services, and marketing, the company aims to keep pace with China's rapidly growing internet user base as well as expanding its reach globally.

4. PREPARING BUSINESS FOR THE FUTURE

Reshaping how you work International expansion required that Tencent address the same challenges as domestic companies from other countries must do when they go overseas. Like their international counterparts, Chinese companies need to establish and maintain an emotional bond with local consumers, across multiple markets. Tencent has understood and addressed the cultural challenges involved by, for example, releasing localized platforms, investing in local companies, making franchise and licensing agreements, and by delivering text, voice, and video in nine different languages. It has also pursued an aggressive acquisition strategy to increase its visibility in the international online world and is, unlike Baidu (the world's leading Chinese language search engine and ranked as the world's fifth most popular website by Alexa.com in 2013), offering English language products and services.

Learn-act-learn-adjust Tencent has also applied learning from its growth inside the company. Some years ago it made the decision to go with an open platform approach to respond to the fierce competition in the industry, and in 2012 it re-organized its business units into six new business groups as well as a wholly-owned subsidiary focusing strictly on e-commerce business. The next big moves for Tencent are introducing mobile social games and micro-payments for services like taxis, among other innovations to generate revenue streams from its mobile app WeChat.

Sources: Think Business, The Economist, Lighthouse Insights, Tencent, Value2020, TechNode, Mayalsian Wireless, Computerworld, eMarketer, Internet World Stats,Chinese Internet Companies and Their Quest for Globalization, http://www.linkedin.com/today/post/article/20131104184701-13518874-who-has-1bn-users-is-about-to-overtake-facebook

4.3 IN BRIEF EXAMPLES OF BUSINESSES PREPARING FOR THE FUTURE

Amazon's growing ecosystem Once a website for simply selling books, almost 20 years later Amazon offers tens of thousands of different products along with the ability to self-publish quickly and at low cost, borrow electronic books through a club, and increasingly a range of B2C and B2B technology-based services. Amazon is in a league (almost) of its own, building on foundations of a superior use of technology and consumer data, and constant focus on building consumer relationships which make it one of the most trusted brands globally. It has built what is best described as its own ecosystem by embracing partnerships and external innovation. Ultimately its success lies in the consumer, and because consumer tastes change rapidly, platforms such as Amazon must adapt almost instantly through innovation. The company's "Earth Kaizen" program offers just one example of innovation to meet consumer demands for sustainable business practices. The program brings together employees at all levels of the organization to work on a large number of environmentally focused projects, each delivering reductions in energy consumption and waste. One project focused on rethinking conveyor belts, led to them being automatically shut down when not in use, resulting in a 30% reduction of kilowatt-hours of power used in one fulfillment center alone. (Sources: "the Age of the Platform" by Phil Simon; Amazon)

SABMiller working to make a difference "Making a Difference through Beer" is SABMiller's slogan and working to make a difference, they are. Sustainable development is integral to how they do business, with a number of initiatives running across its companies and in the countries in which it operates. Their list of 10 sustainability priorities focuses on issues ranging from wellness in terms of responsible drinking, and the fights against HIV/Aids and for human rights, to reducing the use of resources, including water and energy, and efforts towards zero-waste operations. SABMiller aims to reduce water use per hectoliter of lager by 25% by 2015, and energy use by 50% by 2020. Beer brewer Grolsch has changed to lightweight bottle caps, which are 17% lighter and contain 19% less steel, saving over 100,000 kg of steel per year while cutting transport costs and reducing environmental impact. In Africa, Chibuku, which is sold in cardboard boxes, provides an affordable and better-produced alternative to homebrewed alcohol. It costs up to 40% less than mainstream beer, with flavors adapted by market to local tastes, and to use locally produced ingredients such as corn and malted sorghum. In the Netherlands CO_2 emissions were cut by 22% between 2007 and 2012 through initiatives including modifying road transport operations. (Sources: SABMiller, Bloomberg, Innovia Technology, Packaging News)

4. PREPARING BUSINESS FOR THE FUTURE

Disney engages with the internet Animation giant Disney has a poor track record in digital media with a failed internet portal and other online flops, contributing to loss in 17 of 18 recent quarters. But times are changing, and with the famous line of space ranger Buzz Lightyear: "To infinity and beyond" it appears that Disney is launching itself into a new era, trying to win over the internet. The company's latest video game, Disney Infinity, does what no other Disney game has done before by uniting all the Pixar characters, and moving them from strictly console games towards a network of mobile games. Users can access the platform via a single login across all Disney games, connecting them to news feeds, profiles, a place to store badges or rewards, and ways to play with other fans. The vision is to allow a young player to build his or her own world using a console game, such as Nintendo Wii, Playstation 3 or Xbox 360, and then later access the game through the Disney Infinity mobile app by simply logging in with the player's Disney ID. Disney plans to have two to three new characters star in new mobile games each year. The company does not initially anticipate substantial revenues, but at this point reach and engagement is the key. (Source: Fast Company)

GE reinventing itself for another century From the light bulb to locomotives to MRI screeners, nuclear reactors, commercial lending, health care, and kitchen sinks, few companies have the reach and brand recognition of GE. The company is the single surviving company on the original 1896 Dow Jones industrial index, in part due to its long tradition of mergers and acquisitions. In 2009 GE announced that it would bring back jobs that in the past had been moved to cheaper factories overseas. The result has been cheaper and faster production due to a domestic supply chain. Over the past decade GE has doubled its R&D budget, and is also investing in the "industrial internet," an effort to harness big data to make more efficient machines. GE Open Innovation has also launched two open innovation quests to bring the additive manufacturing ("maker") community together to design and create around new challenges. (Sources: Forbes, GE)

IBM keeps on transitioning Once seen as a hardware dinosaur, IBM has since become the model of successful technology transitions in a software-dominated world. Today IBM is defined by innovation and cutting edge technology. To get to this point it used disciplined experimentation, innovating in incremental steps, and testing progress at each stage to ensure that it was able to learn quickly, make good decisions, and get better results at the least expense possible. This included making targeted acquisitions, such as the recent purchase of SoftLayer Technologies to bolster its cloud services portfolio. In 2012, Newsweek voted IBM the greenest company in the U.S. IBM's "Smarter Planet" initiative helps clients measure and reduce their resource consumption, and save money at the same time. It also practices what it preaches: at its Zurich lab water that cools a supercomputer is used to warm nearby buildings. (Sources: Newsweek, Forbes, FT, IBM)

Infosys collaborating for the future The Indian multinational provider of business consulting, IT, and outsourcing solutions has a long list of prestigious awards that attest to its success, from the Global Telecoms Business Innovation Award to being identified as one of the top 25 performers in the Caring for Climate Initiative by the UN. Infosys brings life to great ideas and enterprise solutions through initiatives such as Infosys Labs, which is a global network of research labs and innovation hubs. Infosys Labs collaborates with leading national and international universities, technology partners, and industry research consortiums. In 2012, Infosys Labs published more than 334 research articles. The Infosys Foundation focuses on support to the underprivileged sections of society by heading programs in areas of healthcare, education, and rural development among others. (Sources: Infosys, India Times, Karnataka.com)

Alibaba poised to go public China's online retail market is growing exponentially and expected to surpass that of the U.S. in the near future, with B2B e-commerce giant Alibaba currently controlling almost 80% of the country's internet shopping market. The Chinese company operates two marketplaces: one in English, tailored to global importers and exporters in China, and one in Chinese that focuses on suppliers and buyers trading domestically in China. It has also launched B2B sites in six non-English language versions, including Spanish and Russian. The company's online marketplace, Tao Bao, continues to grow: similar to eBay, it has an offshoot called T-mall, where domestic and a growing number of foreign companies such as Marks & Spencer can set up online storefronts to try and tap into the Chinese market. Other services include AliPay, AliExpress for consumers, Juhuasuan, which is a group-shopping platform in China, and Alibaba Cloud Computing. Alibaba plans to go global and public, the latter with an IPO expected in 2014 that some say could rival that of Facebook's. (Sources: Alibaba, CrunchBase, BBC, Reuters)

4. PREPARING BUSINESS FOR THE FUTURE

Cemex betting on collaborative innovation Through a range of acquisitions, Cemex grew itself out of the Mexican market and onto the global scene establishing a production network across North America, the Caribbean, South America, Asia, Europe, and Africa. However, the company fared less well in the recent financial crisis, with its share price dropping dramatically as both Citigroup and Credit Suisse cut their ratings. The sale of its entire Australian operations allowed Cemex to stay afloat by refinancing its debts. Faced with the need to improve effectiveness and efficiency the company's innovation team introduced an internal collaboration platform called Shift, designed to make the company more innovative, efficient, and agile by letting employees share opinions, information, experiences, knowledge, and best practices – in essence, a social network with a business focus. Less than two years after the introduction of Shift, Cemex has seen positive changes as ideas and suggestions bubble up through the network. Communities of interest have formed to tackle challenges common to their locations, markets, and skills. Projects are moving forward without the traditional barriers such as live meetings. The payoff is lower cycle times, faster time to market, and real-time process improvement. (Sources: Cemex, Reuters, Business Day, Open Source)

Facebook, what's next? After a tumultuous time with its IPO and the controversies surrounding the company in 2013, Facebook's Q4, 2013 was a success and topped all estimates. 53% of its revenue came from iPads, smartphones and other mobile devices. (Source: Business Insider) Although some may claim that Facebook is merely riding the wave of users moving to mobile computing, it is nevertheless essential for the company to continue to have a good handle on advances in technology usage. So far it has proven to have it. In terms of advertising, Facebook's level of targeting is unparalleled versus competitors. The retargeting platform Facebook Exchange (FBX) with its real-time dynamic ads has been proven to outperform static ads: click-through rates are 1.9 times higher, conversion rates have doubled, cost per click is 16% lower, cost per acquisition is 52% lower, and return on investment is 1.8 times higher. (Sources: Yahoo Finance, Inside Facebook) However, the big question is whether Facebook knows its users' needs as well as it knows its advertising technology. Rumors of the network's impending demise may be overdone, but it is clear that it is losing traction among younger users. Facebook: What's next?

4.4 FOOD FOR THOUGHT ON THE FUTURE LANDSCAPE OF BUSINESS

The tech visionaries reinventing the world

When Elon Musk, CEO of electric vehicle leader Tesla Motors, suggested the "hyperloop" to connect Los Angeles and San Francisco moving people at speeds up to 700 miles an hour rather than an expensive high-speed train link, critics immediately said that it would not work. The concept underpinning the idea has been around for many years and the technology challenges remain substantial – plus, they said, "Musk is not going to take it forward himself, which means of course that he does not believe in it." His response was that he simply did not have the time to focus on this as well as building up his other businesses – rather he wanted to start a debate around a potentially transformational idea in personal transport.

Musk is not alone in proposing transformational ideas. A number of technology's best-known billionaires are turning their attention to some of the world's biggest challenges including resource scarcity, transportation, energy, space, and healthcare, seeing nascent market opportunities, and in the process pushing forward the frontiers of science, technology, and human capacities. The question is whether they have the appetite and resources to push such radical ideas through, reshape industries, and build popular support for dramatic change. Or is it simply hubris? Whether or not these so-called visionaries succeed, the debates around the ideas that they are promoting could well challenge how the world operates in future.

On the space front, pioneer Peter Diamandis, has co-founded Planetary Resources which aims to mine asteroids, as well as creating the X Prize Foundation for the first privately backed suborbital flight. His partners in the venture include Google billionaires Larry Page and Eric Schmidt. Meanwhile Musk is moving on to the challenge of space flight to Mars after his company SpaceX became the first to launch a privately-funded rocket to dock with the International Space Station. Another tech leader chasing his dreams of new era in space is Jeff Bezos, CEO of Amazon and founder of Blue Origin, a company dedicated to help enable "anybody to go into space." The company is committed to decreasing the cost and increasing the safety of spaceflight with news reports in 2013 suggesting that Bezos is discussing business opportunities with Virgin Group founder Richard Branson, who is Chairman of Virgin Galactic, another company aiming to open up space travel to paying customers.

Personal transport closer to home could be radically reshaped by the impending era of intelligent, electric and, driverless vehicles, with again the founders of Google making an appearance at the forefront of driverless technology, alongside Musk's Tesla Motors electric vehicles. Sergey Brin of Google is also focused on the challenge of food scarcity, largely funding a project to grow beef in a laboratory – the first taste of which was unveiled in London in August 2013.

Peter Thiel, a co-founder and former CEO of PayPal, concentrates much of his philanthropic donations on breakthrough technologies, including anti-ageing research and the technological singularity, when machine intelligence will exceed that of humans. He is also funding the Seasteading Institute whose mission is "to establish permanent, autonomous ocean communities to enable experimentation and innovation with diverse social, political, and legal systems."

These ground-breaking initiatives funded or led by the tech billionaires could change the world, and create whole new industries. With the decline of government funding for advanced research in many countries, the dismantling of corporate labs that used to lead the way and the rise of short-term thinking in both business and politics, the ambition of these entrepreneurs is plugging the gap, pushing the bounds of possibility.

However, The Economist warns that the tech elite may risk public opinion turning against them, as the young and wealthy of Silicon Valley become more involved in politics, more visible through lavish events, and more recognized as paying low corporate tax rates and employing far fewer privileged geeks than companies of similar sizes. This coming "tech-lash" could see the "oligarchs" (and their "troops") regarded with as much dislike as bankers and oilmen, the magazine contends, as the money culture of tech, its links to national security surveillance scandals, and its elite lifestyles infuriate the broader population. Already the bubble may be starting to burst. Residents of San Francisco have been protesting against the cocooned, WiFi'ed luxury coaches used to transport elite techies to the headquarters of Facebook, Google, and others, holding up public transportation along the way even as their passengers push up city property prices beyond the reach of many. Broken windows and eggs in local neighborhoods may be just a first step towards a tech-lash where tech visionaries become regarded as plutocrat illusionists. (Sources: FT, Wikipedia, The Economist)

4. PREPARING BUSINESS FOR THE FUTURE

Responsible capitalism – myths and realities[10]

Many companies have started rethinking their playing field in the light of changing social expectations, with business leaders describing a wide range of approaches, as set out in the business-society ladder.

The Business-Society Ladder

	Focus of societal activities	Responsible unit	Output/impact on the business
Level 1:	Philanthropy or propaganda; meeting legal requirements	CSR as a separate function	Charitable activities and/or "greenwashing" promotions; compliance with regulations
Level 2:	Focused partnerships in areas of significant mutual benefit	CSR as a separate function, with authority in specific areas	Strengthens firm operations; delivers mutual benefits to society and firm within targeted areas
Level 3:	Shaping strategy, business models, and activities to ensure "permissibility"	Core element of top management agenda; CSR integrated into operations and strategies	Reshapes how the business operates; earns the license to operate and grow in the future
Level 4:	Shaping the objectives and direction of the company; aligning the company's core purpose with societal needs	Core element of top management agenda; CSR integrated into operations, strategy, purpose, and direction	Fundamentally reshapes why, how, and where the business operates; delivers shared value/prosperity; impacts all decision-making

Even before we start describing the levels in the ladder above, it is worth noting that there are firms which conform to regulations governing their industry but have little further interest in social responsibility. The only exception to this comes when a chairman or CEO uses his or her role to support pet projects or individual causes.

The leader of one such company told us: "If a person thinks that sustainability is more important than profit, they should quit and work for an NGO. We are not an NGO, we are a company and the best thing that we can do for society is to generate sustainable wealth." This sums up the prevailing attitude in such firms rather nicely.

Level one Companies in this category as well as meeting legal requirements often make a lot of noise about their CSR activities, but these deliver only marginal benefits to either society or the business. Most have established a CSR function but have not given it the power to make any changes to the firm's core activities or operations. They may be involved in corporate philanthropy, although this is likely to be limited to financial donations. CSR activities are usually designed to maximize marketing and public relations opportunities, rather than with a focus on their underlying substance; the results can look like propaganda or "green washing."

[10] *"Ready? The 3Rs of preparing your organization for the future"* by Thomas W. Malnight, Tracey S. Keys, and Kees van der Graaf, 2013

4. PREPARING BUSINESS FOR THE FUTURE

Level two Organizations at this level have a true social responsibility agenda, typically involving active partnering with other stakeholders in areas of significant mutual interest, as well as a philosophy of taking responsibility for its impact on society. These partnerships, which tend to be built around a sustainable agenda, deliver significant benefits to all involved. CSR activities are usually supported or driven by a separate function, as at level one, but at this level the function has real authority and the ability to shape the firm's activities, albeit only in certain specified areas.

There are many examples of level two partnerships at Unilever (tea), Nestlé (coffee), Mars (cocoa), and other companies which purchase significant quantities of farming raw materials. While the firms require sustainable supplies of raw materials to support their businesses, the supplying farms and communities can benefit from investment in improving productivity and sustainability. These partnerships provide a natural linkage to meet the interests of the businesses and society.

For example, Mars, a major global food manufacturer with a strong commitment to social responsibility, depends on a sustainable supply of high-quality cocoa. With demand for cocoa rising, supply is not expected to keep pace given that it is sourced through labor-intensive processes, mostly in developing countries. Farmers there struggle with aging trees, pests and disease, depleted soil, and poor access to training and other resources. In response, Mars has launched a cocoa sustainability program to help farmers produce better crops and make more money for their families. The ultimate goal of this initiative is to create a sustainable supply of quality cocoa, with farmers being empowered to reinvest in their businesses and communities.

Level three At this level, leaders have a clear vision of what it will take for their business to be successful in the future, and are shaping and reshaping their company accordingly. This vision incorporates a strong understanding of the relationship between business and society. At this level, senior management, not a specialized function, has responsibility for the business's overall relationship with society, which means that it is integrated into strategy development and can shape the business's agenda.

The result is that the firm's direct and indirect impacts on society become integral to organizational activity. Often leaders of such companies will talk about these activities in terms of developing permissible business models and earning the license to operate and grow in the future.

Unilever is a good example of level three. The company has made a commitment to halve environmental impact at the same time it doubles its business. A key element of this effort is their Sustainable Living Plan.

Level four Shared value, also known as linked prosperity or a host of other names, shapes the agenda of companies operating at this level. This approach, recently highlighted and popularized by Michael Porter in a Harvard Business Review article, involves rethinking and altering not just what the firm does, but its fundamental purpose, the value it creates, and how this value is shared.

We met many firms whose leaders told us they intended to take this approach, but our experience suggests that many leaders and firms talk about being at levels three and four, while their activities seem more closely associated with levels one and two. Many companies talked about creating shared value scorecards, for example, but these were often applied only after they were sure that they had met the traditional financial and performance scorecard.

We encountered two firms that were clearly operating at level four: Ben & Jerry's, the U.S. ice-cream company now owned by Unilever, and Mahindra Group, a multinational business based in India. They place their relationship with society at the center of their strategies, using it to shape not only how they operate, but also what activities and businesses they undertake.

For more detail on how companies are rethinking their relationship with society, see "Making the Most of Corporate Social Responsibility" by Tracey S. Keys, Thomas W. Malnight, and Kees van der Graaf, which was published in the December 2009 issue of McKinsey Quarterly.

To read more about shared value, see "Creating Shared Value" by Michael E. Porter and Mark R. Kramer, which was published in the January 2011 issue of Harvard Business Review.

4. PREPARING BUSINESS FOR THE FUTURE

Nokia's demise

There was a time that Nokia was synonymous with cell phones and its 13-note ringtone was the soundtrack of the mobile revolution. Yet, in less than ten years it has gone from market domination to selling off what used to be core assets.

Nokia produced everything from paper pulp to rubber boots to cables long before it entered the world of consumer electronics. As a company it has successfully reinvented itself time and again, although it did face serious financial problems in the late 1980s and early 1990s, much due to heavy losses in the television manufacturing division along with a portfolio of businesses that were just too diverse. After a major overhaul to address these issues, in 1992, the new CEO Jorma Ollila made a crucial strategic decision to concentrate solely on telecommunications. The restructuring had left it a streamlined and decentralized company with a deep pool of innovative and creative employees, strong leadership, world-class product innovation, advanced technologies, and economies of scale. In subsequent years it built on these foundations to power, becoming recognized globally as a success story and an excellent example of innovative and disruptive business behaviors.

The company's history in consumer electronics began in the 1980s, when it decided to enter the market, including making telephone handsets. In partnership with a pair of Finnish telcos it paved the way for radical change in the cellular industry, starting the shift from analog to digital technologies by introducing the first ever digital telecommunications network, using GSM technology. In 1991 it finally had its breakthrough when the Finnish Prime Minister used a Nokia phone to place the first ever call on a commercial GSM network — and with that text messaging was also born. GSM's high-quality voice calls, easy international roaming and support for new services like text messaging (SMS) laid the foundations for a worldwide boom in mobile phone use. GSM technology came to dominate the world of mobile telephony in the 1990s, leaving the analog mobile champion Motorola caught flat-footed by the switch to digital networks that offered the potential to streamline diverse and messy analog systems globally.

By 1998, Nokia was the leading mobile phone handset maker in the world supplying more than 22% of the global market, a market share that would reach an all-time high of 40% in 2008. The Nokia phone not only had better functionality, it also had better design than its competitors and was the handset of choice for consumers. Between 1996 and 2001 Nokia's turnover increased by a factor of nearly five, from €6.5 billion to €31 billion.

The turning point in the company's fortunes came in 2007 when Apple introduced the iPhone. Steve Jobs had got everything right: the iPhone quickly became the consumer gadget of choice for the next generation — and even their parents. Nokia fans still bought Nokia's new N95 smart phone but compared to the iPhone the design, content, and operating system were simply not good enough. While Samsung introduced its hot-selling Android-powered models to keep up with Apple at the premium end of the market, Nokia went the other way, deciding to focus on commoditized phones in developing countries. The company increased its market share but unfortunately not its long-term outlook.

In 2008, ironically at the height of its market share, Nokia profits fell by 30% in the third quarter, underlining its losing battle against the iPhone: sales of Nokia smartphones fell by 3.1% during the quarter, compared to growth in sales of Apple iPhones of 327.5%. The financial crisis and global recession also started to bite, hitting mobile phone sales across the board. Posting its first loss in a decade in 2009, Nokia also cut 1700 jobs worldwide that year, the start of slow and painful downsizing which would see a further 1800 jobs cut in 2010, 4000 in 2011, and another 4000 in 2012. In 2010, newly appointed CEO Stephen Elop, formerly with Microsoft, was brought it to try to turn the company's fortunes around.

But it was too late. In 2011 Elop warned that the company faced a "burning platform," announcing a strategic alliance with Microsoft to develop an operating system to compete with iOS and Android. It was to no avail; Apple and Samsung smartphone sales outstripped Nokia's that year. In 2012, with shares down following a profit warning, Nokia slumped to a €1.3 billion loss and shut its last factory in Finland. The writing was on the wall: in 2013 Finland's corporate pride took a massive hit as the country's most beloved company sold its handset business to Microsoft for €5.44 billion (US$7.2 billion). A new chapter with Microsoft is beginning and it remains to be seen if they will do any better.

4. PREPARING BUSINESS FOR THE FUTURE

What went wrong? Was Nokia too complacent given its leading position? Did the company from the small Nordic country that audaciously drove the global switch from analog to digital telecommunications miss the smartphone trend? To some degree, the company could be accused of complacency, as it completely missed the flip phone trend pioneered by Motorola, which too has had its problems in handsets, being bought by Google and less than two years later by Lenovo as of January 2014. Protecting its market position – and the expense of margins – by focusing on commoditized phones was also a potentially costly mistake.

The interesting thing is that Nokia was there for the smartphone trend. And it was early: in 1998 it had the vision of putting the internet in everybody's pocket, while in 1999 a New York Times profile of Nokia's design chief, Frank Nuovo, credited him with the idea of "turning cell phones into fashion statements." In fact, the company was full of visionaries, technologically savvy innovators, and strong leaders with access to some of the best ideas in the market, simply because it had such broad reach and a pedigree of success and innovation. It was a classic business school case. The question is why the early thinking did not translate into a Nokia smartphone with the elegant designs and leading technology that were hallmarks of the company's rise, given the time between articulating what really sounded like an iPhone in 1998 and the Apple iPhone's arrival. Various causes have been cited, including poor execution in terms of design and functionality, and the determination to build its own Symbian operating system which was less robust than those of its competitors, an issue which led to its initial partnership with Microsoft. Perhaps the biggest challenge was shifting mindsets, from hardware to software and content. Nokia did not see what Apple saw – namely that all that the consumer needed was a rectangular screen and the rest was software-driven content, providing everything you needed in your pocket from calendars to music.

Nokia still makes great phones but lost its way, somehow strange for a company with a history that shows a deep-rooted ability to reinvent itself. But this is not really the point – the point is that what happened to Nokia could happen to every business or industry. It is time for all executives to ask themselves simply: What will it take to stop us from missing out the next big thing disrupting our industry?

(Sources: The Atlantic, The Guardian)

Fighting for the future: BRICS versus beyond BRICS

The size and high growth rates of the BRICS and beyond (B&B) economies continue to attract competitors from around the world, as well as to incubate the next generation of global companies. These are crowded, competitive markets. So how do you compete in them?

For some, often developed market players, the opportunity is to leverage existing portfolios of products and services – often adapted (lower price), sometimes not (e.g. luxury goods). This is typically an "export" model, even if production happens in the B&B, and aims to extend existing capabilities and portfolios. The other approach, which we see among many B&B competitors and an increasing number of forward-thinking developed market companies, is to see the B&B markets as catalysts for building long-term growth platforms. This involves local R&D and design for customer needs, deep understanding of the economic systems, and innovative business models. There is a recognition that B&B markets in the future will actively drive future trends, technologies, and innovations. A key challenge with this approach is not only to develop the B&B focus and strategies, but to build an organization and mindset that is flexible enough to manage multiple business models at the same time – as one size does not fit all – and to operate in markets with radically different environments: overcoming infrastructure deficiencies and bureaucracy, navigating sprawling retail and distribution channels, and addressing the cultural challenges of being a global company.

Looking forward, there are three underlying levels of competition, with important long-term implications for the positions of both individual firms and their home economies. First, there is strong competition in the **BRICS (or B&B)** markets to capture today's growth. This competition pits developed market players, often with their developed market products, business models, and mindsets, against strong, increasingly capable, and aggressive home market players. Whereas developed market players often

4. PREPARING BUSINESS FOR THE FUTURE

seek to exploit existing strengths and ways of working, BRICS players are investing to build their positions today in order to own the future.

This battle is for today's growth markets, but is one with asymmetric expectations. Some developed market companies are seeking to counter this challenge by combining their expertise with local players, e.g. in June 2012, Walgreens (U.S.) bought a 45% stake in UK-based Alliance Boots creating the world's largest pharmacy chain. One of the attractions: in September 2012, Alliance Boots revealed plans to buy a 12% stake in China's fifth-largest pharmaceutical wholesaler Nanjing Pharmaceutical. (Source: EIU)

The second level of competition is with **BRICS (or B&B)** players on the global stage. Growth is happening in a vast array of markets across Asia, Africa, Latin America, and the Middle East (the "beyond" markets). Competition in these "neutral" territories again reflects fundamentally different mind sets, business models, strategies, and home economic systems between developed and B&B firms. While they offer important short-term growth opportunities for developed players, they often are the central focus of international expansion for the B&B players, leveraging their home business models. According to one CEO, "Why would I want to invest in the crowded, stagnant markets in Europe when there are much bigger opportunities closer to home?" However, some B&B companies also see potential in competing more aggressively for developed markets, particularly as some, including the U.S., are becoming more attractive as manufacturing centers again as costs come down in the wake of economic slowdown. Some of these B&B corporates are buying their way into developed markets, e.g. Chinese Sany Heavy Industry (the largest Chinese construction equipment group), bought 90% of German firm Putzmeister in January 2012, while China's Geely Holding Group acquired Volvo. In the next five years Chinese acquisitions of foreign companies are set to double, and by 2020 they could quadruple. (Source: BBC) This second battle is about positioning for the next generation of growth markets – and for the consumption potential of developed markets.

The third level of competition is among the **BRICS (or B&B)** players – together with their home political and economic systems – for leadership in and control of future growth technologies and industries. It is no secret that much of the investment in key future technologies, e.g. clean energy, is taking place in the cash-rich BRICS, most notably China and India. On the other hand, the cash-strapped developed markets are often trying to protect old industries and players to prevent further disruption to weakened economies. The role of the state, politically and economically, in both instances is important. Competition between state control (China and Russia), chaotic democracy (India), social democracy (Brazil), and regulated democracy (Europe and the U.S.), will create the seeds and environment for control of key future technologies and markets. This battle is ultimately for control of the engines of future economic growth.

As an executive – wherever you are located – how do these B&B wars impact your organization's playing field today – and in the future? Consider:

1. What role do activities in B&B markets play in your overall strategy, both to meet short-term growth targets and to reinvent the company based on the long-term shifts underway?

2. What are the primary barriers you face, in terms of products, business models, and mindsets, in successfully preparing your organization to compete in an economic future led – or at least co-led – by B&B markets?

3. What would be the implications of moving your headquarters to China, India, or Brazil to prepare your leaders and your businesses for the future?

Answering the first question requires exploring how much your organization perceives B&B markets as add-on, short-term growth opportunities for current business models and products versus using these opportunities to fundamentally rethink the business for the future. The second requires considering what specific elements of your current operations are focused on holding onto the past as opposed to preparing for the future. Answering the third question challenges leadership to consider how its base impacts its worldview as it prepares to lead the organization to the future.

4. PREPARING BUSINESS FOR THE FUTURE

Preparing for the digital generation

For the digital generation flexibility, mobility, and immediacy are king. Their digital attitudes and behaviors are permeating every facet of life and work, embracing the virtual, living in real time. They are coexisting with, if not thriving on, social networking, the cloud, and cyberspace demands that are often seen as overwhelming and beyond the "normal" human capacities of many in older generations. Flexible and mobile ways of working are becoming more common, as the younger generations challenge conventional and stationary working patterns and management methods. For more traits and information about the new digital generation see the section on generational shifts in Chapter 4.

Forget retaining, inspire! That is exactly what GE has in mind to attract and develop the best of the next generations. Some of the recommendations from GE's Global New Direction Group are: 1. Leveraging gaming technology to create a new interactive channel that connects the world to GE in a fun and engaging way, helping to educate prospective employees about the company and its economic and social values. 2. Creating a personalized suite of benefits, providing greater flexibility and choice to better meet the needs of a global, diverse workforce. 3. Enhancing performance-management systems with new tools to help employees navigate their career at GE and identify a wider range of opportunities across the company. Processes that allow for more just-in-time feedback and coaching, that the next generation considers to be highly desirable, round out the system enhancements. 4. Expanding leadership development and accelerator programs, connecting participants across those programs in order to support a broader base of culturally adaptive global leaders. (Source: HBR Blog Network) How can your company implement better strategies to attract, develop, and retain the next generations?

4.5   SUMMARY: 8 PRINCIPLES OF PREPARING FOR THE FUTURE IN ACTION IN BUSINESS

The case studies, in brief examples, and food for thought topics offer interesting stories, but the question is what leaders can learn from how these businesses are preparing for the future today. Using the 8 principles outlined in Chapter 3, the following insights stand out:

1. Embrace ambiguity: don't just think outside the box, throw away the boxes

Many, if not all of these companies **accept cross-industry competition** as a way of life, e.g. BMW's revolutionary i3 and i8 cars, which combine intelligence, new energy solutions, and a clear understanding that what they are doing is meeting the end-users' personal transportation needs, not making cars. DSM highlights the need to **get out of the comfort zone**. Having reinvented itself multiple times in its long history, it is pushing to do so again. Disney is also – after some false starts – pushing itself to succeed in the uncomfortable space of the internet, recognizing that failure to engage is not an option.

2. Think first from the outside-in, then inside-out

A **deep understanding of trends** impacting the world is the starting point for the leaders driving the preparation of their firms for the future. In BMW's case extensive work was done, involving many executives, highlighting another key insight: **look globally and look outside the boundaries of your own industry and markets**. As challengers from rapidly developing markets, Tencent, Infosys, and Alibaba have also embraced the global view, with Tencent's localized platforms demonstrating that there is a need to **balance global and local offerings**.

3. Identify and address root causes, not symptoms

From Amazon to Alibaba, these companies have a deep and unwavering **focus on consumer, customer, and end-user needs** which serves as their starting point for action and innovation. Many have built **strong technology foundations** to underpin growth, not just in the digital world where Amazon has emerged as a leading cloud player, but also in the physical world, where BMW's, DSM's and GE's commitment to pioneering and applied research is critical. However, they see **technology as an enabler** to serving customer and consumer needs, rather than an end in its own right – which is perhaps an insight Nokia missed.

4. Practice two-directional thinking

Two directional thinking means accelerating actions today to provide a strong foundation for growth while simultaneously taking steps to prepare for the long term. BMW clearly embodies these principles, with a **clear business metrics for performance today** (all cars should be profitable) while exploring and **shaping the future** of personal transportation. DSM also applies tangible metrics to its innovation efforts to ensure they are supporting its ambition, while SABMiller applies full business rigor to its sustainability efforts. In addition a number of companies show the importance of **redefining the business while it is still doing well**, with DSM's CEO explicitly stating this as a goal, while Tencent, IBM, and Infosys recognize the role of partnerships and acquisitions in staying ahead of change. **Timing matters** in taking action.

5. Manage in relationships/networks versus transactions

The majority, if not all, of the companies above **use partnerships** at various stages of the value chain, from BMW for its energy and carbon fibre needs to Tencent using local partnerships to expand its offerings and reach worldwide. In Tencent's case **taking an open platform approach** has allowed it to respond effectively to competition and to innovate rapidly. GE too is opening up its innovation platforms to embrace the maker movement. Taking collaboration seriously too in the drive not just for ideas, but also for efficiency and increased speed to market is Cemex which is **driving both internal and external collaboration** initiatives to share and capitalize on knowledge and ideas.

6. Focus on co-creation

Co-creating solutions to consumer and customer needs extends and deepens collaboration and relationships within a value creation network. While GE embraces the maker movement, Disney and Tencent are **tapping into the needs and behaviors of the next generations** of co-creating consumers through game-based approaches. BMW's focus on intelligent machines and connectivity also reflects its understanding of these emerging generations, who want to be involved not only in personalizing their transport experience but shaping its design. In many cases, it is clear that the mindset of **"not invented here" is alien** to these companies – their open approaches to partnerships, acquisitions, and innovation suggest that if it can't be done in-house there are solutions to be found outside by working with others.

7. Align purpose and profit

Profit is important, as it means the company stays in business. But **so too are sustainability and corporate responsibility**, as these allow companies the licence to operate, innovate, and stay ahead. What is perhaps most interesting in the case studies is that **sustainability and responsibility are becoming embedded as part of business as usual**, rather than being seen as a separate unit or set of initiatives. For SABMiller managing water resources is a critical area as it is a major component of their products, but their sustainability agenda is much broader, as is that of DSM. Both these companies, however, highlight the importance of **clear and measurable goals** for their efforts.

8. Embed continual challenge, avoid complacent compliance

Continuous, focused, and measurable experimentation is the hallmark of the innovation efforts of companies including Amazon, BMW, Tencent, and IBM. None are content to rest on their past successes, recognizing not only that change is happening faster than ever, even as product lifecycles shorten. In many companies there is **strong commitment to and funding of R&D and innovation** efforts focused on the future, while Cemex's internal collaboration efforts and Amazon's "Earth Kaizen" remind us that **daily, incremental challenges to the status quo** are equally important and can yield positive results.

Even as the companies profiled offer important insights and lessons for others preparing for the future, it is clear that they do not have all the answers. Their leaders are still facing the same challenges as every other company, including:

- Rethinking education and talent management and development
- Driving real transformation versus following hubris
- Dealing with disruption, whether self-induced or external
- Figuring out where corporate responsibility starts and ends
- Getting to grips with next generations

5. PREPARING GOVERNMENTS FOR THE FUTURE

5. PREPARING GOVERNMENTS FOR THE FUTURE

Chapter five focuses on how governments are translating macro implications into specific insights and actions to prepare for the future. As in the previous and subsequent chapters, the first subsection provides some context, looking at the key trends that are impacting the landscape within which each type of organizations is operating.

The second subsection focuses on detailed case studies, offering insights into how different governments are approaching the challenges of preparing their countries for the future. Each detailed case study, explores the organization's thinking and actions using the lens of the 3Rs model below: what are the key trends and implications impacting the organization; how did these drive rethinking the playing field; how did the organization redefine their ambition (vision, purpose, targets, measures) as a result; what were the options they considered in building an agenda for action; how did they reshape how they worked; and what is the ongoing process of learn-act-learn-adjust.

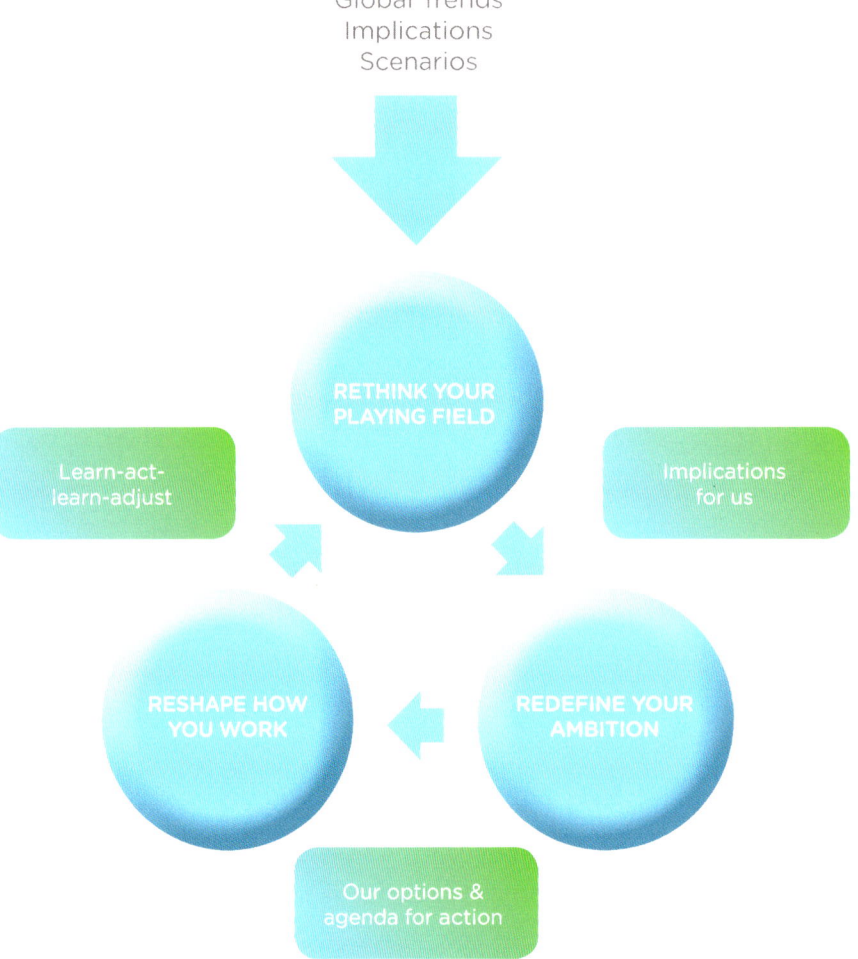

The third subsection provides some in brief examples of how other organizations are preparing for the future in specific areas, e.g. addressing the issues of cyber security, and driving innovation, often through new technologies. The fourth highlights food for thought examples, which are designed to provoke thinking on some of the key challenges facing organizations in the future, which many governments are grappling with, e.g. whose responsibility is it to address societal challenges, and decoding and addressing the agenda of China. Finally, in subsection five, we draw together some insights to take away from these examples using the 8 principles introduced in Chapter 3.

5. PREPARING GOVERNMENTS FOR THE FUTURE

5.1 THE SHIFTING LANDSCAPE OF GOVERNANCE

Governments worldwide vary dramatically in size, their underpinning economic, political, and social systems, and in the opportunities and challenges they face. To be able to understand the implications of global trends and how to address them, a first step is to understand the situations and characteristics of the economies and societies that governments represent today.

Type of economy	Characteristics	Size and growth expectations	Economic systems	Example economies
Developed markets	• Advanced infrastructure and technologies • Industrialized, well developed service sectors • High income economies • High standards of living • High educational levels • Largely democracies • Leaders in the world's major geopolitical, economic, and social affairs	• Small to large populations and markets • Resource bases varied • Slow to modest growth	Market-led, capitalism, mixed economies	U.S., UK, Germany, France, Japan
BRICS	• Regional economic powerhouses, China globally • Undertaking domestic economic and political reforms • Seeking greater influence in global geopolitical, economic, and social affairs in line with their size and growth • High levels of inequality • Development needs include physical infrastructure, education, technology • Increasing consumer spending power • Varied governance from state control to democracy	• Large populations and markets • Resource bases varied • Among the world's fastest growing economies	Transitional economic systems, moving towards market openness, but often with high levels of state intervention	Brazil, Russia, India, China, South Africa
High-growth markets beyond BRICS	• Undertaking domestic economic and/or political reforms • Untapped potential requires foreign capital investment • Development needs include: infrastructure, education, and technologies • Low economic power in international markets • Low standards of living and education, high inequality • Mixed governance models	• Large populations and markets • High potential of becoming, along with the BRICS, the world's fastest growing economies in the 21st century	Transitional economic systems, often high levels of state intervention	Indonesia, Mexico, Turkey, Iran, South Korea, Egypt, Nigeria, Thailand, Vietnam, Pakistan, Bangladesh, Philippines, Argentina

5. PREPARING GOVERNMENTS FOR THE FUTURE

Type of economy	Characteristics	Size and growth expectations	Economic systems	Example economies
Less developed markets	• Underdeveloped • High levels of poverty and inequality • Lack of capital, dependent on foreign investment/aid • Low levels of infrastructure, technology, and education • Dependence on agriculture • Frequently politically unstable • Corruption a major issue	• Medium-sized but fast-growing populations • Potential fast growth markets with GDP's between 4.0-7.5% in 2018	Transitional economic systems, some market openness, but highly dependent on state governance	Myanmar, Cambodia, Ethiopia, Mali, Sudan
Cities	• Largest and fastest-growing economic centers globally • Home to the corporate giants of today and the future • Increasingly important trade hubs and talent hubs • Drive global trends in consumption, working patterns, environmental awareness, design, culture, and more	• Home to around 38% of the global population, but generate as much as 72% of global GDP • Cities could inject up to US$30 trillion into the global economy by 2025	Highly market-orientated, may differ in economic system versus home country (e.g. free trade zones)	Shanghai, Beijing, Tianjin, São Paulo, Guangzhou, Shenzhen, New York, Moscow, Tokyo, Istanbul, Los Angeles, London, Singapore

Sources: University of Iowa, McKinsey Quarterly's City 600 index, Corporate Clout 2013: Time for Responsible Capitalism, IMF, several news sources

In addition, resource positions will play a significant role in terms of the challenges and opportunities that each type of government will face. Although increasing populations with strong projected increases in GDP per capita appear to be attractive future markets, in assessing their potential, the impact of increasing pressures on ecological and natural resources of these growing populations needs to be taken into account. Many of the countries with the fastest growing populations also face ecological/resource deficits that could negatively impact future economic growth potential as well as social development.

5. PREPARING GOVERNMENTS FOR THE FUTURE

Growth versus natural resource assets (estimated absolute growth in population from 2012 to 2100 versus ecological reserve/deficit)

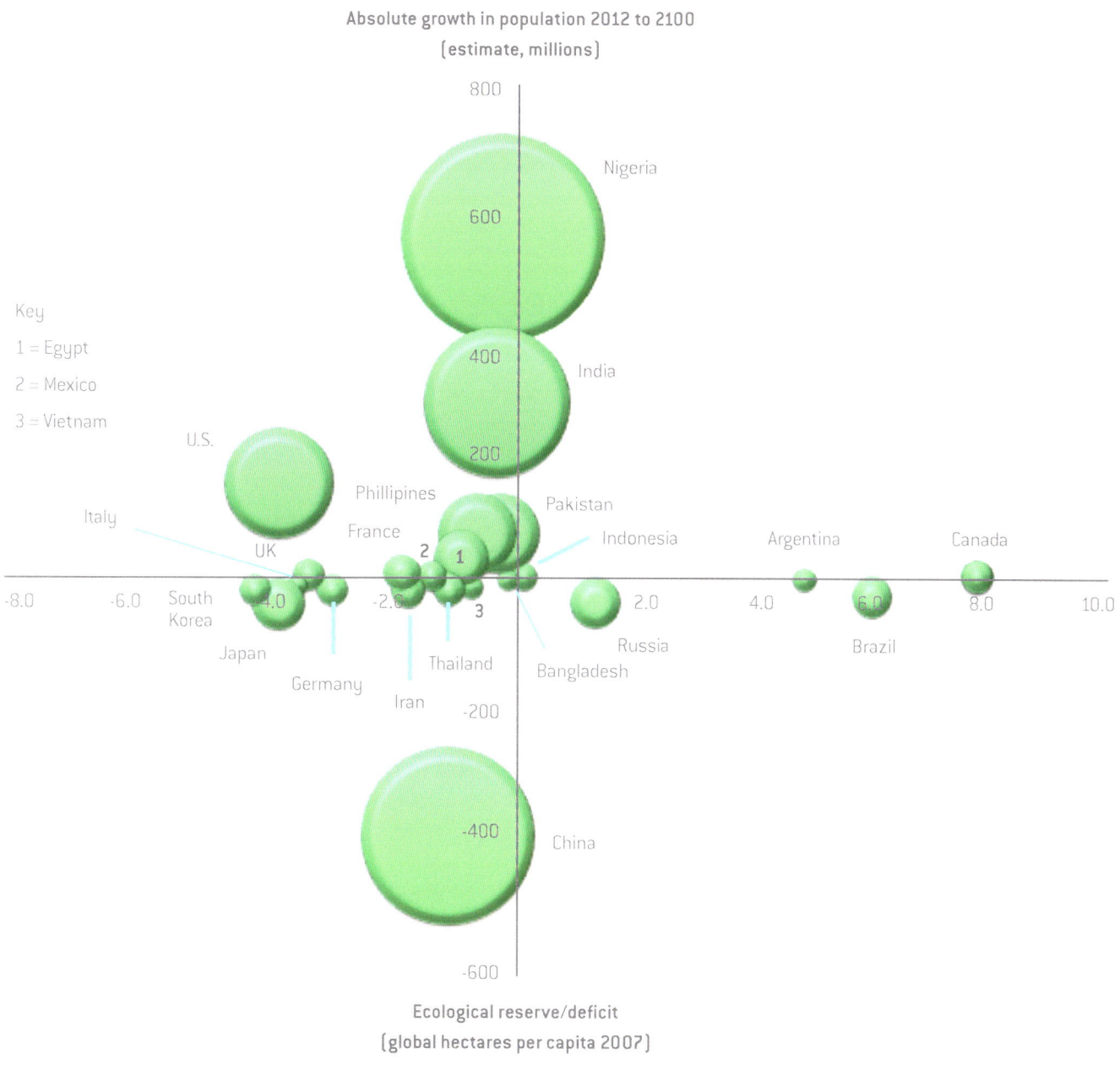

Absolute growth in population 2012 to 2100
(estimate, millions)

Key
1 = Egypt
2 = Mexico
3 = Vietnam

Ecological reserve/deficit
(global hectares per capita 2007)

Sources: UN, Global Footprint Network

5. PREPARING GOVERNMENTS FOR THE FUTURE

Cities are included as a type of "government" player, given that many of the world's current and emerging mega cities will play a huge role in future economic growth. Rapid urbanization across the globe is making cities increasingly important global generators of growth and wealth – and it is the emerging market cities that will win the race. McKinsey Quarterly's City 600 index suggests that developed market cities will create 17% of global GDP growth in 2025, down from 36% in 2010 while emerging market cities will create 47%, up from 18% in 2010. Overall, cities could inject up to US$30 trillion into the global economy by 2025. Despite these forecasts, few companies focus on the growth potential of cities.

Contribution to GDP growth* at real exchange rates by geography, 2010-2025

100% = US$50.2 trillion

Developing 74%   **Developed** 26%

Emerging 440, 47%   **Developed 160,** 17%

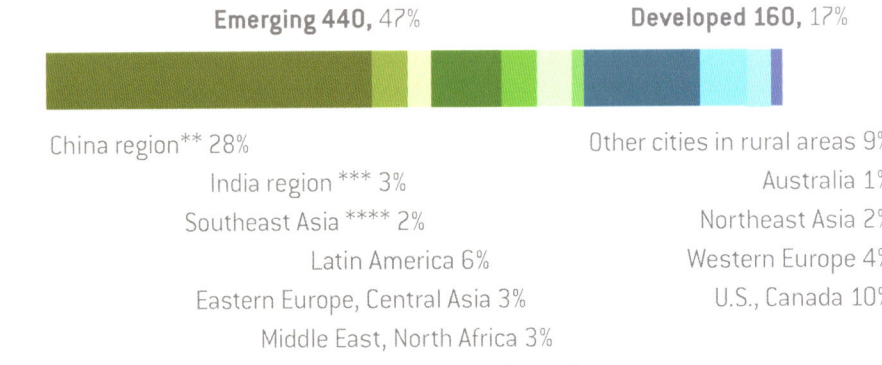

Other cities in rural areas 27%

China region** 28%
India region *** 3%
Southeast Asia **** 2%
Latin America 6%
Eastern Europe, Central Asia 3%
Middle East, North Africa 3%
Sub-Saharan Africa 1%

Other cities in rural areas 9%
Australia 1%
Northeast Asia 2%
Western Europe 4%
U.S., Canada 10%

*Predicted real exchange rate; figures may not sum to totals, because of rounding

** Includes cities in China (including Hong Kong and Macau) and Taiwan

*** Includes cities in Afghanistan, Bangladesh, India, Pakistan, and Sri Lanka

****Includes cities in Cambodia, Laos, Malaysia, Myanmar, Papua New Guinea, Philippines, Singapore, Thailand, and Vietnam

Source: McKinsey Quarterly

5. PREPARING GOVERNMENTS FOR THE FUTURE

Globally, the economic power shift is accelerating from West to East and North to South. The key, however, is to look beyond the BRICS to those markets that will lead the next wave of economic growth and development, as in the long term, the BRICS markets may show slower growth, although they will obviously continue to be important in terms of sheer size. In the short term, competition in the BRICS is intense – and may not offer the potential of less crowded markets. Of course, careful research is critical in order to identify the most promising growth opportunities for your business.

Investors, consultants, development agencies, and businesses each have their own opinions about which markets – and why those – will be the next most important growth markets. Some of these opinions converge, others do not. One of the most widely publicized lists is probably the N-11, coined by Goldman Sachs' Jim O'Neill, who gave us the acronyms BRIC (Brazil, Russia, India, and China) and MIST (Mexico, Indonesia, South Korea, and Turkey). Our Global Trends analysis suggests a slightly longer list, based on market size, population, and economic growth, income per capita, global focus/influence, and resource strength.

Company	Emerging markets (beyond BRICS) that are anticipated to offer future growth potential
Goldman Sachs	N-11: Bangladesh, Egypt, Indonesia, Iran, Mexico, Nigeria, Pakistan, Philippines, Turkey, South Korea, and Vietnam
Ernst & Young	Argentina, Chile, Colombia, Czech Republic, Egypt, Ghana, Indonesia, Kazakhstan, Korea, Malaysia, Mexico, Nigeria, Poland, Qatar, Saudi Arabia, South Africa, Thailand, Turkey, Ukraine, United Arab Emirates, and Vietnam (Rapid growth market, BRIC omitted)
Economist Intelligence Unit	CIVETS: Colombia, Indonesia, Vietnam, Egypt, Turkey, and South Africa
Yahoo	Turkey, Philippines, Thailand, Poland, Columbia, South Korea, Nigeria (as part of the BRIC India is omitted here). Rank among the top performers in 2012, and is thought to be breakout nations
Forbes (Contribution by McKinsey & Company)	Argentina, Colombia, Indonesia, Mexico, Philippines, Poland, South Africa, South Korea, Turkey, and Ukraine
Global Trends	Indonesia, Mexico, Turkey, Iran, South Korea, Egypt, Nigeria, Thailand, Vietnam, Pakistan, Bangladesh, Philippines, and Argentina

Despite growth potential and market attractiveness, it is important to recognize that governments worldwide are facing increasing challenges, not only in developing/renewing essential infrastructure and developing societies, but also in terms of their own legitimacy with citizens.

Distrust in governments continues to decline, in cases to historic lows, according to the 2014 Trust Barometer from Edelman. The Trust Barometer also revealed a historic gap of 14 points globally between trust in government and business, a development that can be attributed to the continued destruction of trust in government that began in 2011, and a steady rise in belief in business since its nadir in 2008. Government officials and regulators remain the least credible spokespeople.

At the same time, over half the world's people live in countries that are not free in terms of political rights and civil liberties. Freedom House reports that 2013 was the eighth consecutive year where more declines than gains were noted worldwide. The data also shows a stepped-up campaign of persecution by dictators that specifically targeted civil society organizations and independent media.

5. PREPARING GOVERNMENTS FOR THE FUTURE

Increasingly people have been turning to communities of choice to get their voices heard — and recent years have witnessed a dramatic shift from raising voices to taking action, with revolution and popular protest in countries from North Africa and the Middle East to Ukraine and Brazil. Even where dictatorial governments have been replaced through popular uprisings, the world and the countries involved are struggling with the way forward, and some countries have even had setbacks for their freedom. Syria continues to suffer under the hand of President Bashar al-Assad, with thousands dead and millions displaced.

The knock-on impact on other countries with highly centralized political control is also a consideration, especially those rapidly developing economies, which are increasingly driving the global economy. An example is the 2012 parliamentary elections in Russia where the government faced massive protests because many both inside the country, as well as international observers, deemed the election practices unfair.

The impact of the voice of the people is not just confined to the developing world. In most developed economies, the dismal level of trust from voters, plus falling tenures among politicians and converging policies among parties, suggests the potential for governments to drive development and prosperity at home, let alone tackle global issues, is falling. Despite the fact that the democratic governments of the world are designed to be elected by and serve the people, many voters have lost faith in the ability of their governments and leaders to deliver on their promises.

Many governments are now seen as barriers to growth and prosperity rather than enablers of positive development — for example, the continued partisan infighting in the U.S. With the perceived failure of politicians, citizens are becoming increasingly active on pressing issues, protesting against poverty, corruption, poor infrastructure, and education, high unemployment, and the greed and the influence of banks and businesses on governments and the economy.

Nationalism and protectionism are squarely back on the agenda in the developed world as politicians try to appease voters who have already ousted the leaders of heavily indebted PIIGS countries (Portugal, Ireland, Italy, Greece, and Spain) and are facing continued austerity, recession and unemployment. Ongoing debates in Europe around the Eurozone and sovereign debt crises could potentially mean changes to the EU treaty and greater integration of fiscal and economic policies, changes which are already generating resistance in countries, most notably the UK.

While the nation-state remains the preeminent unit of organization, these alternative communities that frequently cross borders are likely to have an increasing voice in how we govern ourselves in the future. Against this backdrop, the need to find hybrid models of governance reflecting a balance between states, individuals, and communities of choice — within and across national borders — becomes increasingly critical.

5. PREPARING GOVERNMENTS FOR THE FUTURE

5.2 HOW ARE GOVERNMENTS PREPARING FOR THE FUTURE? CASE STUDIES

Singapore Economic Development Board: Building Singapore as the Asian capital

Implications of global trends for Singapore "In today's world economy, Asia presents huge opportunities. It is not just one or even a few economies that are experiencing this growth, it is 'pan-Asian,'" Leo Yip, Chairman of Singapore's Economic Development Board (EDB) stated in a 2011 interview. For the growing city-state this presents significant opportunities to benefit from the region's growth as well as challenges in terms of how to position the country in the eyes of global companies from developed nations looking to grow in Asia, and also of Asian companies looking to expand internationally.

Rethinking your playing field As the global economy shifts from West and North to East and South, Asia is no longer being viewed simply as a production base, but as an attractive market in its own right with some 3 billion potential consumers. Given this, Yip discussed the need to constantly rethink: "How we can add value both for global companies looking to penetrate the Asian market and for Asian companies wishing to expand beyond it." It's about building on the country's strengths over time, but persistently moving up the value ladder: "We've been deliberately developing Singapore as a business-friendly and strategic location, and this has worked well for us. In the early days of economic development in this region, Singapore was a popular location for off-shore manufacturing. Then it moved up the value ladder. Today, I think we can consider ourselves a global business city: global business is conducted here according to international standards. We have a global business infrastructure, with a good representation of multinationals. We understand the global economy, and we understand Asia – a rising Asia."

Redefining your ambition Singapore has positioned itself as a global/Asian interface: a strategic business location offering a strong base for multinationals to grow across the entire region. However, Yip notes, "To grow and innovate in Asia, however, you first need to understand Asian markets and consumers, before translating that knowledge into the development of products, services, and solutions that will be commercialized in Asia for Asia. "Business, innovation, and talent are the three key areas in which Singapore should continue to build capabilities that are valuable to global companies." The question is how to differentiate Singapore versus other cities in the region that have similar ambitions.

These ambitions are reflected in how the EDB looks at success. Annual key performance indicators (KPIs), include the amount of investment brought in, and the number of new strategic bases ("homes") that companies establish in Singapore. Another encompasses key capabilities from innovation to talent. In the medium term, success is more about global competitive positioning, with the EDB looking at Singapore's comparative position as a global business city versus Shanghai and others based on a range of competitive indicators. In addition, he noted, "We have also asked how the rest of the world, namely the global, the non-Asian, and the Asian-global business worlds, will perceive Singapore, and whether the indicators would have moved up or come down."

Creating options One route towards differentiation that the EDB is pursuing is aggressive development of world-class human capital. Even as local universities move up the global rankings, they are actively trying to attract "the global best" educational institutions and talent to Singapore, often in partnership with local universities. For example, the EDB facilitated partnerships with Duke University (U.S.) and Imperial College (UK) to set up new medical schools. They also partnered with Yale (U.S.) to set up a liberal arts college. The aim: to achieve global levels in the shortest possible time by bringing in the best global partners, while simultaneously building capabilities in leadership development by leveraging Asian understanding and global thought leaders.

Another challenge that the crowded island nation faces is scarcity of land. To create the options that will allow it to drive future success, the government has a systematic and holistic land planning approach, which involves the whole government every few years. Yip explained: "During these sessions, we look together at demand and supply for land, and work out how to optimize them. In other words: What do we want to or not want to use the land for? So we're making decisions about value generation and the kinds of economic activities we want to promote. Optimizing land use is critical. It may mean, for example, increasing existing three-story buildings to 30 stories; rebuilding low-rise industrial parks; or moving the port somewhere else, away from its current position in the center."

5. PREPARING GOVERNMENTS FOR THE FUTURE

It's also critical to test these options, including demonstrating the application of many sustainable and environmentally friendly technologies, for example energy management and efficiency, transport management, water management, and industrial energy efficiency. These are tested as part of an urban management system, the idea being to use "Singapore as a Living Laboratory." Singapore has also embarked on a National Innovation Challenge on Energy, calling for big ideas – based on technologies from anywhere in the world – to achieve its national goal of greater energy resilience.

Reshaping how you work As both a leading city and a leading nation, Singapore benefits from the interactions between urban and national systems. However, to succeed in becoming a global center for the companies that it wants to attract it needs to reshape how it works in terms of building new capabilities and taking the close working relationship between government and the private sector to the next level. In terms of new strengths, Yip identified that these would include consumer insights and the country's innovation capability.

At the EDB level, he also identified the need to have a strong and steady pipeline of talent flowing into the organization and to raise the game in terms of leadership competencies. Within the framework which the EDB has developed, one important competency looking forward is strategic influencing, training people to be able to strategically influence others from the C-level to the working-level executives with which the organization engages.

He explained, "Today, when we sit down with a company, we discuss strategy. Forty years ago, we may have offered just a manufacturing location. But today, we also want to understand the company's strategy and how we can add value and new dimensions to it. Then we try to work out how we can help the company further the execution of that strategy from a base in Singapore. That's a much broader and deeper level of engagement."

Learn-act-learn-adjust With 25 offices around world in 2011 and more planned, another critical challenge for Yip and his organization is the rapid evolution of Asia's rise. To be able to work with companies in a strategic context, executives need to stay on top of the changes in Asia. One way the EDB does this is bringing all its overseas officers to Asia so that its people based in the U.S. and Europe also spend some time in the region.

From a personal perspective Yip noted that "The purpose [of extensive travelling] is beyond marketing – it is also to gain the perspectives, the sensing, and the understanding, and the chance to develop my own insights. I think that's primary, because the strategizing, execution, capability building, systems, and processes flow from that. They flow from the world view that you develop and that you have to keep refreshing. You need to take a couple of steps back and say, 'This is what I'm sensing now. How do I bring that sensing to bear in an insight, leading to a strategic viewpoint?'"

Sources: *"Ready? The 3Rs of preparing your organization for the future"* by Thomas W. Malnight, Tracey S. Keys, and Kees van der Graaf, 2013; LCF interview with Leo Yip, Chairman, EDB – Singapore Economic Development Board, IMD

Enterprise Ireland's Leadership for Growth Program: realizing the potential of government to drive growth

In 2010, the Irish economy was facing significant challenges due to the global economic and financial crisis. Banks were in need of bailouts, growth was stalled, and the competitiveness of the economy which had driven growth in previous decades was in question. Against this backdrop, clearly boosting the traditional strength of the agri-food and fisheries sector would be critical. The sector contributed gross annual output approaching €24 billion, directly employed over 150,000 people, provided the outlet for the produce from Ireland's 128,000 family farms, represented 60% of manufacturing exports by indigenous firms, and domestically sourced 71% of its raw materials. Even with global demand for food rising – and expected to continue to do so – the question was how the sector could innovate and grow globally.

5. PREPARING GOVERNMENTS FOR THE FUTURE

Enterprise Ireland, the government organization responsible for the development and growth of Irish enterprises in world markets, is a key player in addressing the tremendous opportunities and challenges for the sector. Its mandate is to work in partnership with Irish enterprises to help them start, grow, innovate and win export sales on global markets, thus supporting sustainable economic growth, regional development, and secure employment.

Frank Ryan, former CEO of Enterprise Ireland, was convinced that "food and agriculture will lead the economic comeback of Ireland" and moreover, that such growth will come through global export. Julie Sinnamon, current CEO of Enterprise Ireland noted in 2011: "Breaking into key markets in Asia will take time. It will take years for some companies to breakthrough after they have established a presence." But she added the potential for food exports, in particular, was "enormous." (Source: Irish Examiner, September 2013)

Implications of global trends for the food and agriculture sector in Ireland Achieving robust economic growth would mean helping the sector to build on its strengths, and also overcome major challenges that were inhibiting growth in the short term. The industry was characterized by lack of scale, high fragmentation, low investment, and an over-reliance on commodity and private-label products. At the same time global trends implied that the sector would need to innovate and expand its horizons to win amid the growing global demand for food. These horizons would likely include looking for opportunities in new high-growth markets in Asia and Africa, where an emerging middle class of some 3 billion is spending more on food and drink, versus relying on maturing Western markets. Making such moves would require addressing the contradictions inherent in the "globalization" of products and brands, with localization of tastes and traditions.

Shifts in the food and agriculture value chains also needed to be addressed, as major players were becoming more concentrated worldwide, both in production and in retail, often aided by technological advances. Commoditization was also an issue, but one that could be addressed by understanding and addressing the needs of ever more demanding, connected, and educated consumers. Questions around who "owned" these consumers – the retailer, the producer, or even the consumer themselves – reflected the growing shift in power along the value chain. Yet, new demands also offered potential for differentiation and higher value-added products and services as concerns were growing around health & wellness, environmental and natural resources, even as the focus grew on taste/pleasure, indulgence, freshness, natural authenticity, convenience, choice, and functional benefits.

Rethinking your playing field The substantial opportunities and challenges led the Irish Minister of Agriculture, Fisheries and Food to commission a team of industry participants to develop an action plan, known as Food Harvest 2020. It contains ambitious targets:

- Increase the value of primary output in the agriculture and fisheries sector by € 1.5 billion by 2020 › 33% increase versus 2007-9 average
- Increase value-added output by € 3 billion by 2020 › 40% increase versus 2008
- Achieve an export target of € 12 billion by 2020 → 42% increase versus 2007-9 average

To achieve these goals, the plan states, "there is an ongoing need to attract the best people to the sector and to enhance the leadership and management skills of those working in the industry."

Redefining your ambition How could this plan ignite a similar ambition in Ireland's agriculture and food industry? Can ambition be taught? Is there a way to make CEOs dream even bigger? Can you build the skills and leadership they need to deliver those dreams?

These questions drove the creation of Enterprise Ireland's Leadership 4 Growth (L4G) program for the agri-food and fisheries industry, after success with a similar approach in other industries. L4G was designed as a high-impact, nine-month development journey to help Ireland's leaders in the industry to explore new directions for their business models, strategies, organizations, and cultures. A collaborative approach to executive development, developed together by Enterprise Ireland, IMD

5. PREPARING GOVERNMENTS FOR THE FUTURE

business school and the Irish Management Institute (IMI), L4G is partially funded by government investment and has as its long-term goals:

- Individual and organizational development
- Lay the foundation for developing new capabilities and mindsets
- Enhanced firm (and national industry) competitiveness
- Attract talent and investment into the sector

Creating options In the short term, the program benefits the individual companies participating by:

- Awareness and insights on strategic, organizational, and leadership challenges and opportunities
- Tools, examples & focused exercises to inform and support the building of personal and organizational action agendas
- Building common understanding, vocabulary, and structured approaches and toolkits with management teams
- Specific ideas, alternatives and options to move the company forward
- Build and strengthen networks, relationships, partnerships

For each company and CEO participating there are no "right" answers to their opportunities and challenges — the key is to develop a vision, strategy, organization, and culture that enables the participant and his or her team to create options and an agenda for action that engages the whole organization.

Reshaping how you work Delivering a program that is customized to the needs of approximately 40 CEOs with different situations, needs, and opportunities and challenges — at the same time — required a new approach, both for Enterprise Ireland and its educational partners. The journey was built around a combination of learning and action, pairing three residential modules at IMD's Lausanne, Switzerland campus with Insight Days in Ireland, where the learning is extended to each participant's senior team, building broader engagement and offering the CEO critical input along the way. This engagement was supported by a virtual classroom including program materials and video tools that allow the CEOs' extended teams to participate actively through the journey. Tying the learning and action together is an expert team of local Business Advisor Coaches, facilitated by IMI, who support and challenge their small group of participants throughout the journey.

Building the relationships, both to co-create and manage the journey, required time and input from all involved. A collaborative partnership was essential — and this extended to the participants, whose work in peer networks also served to set the bar high for developing and implementing new ambitions and agendas.

It also required moving away from a traditional modular format of learning topics to a mix of tools, learning and inputs that delivered both greater and earlier impact for the companies involved. Rather than a lecturer, the IMD Program Director, Tom Malnight, describes his role as "a colleague, challenger, and partner in the journey."

Learn-act-learn-adjust A critical component of the program — and its ability to drive impact — is the timeframe of the journey. Modules, insight days, and coaching take place over nine months, with time between each to allow participants to start to apply tools, ideas, and concepts with their teams, allowing them to test and learn over time.

The L4G program is now in its third year, with a fourth journey planned in 2014. Even though the results both for individual companies and the sector as a whole will take time to show, leaders begin making the day-to-day changes immediately that impact culture, ambition, and performance. "I believe we are a different company than when I started this journey," declared one participant to his classmates on the last day of the program, describing the new alignment among his leadership team and newfound pride among his company. Many more have also remarked on the ongoing learning as they move from the start of their journey at L4G to the bigger journey of implementing their ambitions.

Sources: www.enterprise-ireland.com; www.imd.org

5. PREPARING GOVERNMENTS FOR THE FUTURE

Denmark: an ambition to be carbon neutral by 2050

Today 80% of the Danish energy supply is based on fossil fuels. However, the Danish government has decided that by 2050 Denmark must be independent of fossil fuels and its vision is widely supported by Danish municipalities, enterprises and organizations. This is for Denmark, as it would be for any other country, a very ambitious goal. Why? To become carbon neutral means that the entire energy system in Denmark needs to be reshaped, all this without interfering with the economic growth needed to sustain and develop the Danish welfare state and social systems.

Implications of global trends for a green future in Denmark Global climate changes and long-term pressure on current energy resources, in particular oil and natural gas, are key factors in the discussion of climate and energy politics in Denmark and worldwide. The Danish and the international community face substantial challenges: *First*, man-made climate change needs to be reduced, requiring a reduction in CO2 emissions. The question of pollution, particularly CO2 emissions contributing to climate change has already made many governments put in place targets to generate substantial percentages of electricity from renewable energies such as solar, wind, and biofuel sources. However, in 2014, many countries in the EU are seen as reducing their commitments in this area. *Second*, global population and economic growth in the decades to come will require significantly greater amounts of energy pushing up prices of fossil fuels, even taking account of new resources such as shale oil/gas. *Third*, domestic energy security is top of mind for many governments who wish to reduce their dependence on energy supplies from countries that have significant control of the energy market and/or may be less stable.

Rethinking your playing field To meet the ambitious goal of making Denmark carbon neutral by 2050, in 2008 the Danish government appointed a Climate Commission compromised of 10 scientists, each with expert knowledge in the fields of climate, agriculture, transportation, and economics. The goal of this commission was to propose how Denmark can phase out fossil fuels in the future. In 2010 it delivered the report "Green Energy – the road to a Danish energy system without fossil fuels (Grøn energi – vejen mod et energisystem uden fossile brændsler)." In the report the commission stated that even as Danish energy demand is expected to double there are ample renewable resources to cover the rising need.

Potential renewable energy from Danish sources, in PJ

	Current production	Total potential resource	How much of consumption in 2050 can the energy resource technically cover?
Wind	26	1.220	>250%
Wave power	0	40	<10%
Solar electricity and heating	1	250	<50%
Biofuels and waste	89	250*	<50%
Total renewables**	123	1.760	>300%

* Incl. 20 PJ fossil fuel waste

** Heat from geothermal installations and heat pumps is not included in the estimate, as the potential is hard to determine

Source: "Green Energy – the road to a Danish energy system without fossil fuels," Danish Climate Commisson

5. PREPARING GOVERNMENTS FOR THE FUTURE

Redefining your ambition One thing is believing and making sure the Danish society has the necessary and potential resources to make Denmark a 100% sustainable energy system; another and much harder task is to implement the ambition by convincing its population and business communities to convert to the use of renewables. It requires one very important thing, namely a change in behavior, a change that can be achieved either through incentives or legal regulations.

The Climate Commission made 40 recommendations to the Danish government in terms of driving the required changes, a selection of which are:

General
- That a new tax be introduced on fossil fuels, which will ensure that the market mechanism becomes the driver of choice. A clear message on the gradual, projected increase of the tax provides a secure environment for investment decisions
- Funding for research and development to be maintained at the current year's level, with stable funding over five to ten year intervals

Energy efficiency
- A new "energy savings account" introduced for all buildings. The account is linked to the individual building. The lower the building's energy efficiency the higher will be its required saving. The savings are available for projects, which improve the building's energy efficiency
- Higher incentives for the use of heat pumps
- No new oil heaters after 2015

Transport
- Duty reductions on electric cars extended after 2015 until a critical mass of 100,000 cars is reached. Duty reductions to encompass plug-in hybrids
- A single plan for an infrastructure to allow charging of electric cars
- Demonstration of the use of biogas in heavy load transportation

The total energy system
- A complete plan for an intelligent electrical grid in Denmark (smart grid)
- Extension of offshore wind turbine capacity by 200 MW/year from 2015 to 2025

Other
- Strengthened international efforts for continued energy efficiency improvements
- Efforts in relation to other sources of greenhouse gases (primarily from agriculture)
- A statutory framework for the vision of Denmark becoming independent of fossil fuels complemented by regular reviews of progress towards the ultimate goal

5. PREPARING GOVERNMENTS FOR THE FUTURE

Creating options While Denmark is fighting to keep its position as a strong economy globally it has positioned itself as the "World's Greenest Economy" and believes that export of sustainability knowledge and technology is a competitive resource that could generate much needed revenues for the Danish welfare model. However, the competition is fierce as many other countries, e.g. Germany, Korea, China, U.S., and Sweden, also are concentrating on green technology. This raises the question of who will be the winning countries/companies in this field.

Denmark has a large number of businesses with strong competences in areas such as wind turbines, district heating, process optimization, insulation, and the manufacturing of biofuels. For some parts of the Danish business community, addressing the major climate and energy policy challenges could, therefore, serve as an important lever for green growth. It could also provide valuable opportunities in the global market, where there is a growing demand for innovative solutions within green energy.

Reshaping how you work One of the first recommendations from the Climate Commission, and perhaps the most important, was the establishment of an overall legal framework for making Denmark carbon-neutral by 2050. To keep its place as the "World's Greenest Economy" and to make sure that the result of the commission's work was not just an aspirational but empty statement about a long-term goal of a 100% sustainable energy system, it was critical that the Danish government act on the commission's work. It did. In 2012, the Danish government signed an historical agreement with ambitious energy policy initiatives for the period 2012 to 2020, including a continuous review of progress. It also ensures that at the end of 2018 complementary initiatives will be discussed for the period after 2020.

Learn-act-learn-adjust The guiding principle of the Climate Commission has been that it cannot, and should not, identify exactly what the energy system will look like in 2050 or identify which technologies and solutions are best. There is no guarantee that today's fossil-free technologies will mature further. New technologies will emerge, so a critical challenge for the Danish government is, through its legal framework, to continuously be informed about and take advantage of new, perhaps unanticipated breakthroughs. Another challenge is to ensure that Danish society and business communities are able to develop, with for example well-functioning homes, transport needs met, and plentiful job opportunities. Transforming the Danish energy system must support this development, not be a barrier to it. These challenges will therefore requiring constant monitoring of and learning from progress towards the country's green ambition.

Sources: Danish Energy Agency (Energistyrelsen), Politiken, 2050 Something's Green in the State of Denmark

5. PREPARING GOVERNMENTS FOR THE FUTURE

5.3 IN BRIEF EXAMPLES OF GOVERNMENTS PREPARING FOR THE FUTURE

Rethinking waste in South Korea As landfills multiply and the steady stream of waste seems never ending, we will inevitable run out of space to "store" what we no longer use. The philosophy of zero waste is to redesign the whole life cycle of resource use, including product design, use, and disposal, so that all elements of a product can be reused, eliminating waste. In South Korea, the KWMN (Korea Waste Movement Network) was set up as a core-networking group, bringing together many NGO groups. It initially worked to reduce the use of disposable tableware in fast food chains with projects such as "Bring Your Own Cup." The group now also leads committees on packaging, toxic waste, and policy guidance. In 2010, the Ministry of the Environment approved a key KWMN initiative, leading to South Korea's major superstores declaring a "No Disposable Plastic Bags" policy. By late 2011 more than half of shoppers (55.1%) were using their own tote bag, cardboard box or simply moving groceries directly from cart to car. Since then more stores have joined the initiative.

Waste is also a focus for industrial players. In the automotive industry, General Motors has declared the Cheongna proving ground landfill-free, bringing the company's total to 33 sites throughout Asia that recycle, reuse, or convert to energy all their daily waste. At Cheongna materials required for vehicle development and research, including batteries, plastic, chassis components, packaging, and chemicals are recycled. (Sources: KWMN, General Motors, Plastic Free Times)

Africa's wired future – digitizing Rwanda ICT technologies are reaching every corner of earth, including resource-poor Rwanda. The country aims to transform its agrarian economy into a knowledge-based economy by 2020 using ICT. The country has invested in education, made partnerships with foreign universities, and is expanding its ICT environment by installing fiber-optic cables. Services such as E-Soko, a mobile service that allows farmers to check market prices for their products, have already improved the daily life of many Rwandans. With these new technologies, Rwanda hopes to capitalize on its central location in Africa to act as a hub for banking, financial, and outsourcing services. (Source: WEF, Global Information Technology Report 2013)

Nigeria as a hub for innovation Nigeria is poor but progressing: it has an abundant supply of oil to anchor the economy, a growing population of more than 160 million people and current real GDP growth of 6.4% expected to rise to 7.2% in 2014. Its growth potential reaches far beyond oil and resources, with sectors including telecommunications, constructions, wholesale and retail trade, hospitality, manufacturing, and agriculture also driving economic development. Its next frontier: becoming a hub for innovation and new technologies.

A newly opened Co-Creation Hub (CcHub) in Lagos is a state-of-the-art space for innovation. Here, developers come together to create and develop technology such as mobile phone apps, teaching tools, movie editing, and special effects software. It also aims to achieve government funded installation of fiber optic cables and free Wi-Fi access in the area surrounding the hub. The government is supportive, recognizing the need to boost broadband penetration in the state, especially in support of education. Beyond the capital, the state of Abia has announced the building of an open access fiber optic network. Lagos-based Broadbased Communications will bear the costs and provide technical expertise for the project, with the government providing the right of way. The project aims to provide connectivity for "everything-e" from e-learning to e-commerce and e-government. (Source: CNN, All Africa)

Cyber warfare departments Cybercrime and cyberattacks have become a real threat to individuals as well as governments, whether from cyberattacks on Iran's nuclear enrichment program, or from whistleblower Edward J. Snowden's revelations of unauthorized government surveillance of citizens and organizations in the U.S. and around the globe. Throughout the world, nations are willing to pay big money to hackers to acquire information that they can use against the computers, software, and information networks of their perceived "enemies" or even "friends."

Faced with this rising tide of cybercrime, both the European Commission and the White House are trying to set out a series of new rules. In 2013, U.S. President Barack Obama released an executive order intended to plug the gap left by the failure of a divided Congress to pass cyber security legislation that matches the growing threat. According to a secret presidential directive obtained by the Guardian, Obama has ordered his senior national security and intelligence officials to draw up a list of potential overseas targets for U.S. cyberattacks.

As for the European Commission, their cyber security strategy is at an earlier stage. It wants member countries to introduce laws compelling important firms in industries such as transport, telecoms, finance and online infrastructure to disclose details of any attack they suffer to a national authority, known as a CERT (Computer Emergency Response Team). Each CERT will be responsible for defending against online attacks and sharing information with its counterparts. The EU's Cyber Security Strategy has however received a lukewarm reception with worries that the proposals are too vague and open-ended and lack protection for personal data. Despite governments attempting to prepare for a new world of cyber security, there seems to be some way to go before we can feel safe behind our computer screens. (Sources: New York Times, HNGN, the Economist, the Guardian, Naked Security)

Building a "Big Society" The UK's "Big Society" was the flagship policy idea of the Conservative Party in 2010. It aims to empower local people and communities by involving them in projects for renewable energy, neighborhood developments, sustainable transportation, youth and school, volunteering and more. The first ever audit of the changes made so far shows a high level of public interest and a degree of community involvement in social action through giving and volunteering. However, in striking contrast, the decline of public engagement with national political parties and trust in national politicians is a huge challenge. The voluntary sector is also facing a cut in statutory funding of £3.3 billion between 2010-16, a gap which is unlikely to be filled by increased donations. (Source: Civil Exchange, "The Big Society Audit 2012")

Jet fuel from seawater – the new alternative to fossil fuel Refuelling navy jets, at sea and while underway, is a costly affair on many levels. The U.S. Naval Research Laboratory is developing a technology to extract carbon dioxide and produce hydrogen gas from seawater, subsequently catalytically converting the CO_2 and H_2 into jet fuel by a gas-to liquids process. The potential payoff is the ability to produce JP-5 fuel stock at sea reducing the logistics issues of fuel delivery with no environmental burden, while also increasing the Navy's energy security and independence. (Source: NRL)

Vietnam's hybrid model In the past 20 years Vietnam has gone from being one of the poorest places on earth to one of South-East Asia's success stories. The transition of the country's political system from state dominance towards a hybrid mix of Marxism and capitalism has brought enormous economic progress, and the Vietnamese economy has weathered the current global financial crisis relatively well due to consumer spending, exports, and a vast flow of foreign direct investment (the 2013 target is US$13-14 billion). In a meeting between Vietnam's President Truong Tan Sand and U.S. President Barack Obama, the two countries pledged to deepen trade and military ties even as they tangled over human rights. The meeting followed a difficult period in which Vietnam's Communist government has cracked down at home, imprisoning bloggers, religious leaders, and dissidents, and curtailing labor laws. Whether Obama is able to help Vietnam become a modern democratic country is yet to be seen. (Source: Thanh Nien News, New York Times)

5. PREPARING GOVERNMENTS FOR THE FUTURE

5.4 FOOD FOR THOUGHT ON THE FUTURE LANDSCAPE OF GOVERNMENTS

South Africa – whose responsibility is it to address social challenges?

Overwhelmed and under-resourced governments can be found around the world. Often these are nations with high growth prospects, but facing challenges of preparing their populations, economies, and societies both for rapid development and a greater role on the world stage. Many can be found among the BRICS and beyond markets discussed above, with many in Asia and Africa. Typical challenges include educating a growing younger population, often from a low base, e.g. Nigeria and South Africa; developing the infrastructure required to compete globally, e.g. India; moving up the manufacturing value chain away from reliance on raw material exports to drive a more vibrant economy, e.g. Brazil; and tackling poverty and youth unemployment in many countries. While many of these challenges are economic, the economics drive the development of societies themselves. The big question for those governments that do not have the resources or skills to tackle everything at once is whose responsibility is it to address these issues anyway?

South Africa is a land of contradictions, rich in opportunities and resources, but struggling with many of the issues above. It enjoys the global possibilities of resource development, if these resources can be developed in an appropriate and sustainable way. It has the potential to be a showcase for the rest of the world in using education as a tool to fight poverty, to bridge the gap between rich and poor and to develop a middle class as a critical step in nurturing sustainable economic growth. But it can only do this if leaders across society work together to achieve the country's potential.

Key, interlinked challenges include education and poverty. According to Mike Brown, CEO of Nedbank, "We effectively have a two-tier educational system: a private school educational system that can compete with any system in the world, producing fantastically qualified people who are eminently employable in any of the world centers; and a public school educational system that consumes around 20% of the total budget and has many challenges with few pockets of excellence. Our national budget is around R950 billion, so there's around R200 billion going into education, and it's just not producing the goods." (Source: Interview with Mike Brown, IMD LCF Interview Series 2011-01)

So who is responsible for addressing these challenges? In South Africa, business leaders are increasingly stepping up to help the government in its efforts, recognizing that economic and societal development is a prerequisite for business success.

Tongaat Hulett is an agricultural company, but its purpose is more than producing and selling food. Governments cannot solve the world's problems alone, so it is business's responsibility, Peter Staude, the company's CEO said, to help create the environment for success.

"We are not only in agriculture and food, but also in land development," the South Africa-based CEO said. "We sometimes expand on our business description by saying we want to create successful rural communities in the areas where we operate. We want people who live and work in those rural areas to say, 'This is a great place to work, a great place to live, and a great place to bring up kids.' This is the direction we're working towards for all sorts of reasons."

The company's purpose shapes where Tongaat Hulett operates, what it does – for example, it is moving into long-term partnerships with governments to help develop land and energy resources – and how it operates. Staude's personal purpose aligns with that of his company: "I want my organization, my country, and my region to perform. I am really passionate about this region and its people. I see all this possibility, I see the many people that really want to improve their lives and their economic reality." (Source: *Ready? The 3Rs of preparing your organization for the future* by Thomas W. Malnight, Tracey S. Keys, and Kees van der Graaf, 2013)

5. PREPARING GOVERNMENTS FOR THE FUTURE

Another innovative approach to developing Africa's young talent on the global stage is demonstrated by African Fashion International. The company works in partnership with the government to develop and promote the best design talent not just from South Africa where it is headquartered but from across different parts of the African continent. It has created leading, world-class platforms aimed at driving the growth of the industry and the support of these designers, through events (with corporate sponsorship), seminars, showrooms, trade exhibitions, and educational programs that help the designers both to learn about the industry of fashion design and running a business.

Core to the effort are the career education programs including AFI Fastrack™, the national graduate fashion platform offered by AFI. This initiative offers emerging designers a chance to be exposed to the market though the fashion week vehicle. It provides growth opportunities to participating designers through seminars, workshops, and career education. AFI The Next Generation is the second-phase development platform. It offers graduates from the AFI Fastrack™ program an opportunity to further their fashion businesses through continued growth opportunities such as mentoring by designers who have already established successful businesses.

In highlighting the importance of developing the African fashion industry and young talent, AFI's website quotes Dr Precious Moloi-Motsepe as saying: "Sustainability of the clothing and manufacturing sector in South Africa will need an infusion of local fashion talent that brings diversity and authenticity to the global fashion landscape. Africa cannot compete with companies in the East, as they are able to produce large volumes at low cost. Where we can compete is in high value added products. We are blessed with a talent pool that can add value in design aesthetic and unique hand finish. The development of young fashion designers is vital to creating a sustainable and commercially viable industry."

Discussing the role of business in society more broadly in the interview, Dr. Moloi-Motsepe said: "I think business in South Africa is very engaged with government, has seen the advantage of being actively engaged in government. If you think of when black economic empowerment was introduced, there were a lot of companies that were already practicing that, and were not doing it to score points. So that was good.

"Does business do what it's supposed to do to make sure that society grows? There's still a need for more of that. The focus globally has always been on making a success of the business outside of the broader community and the broader society, and I think there is a need to think much more broadly than just how successful a company is. We need leaders that will start thinking about the success of a company and its relationship to the success and development of the society. Developing nations like South Africa have an opportunity to push that agenda of successful companies being accountable and contributing towards the growth and development of society."

The creation of AFI was a contribution to the need that Dr. Moloi-Motsepe recognized in creating jobs and developing industries where South Africa could be a global player. "African Fashion International sees itself as playing a very important role, firstly, in helping to grow and develop South Africans, and also in bringing that back to people who unfortunately are out of work and do not have an opportunity to go back and learn and be able to take up new jobs. We have many, many, many of those.

"So what we do is develop the creative industry of fashion designers, because we believe that it's a talent that most South Africans have, and Africans have become a source of inspiration for the world in terms of design – and we have extended our work from South Africa to different parts of the African continent. So we use that, the design component, and support the designers. Some of them really haven't even been through school, so we help to make sure that their inherent talent is realized. When they grow and become successful they're able to set up their own enterprises where they can give jobs to local communities.

"One thing that we are really passionate about is to bring back the pride of being South African, to help people do something for themselves. It's really about helping these marginalized people, often women and young people, to develop that self-confidence and to find their purpose in life. With this they are able inspire others in their communities."

(Sources: http://www.afi.za.com; interview with Dr. Precious Moloi-Motsepe, Executive Chairperson of AFI in 2011 by Thomas W. Malnight and Kees van der Graaf)

5. PREPARING GOVERNMENTS FOR THE FUTURE

Is China forward thinking or exploitative?

Sixty years ago, China was a poor agrarian economy struggling with internal social and political turmoil. Today it is the world's second largest economy and on track to become the biggest, as well a major geopolitical and military power. Working its way out of poverty, China has shown impressive, consistent growth for decades. With a vast but ageing population – just short of 1.4 billion – the need not only to meet basic needs such as food and shelter, but also to improve living standards has made this nation one of the world's most hardworking, with an intense focus on societal and economic development. It is also now stepping up to a greater role in global affairs, economically, and geopolitically, commensurate with its increasing size and influence – and reflecting its long history of being a world power before the rise of the West a little over two centuries ago. In fact, the U.S. is no longer being viewed as the leading global superpower – many nations believe that China has already taken that place.

The question is whether this colossus of a nation is being forward thinking in its engagement with the rest of the world or whether it can be accused of being exploitative. The same question may also be applied to the government's relations with its own citizens.

November 2013's Third Plenary Session of China's central government outlined ambitious social, economic, and political reforms, which will be important in addressing the country's internal issues of government bureaucracy, widening regional and rural-urban economic imbalances, the need for more market-orientated allocation of resources to improve efficiency and the need to stimulate domestic consumption to reduce reliance on the export-led growth model of recent decades. Under the new leadership of President Xi Jinping, the challenge will be not only to establish his administration's power, but to implement these reforms against a backdrop of slower economic growth, a weak financial system riddled with local government debt, powerful but inefficient state owned enterprises, rampant pollution and environmental degradation and the potential for social and political unrest.

Even as it tackles these significant internal challenges, China is also looking outwards, seeking to broaden its role and influence in its immediate region as well as globally. It is also building trading and investment relationships, which will allow it to access the resources it requires to maintain its growth trajectory. However, resources alone are insufficient: China's focus on developing its own capabilities, industries, and companies into global leaders means huge investments in new technologies, research and development, and education. For example space, green technologies, renewable energy, and ICT sectors are all receiving significant attention. So how are China's relationships evolving with the rest of the world?

While the rest of the world is focusing its attention on terrorism, spying, climate change, financial meltdowns, Syria, and Ukraine amongst other pressing issues, the Chinese have been busy building influence – or seeking to do so – in their neighboring regions, which are like China, vast. Old disputes over territories in the East and South China Seas have been resumed with vigor, backed up by an increasing naval military buildup, creating tensions with many of China's neighbors including Japan, South Korea, Vietnam, and the Philippines. For example, the Scarborough Shoal off the Philippines in the South Sea has been claimed by the Chinese, while the unilateral declaration of an air defense identification zone which extends to the disputed island chain known Diaoyu in China and as Senkaku in Japan has exacerbated an already extremely tense situation. The latter has been inflamed further by China's Hainan province declaring new fishing rules in January 2014 requiring foreign fishing vessels to obtain approval before entering the disputed waters, as the local government maintains they are under its jurisdiction. The escalation is viewed with disquiet in many corridors of power, as the risks of unintended conflict situations are high. But what is the cause of China's perceived aggression? Part comes down to history of the region, with a number of outstanding border and territory disputes running over decades in South-East Asia, part is attributed to a new president and administration establishing legitimacy domestically in a nation with high anti-Japanese sentiment – and part comes down to a fight for control over valuable resources which are anticipated to be within the disputed territory.

The quest for resources is a recurring theme. In recent years China's enormous growth machine has invested heavily,

5. PREPARING GOVERNMENTS FOR THE FUTURE

particularly in Africa, to access natural resources. While part of such investments, for example in infrastructure such as railroads, airports, and roads, contributes to development in the local countries, often these projects rely on imported Chinese labor rather than providing local job opportunities. In addition, the considerable exports of natural resources do not necessarily help Africa to develop, with the substantial investments by China and other foreign countries being likened to a new wave of colonization. Whether China's growing presence is good or bad for Africa seems to be difficult for even the most experienced analyst to decide. Is China just being a neutral, business-oriented country exploring new market opportunities and sources of supply, particularly as the days of China as a cheap manufacturing country are numbered? What is the role of Chinese state-owned enterprises in the mix and what are their motivations? While China may be the biggest investor in Africa, it will continue to face tough competition from other players such as India, Brazil, and Japan which are also actively seeking business opportunities on the continent and often are more focused on engaging and developing the local economies through their efforts. (Sources: Africa Research Institute, CNN) Let us also not forget that even as China buys resources from other countries, it has proven less willing to share its own: as the virtual monopoly producer of rare earths, which are vital for many modern products from cell phones to wind turbines and consumer electronics, China has at times restricted exports both to benefit domestic manufacturers and for leverage in geopolitical disputes.

A critical source of China's ability to invest, not just in Africa but worldwide, is its substantial foreign exchange reserves, built up over years of trade surpluses. China is increasingly a source of funds for the world, as was seen during the global financial crisis. State entities are becoming more global in their investment outlook, but key drivers of Chinese expansion abroad are the fast-growing companies, which are building their reputations and businesses on a global scale. Chinese technology company Lenovo, which bought IBM's PC business in 2005 and expanded it successfully, has in the last full week of January 2014, gone on another spending spree, agreeing to purchase IBM's low-end server business for US$2.3 billion and Google's Motorola mobile phone business in a deal worth US$2.9 billion over three years. "We dream to become a global player," Lenovo CEO, Yang Yuanqing said in an interview. "You must be a global player to have global presence. Only being in China and emerging markets is not enough."

He is not alone in targeting Western companies: in 2013 Chinese pork producer Shuanghui International bought U.S. meat giant Smithfield Foods for US$4.7 billion, aiming to export more of the company's output to China to feed rising demand. The U.S. was the leading target of Chinese investors, receiving over US$14 billion in 2013. (Sources: AEI Ideas, BBC, Bloomberg)

While China is buying up Western companies, advanced technologies, and resources, as a part of their globalization strategy, the business environment in China is getting increasingly difficult. Foreign companies that once had leverage there are being challenged over practices that once were acceptable but no longer are, e.g. Tim Cook, CEO of Apple was forced apologize for "arrogance" in the application of a warranty program for its iPhone4 devices, while GlaxoSmithKline has been held accountable for bribing doctors and hospitals to prescribe its drugs. Heads of state are no longer immune either with French President Hollande and British Prime Minister Cameron feeling the heat from the Chinese and now trying to play the Chinese game. (Source: FT) Does this cracking of the whip reflect increased confidence among its leaders of China's position in the world?

Clearly there are pros and cons for the rest of the world of Chinese expansionist strategies, economically, politically, and militarily. The world has benefitted immensely from the country's growth, even while criticizing its methods including human rights abuses, suppression of dissent, and environmental damage, and expressing fears over the risks that a China dominant in technologies critical for the future may pose. This poses two questions: *One*, is the rest of the world complicit in China's expansion and therefore wrong to complain when the country seeks to develop itself economically and politically and to secure needed resources on behalf of its citizens? *Two*, should the Chinese be listening more closely to the voices of the world's societies, in order to achieve a rise to power that is in equilibrium with its and the world's interests rather than risking conflict?

The answers to these questions are not clear, but what is clear is that China's ascendance comes with a very high price tag at home. China now accommodates 157 billionaires, the second-highest number in the world after the U.S. with 515 billionaires, adding ten in 2013. (Source: CNBC) Despite the massive growth in wealth and a rising middle class China is struggling with widening income inequality on top of toxic corporate and local government debts. Even more worrying is the environmental and health price tag. Despite heavy investments in green energy pollution permeates rural and urban societies; images from NASA's Earth Observatory satellite show a choking layer of smog descended over Beijing and its surroundings. It is not only the air: China's soil and water are equally polluted. Rapid industrialization, a reliance on coal, and disregard for environmental laws have degraded agricultural land and water supplies such that in some parts of the country land can no longer be used for food production. The bigger cost? An increasing number of Chinese now suffer from cancer, chronic respiratory, and cardiovascular diseases. Inequality, pollution, and health represent just some of the internal challenges for China's leaders – and potential sources of social and political unrest. Add to this a rapidly ageing population, the financial system, reforming the state owned sector, corruption, and ethnic and cultural tensions in Tibet, Nepal, and other parts of the far-reaching Chinese nation.

Is China forward thinking or exploitative? China is certainly thinking ahead and making its voice heard as a potential superpower on the international stage, even as questions remain over whether its domestic interests need to be better balanced with greater global interests. Perhaps the more interesting question is closer to home: Will it remove censorship and restrictions on freedom of speech/internet/association to let the voices of its own citizens be heard in thinking ahead?

5.5 SUMMARY: 8 PRINCIPLES OF PREPARING FOR THE FUTURE IN ACTION IN GOVERNMENTS

As with businesses preparing for the future, governments also need to consider what insights can be found in the case studies, in brief examples and food for thought topics to help them in their endeavors to prepare for a successful future. The following insights stand out:

1. Embrace ambiguity: don't just think outside the box, throw away the boxes

While national boxes are hard to throw away, the rise of cities as drivers of economic development and the increasing global mobility of people, knowledge, communications, and transport is helping to foster a greater awareness in governments of blurring boundaries between key stakeholders. However, there is still caution and concern at national levels about protecting the self-interest of both citizens and, in some cases, governing bodies, for example when looking at cyber security or freedom of speech. The **uneasy balance between openness and control** means that there will be boxes and boundaries for many years yet. However, there are promising signs in some of the above examples of how governments are seeking to **learn on a global basis**, e.g. in terms of technology advances, and education standards and practices. In addition, the **rise of public-private partnerships** domestically is opening the way to more dynamic and flexible models of economic and social development, as well as governance of key projects.

2. Think first from the outside-in, then inside-out

Many governments – at least government agencies, if not politicians who tend to have a shorter-term view – are **looking deeply at the trends and behavior changes** which are happening both **in their markets and in the business value chains** their nations support. Countries such as Denmark are **tapping into the private sector and academic expertise** required to achieve their green ambitions, actively seeking new perspectives and options, while rapidly developing economies in Africa, including Rwanda and Nigeria, are **looking at the leapfrog potential of new ICT technologies**. In the majority of cases, these nations are **taking a global perspective** recognizing the need to learn from the best knowledge and experience worldwide.

3. Identify and address root causes, not symptoms

A **strategic focus on future needs** of the societies, global markets, and business constituencies they serve, and the **capabilities required to meet these needs**, is increasingly evident from Singapore to Ireland to South Africa. The aim is to **build sustainable economies and societies**, actively **moving up the value ladder** and in many cases positioning the country's competitiveness in its chosen fields on a global scale and **addressing global challenges** such as energy in Denmark and food security in China. A core underpinning for many of the governments is a **focus on world-class education**. Talent, knowledge, and technological advances are seen as critical to achieving ambitions and long-term development.

4. Practice two-directional thinking

Like some of the businesses discussed in the previous chapter, some governments are taking an active role in **shaping the future** of global industries and markets. China's ambitions in space and clean technologies (despite massive and ongoing pollution issues) are well known, while Nigeria wants to position itself as an innovation hub and Rwanda wants to become a digital hub for Africa. Achieving these aims demands **long-term thinking**, something which rapidly developing nations have often been better at than developed ones, although the horizons of both Denmark and Ireland can be seen to be a couple of decades or more ahead, rather than a couple of years. As with businesses, such long-term thinking needs to be balanced with acceleration of **addressing short-term issues and measuring progress**, as Singapore does in terms of monitoring its ongoing competitiveness.

5. Manage in relationships/networks versus transactions

Governments are operating in an environment where trust in institutions is low and has been falling, and where the voice of other stakeholders from citizens to NGOs is increasingly powerful. Many are now realizing and reaping the benefits of **building relationships with key stakeholders to bring new perspectives, resources, and knowledge** to address critical issues and achieve shared ambitions. Partnerships with the private sector and academia are important in Singapore and Ireland, **driving new ways of working and business models**, while South Korea's success in addressing waste is built on broad partnerships between business, government, and civil society.

6. Focus on co-creation

Similarly, South Africa's search for sustainable development and focus on building new capabilities such as design and creativity is blurring the roles of business and government, **building shared value by working together to co-create future capabilities**. While nationalism and protectionism are increasing challenges for governments around the world, nations such as Singapore are leading the way in **creating hubs of knowledge, talent, and technology** to serve and co-create with the broader Asian region, as well as globally. Rwanda and Nigeria too have their sights set on developing mutually reinforcing clusters of ICT and innovation enterprises, both on a domestic and regional level, which will demand close interactions between the public and private sectors, as well as with entrepreneurs, academia, and civil society.

5. PREPARING GOVERNMENTS FOR THE FUTURE

7. Align purpose and profit

Arguably, governments are more interested in purpose than profit. Their remit is sound governance of the national interests of societies and economies. However, the financial crisis and its aftermath in terms of high national debts and weakened financial institutions in many countries has highlighted the need for **sound financial management of national accounts**, as well as for ensuring a country **improves its ability to add value** on products and services, and through globally competitive resources and capabilities. Rising income inequality further reinforces these requirements in preparing countries and their citizens for the future. The result has been an increasing willingness by forward-thinking governments to look at **new models of cooperation with business** and new ways of working to achieve social and economic goals, for example in Singapore and in South Africa.

8. Embed continual challenge, avoid complacent compliance

Democratic governance systems have continual challenge of political ideas at their heart, although this can be counter-productive when short-term political gains (and retention of power) obscure long-term development needs. It is often easy to take the popular route and leave the long-term problems for the next administration. The challenge for democratic governments is to **establish a path**, as Denmark is doing, towards long-term ambitions that transcend single party interests. For centrally controlled and hybrid governance models the challenge is to **encourage other voices to challenge conventional thinking** – or even allow them a voice as a first step. For all governments, as the examples above show, the biggest opportunity is to harness the flows of communications and knowledge **to learn globally from the leaders** in many fields, whether technology, education, public-private partnerships, or talent development.

Even as the nations highlighted above offer important insights in preparing for the future, many governments around the world still have a long way to go. Dogged by bureaucracy, and with short-term political horizons in many cases, it is very hard to think differently and to drive behavior changes and action across the complex landscape of stakeholders in pursuit of ambitions, which may not be accepted by all constituencies. In particular, governments face challenges of:

- Balancing protecting national interests with addressing global challenges
- Developing the foundations of talent, knowledge, technologies, and capabilities to underpin sustainable economic and social development
- Driving real long-term transformation in the face of short-term political interests, bureaucracy, and complex societal pressures
- Dealing with inequality and including disenfranchised parts of societies
- Building thriving stakeholder partnerships and relationships, domestically, regionally, and globally to drive mutual benefits

6. PREPARING NGOS FOR THE FUTURE

6. PREPARING NGOS FOR THE FUTURE

Chapter six focuses on how non-governmental organizations (NGOs) are translating macro implications into specific insights and actions to prepare for the future. As in the previous and subsequent chapters, the first subsection provides some context, looking at the key trends that are impacting the landscape within which each type of organizations is operating.

The second subsection focuses on detailed case studies, offering insights into how different NGOs are approaching the challenges of preparing for the future in a networked world of multiple stakeholders. Each detailed case study, explores the organization's thinking and actions using the lens of the 3Rs model below: what are the key trends and implications impacting the organization; how did these drive rethinking the playing field; how did the organization redefine their ambition (vision, purpose, targets, measures) as a result; what were the options they considered in building an agenda for action; how did they reshape how they worked; and what is the ongoing process of learn-act-learn-adjust.

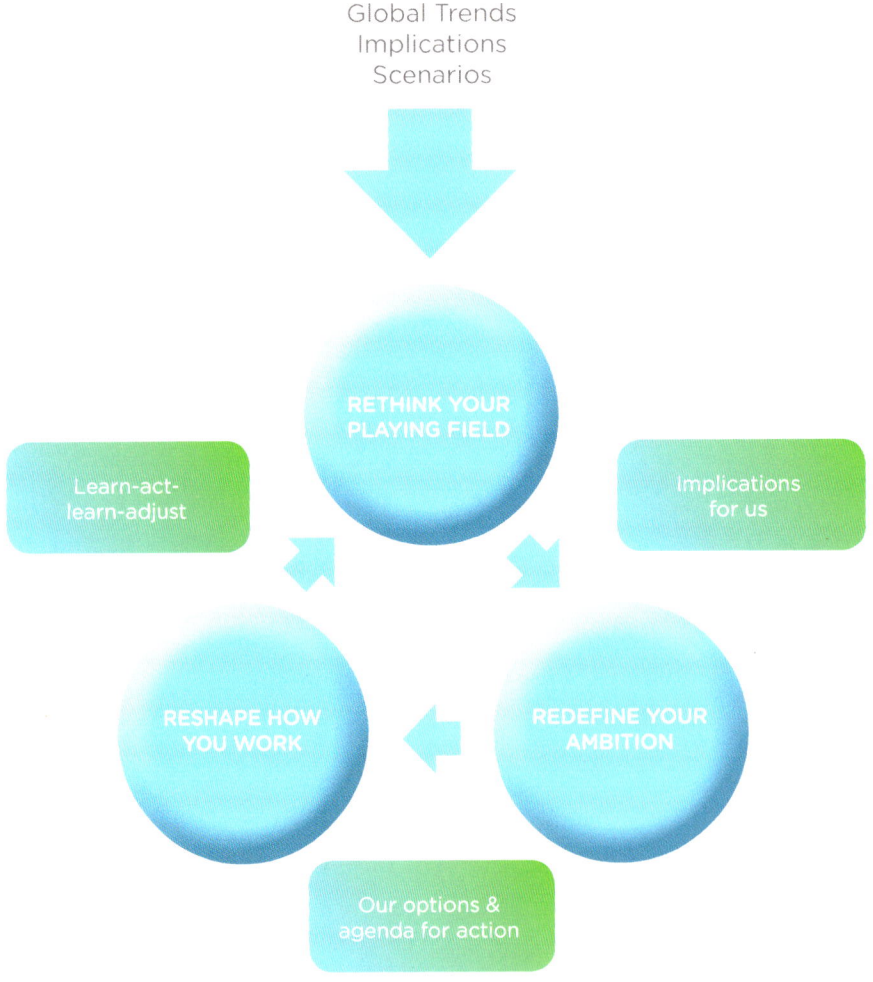

Global Trends
Implications
Scenarios

RETHINK YOUR PLAYING FIELD

Learn-act-learn-adjust

implications for us

RESHAPE HOW YOU WORK

REDEFINE YOUR AMBITION

Our options & agenda for action

The third subsection provides some in brief examples of how other organizations are preparing for the future in specific areas, e.g. tackling the challenges of sustainability and waste. The fourth highlights food for thought examples, which are designed to provoke thinking on some of the key challenges facing organizations in the future, which many NGOs are grappling with, e.g. building philanthropy into the investment agenda, and driving social innovation.Finally, in subsection five, we draw together some insights to take away from these examples using the 8 principles introduced in Chapter 3.

6. PREPARING NGOS FOR THE FUTURE

6.1 THE 21ST CENTURY NGO

A rapidly increasing number of non-governmental organizations (NGOs)[11] is tackling an expanding portfolio of issues from poverty to productive retirement for ageing populations, both internationally and within countries.

While the lack of an official data gathering source means estimates of the numbers of NGOs vary widely, domestic NGOs number in the millions globally. A 2010 estimate of 40,000 international NGOs, based on the growth in the number of NGOs in consultative status with the UN (ECOSOC), shows an increase in these organizations of 60% between 2001 and 2010[12]. The rise in numbers can be attributed to a range of factors, including perceptions of the failure of both governments and markets in adequately addressing the concerns of the individuals and groups who set up and fund the NGOs. A study by Johns Hopkins University reveals that at least 4.6% of the adult population in 40 countries are volunteers or paid staff in non-profit organizations. This represents the equivalent of 48.4 million full-time equivalent workers, and makes an estimated US$1.9 trillion output contribution to the global economy, or around 5% of the world's GDP[13]. Yet these huge numbers have remained largely invisible in official economic statistics even though the sector is the size of one of the bigger economies in the world, France.

NGOs have more power than ever before and a new type of NGO is emerging for the 21st century. 20th century NGOs spent the second half of that century as outsiders, challenging the system, while today and looking forward, NGOs will increasingly be part of the system of social, political, and economic development. Gone are the days of simply highlighting problems around single issues; NGOs now are much more focused on developing solutions around a multidimensional agenda, often with a global view. This requires expanded networks and a shift towards partnerships with all relevant stakeholders, whether public, for-profit, non-profit, or community institutions. Funding is no longer driven largely by guilt or anger but by a focus on investments to create mutual benefits between stakeholders and the societies and communities in which they operate. This also means adopting best practices in transparency, accountability, and governance. (Source: SustainAbility, The 21st Century NGO Project)

NGOs can be broadly grouped into several types: *Operational* NGOs design and implement on-the-ground development-related projects and are often categorized as relief-oriented or development-oriented organizations. *Advocacy* NGOs defend or promote a specific cause, typically trying to raise awareness, acceptance, and knowledge by lobbying, press work, and activist events. *Foundations* provide expertise, funding, and grants to NGOs, as well as often acting as an operational NGO in their chosen fields. In addition, there are a number of emerging organizational and business models including B Corporations, hybrid non-profit and for-profit organizations, philanthrocapitalism (see more below), and crowd-driven philanthropy, an approach to collaboration and innovation that allows ordinary people to do big things even when money is scarce. As social entrepreneurship increases and businesses become more involved in responsible capitalism, look out for more new ways to deliver the aims of NGOs, with a particular emphasis on partnership between a variety of stakeholders.

[11] Apart from NGO, alternative terms are often used include: independent sector, volunteer sector, civil society, grassroots organizations, transnational social movement organizations, private voluntary organizations, self-help organizations, and non-state actors (NSAs). NGO communities display significant differences country by country, reflecting country-specific factors that affect the structure and composition of NGO communities and the role NGOs play in national development.

[12] Sources: Center for the Study of Global Governance - Global Civil Society 2004/5 estimate, UN

[13] Source: Johns Hopkins Center for Civil Society Studies via Slideshare.net

6.   PREPARING NGOS FOR THE FUTURE

Just as NGO organizations are evolving, so too are their aims and how they operate, the evolution of which can be traced over time:

	First generation	Second generation	Third generation	Fourth generation	Fifth generation
	Relief and welfare	Community development	Sustainable systems development	People's movements	Partnerships for social/economic development
Problem definition	Shortage/disaster	Local inertia	Institutional and policy constraints	Inadequate mobilizing vision	Multidimensional agenda; inability of one organization to effect change alone
Time frame	Immediate	Project life	10 to 20 years	Indefinite future	Short- and long-term projects
Scope	Individual or family	Neighborhood or village	Region or nation	National or global	3D worldview: communities at all levels (local, region, national, international)
Chief actors	NGO	NGO + community	All relevant public and private institutions	Loosely defined networks of people and organizations	NGOs, all relevant public and private stakeholders, networks, individuals
NGO Role	Doer	Mobilizer	Catalyst	Activist/educator	Catalyst and partner for change
Management orientation	Logistics management	Project management	Strategic management	Coalescing and energizing self-managing networks	Strategic partnership and technology driven, networks, hybrid organizations
Funding	Donations due to guilt/anger	Donations, community funds	Donations, public funds, international aid, foundations	Donations, public funds, international aid, foundations	Investment, triple bottom line, crowdfunding, foundations
Development education	Starving children	Community self-help	Constraining policies and institutions	Spaceship earth	Mutual benefit, shared value

Sources: Framework from David C Korten (1990) "Getting to the 21st Century – voluntary action and the global agenda," adapted and extended based on SustainAbility - The 21st Century NGO Project, and Strategy Dynamics Global SA analysis

6. PREPARING NGOS FOR THE FUTURE

Factors driving this evolution include rapid advances in technology, notably the internet and mobile communications, which have made it easier, quicker and more effective to find and organize networks and groups of like-minded people and stakeholders, as well as to make issues transparent to a global audience. NGOs are also benefiting from the lack of trust in traditional institutions as they are perceived to be values and issues driven. These groups are increasingly well funded, with governments also provided substantial sums, recognizing that in some instances the NGOs have superior capabilities in tackling issues, e.g. distribution of aid in disaster situations.

However, the economic recession hit the non-governmental organizations (NGOs) doubly hard. The evaporation of wealth is reducing donations in many countries while the human need for help is skyrocketing even as resources shrink. Regardless of this, NGOs are serious business. As interactions with "official" bodies, whether governmental, transnational, or private sector increase, the nature of relationships is changing. The trend is now far more towards informed dialog, with NGOs increasingly willing to move towards partnership with businesses and governments to realize mutual objectives. The caveat is that businesses have also become targets of NGO activity, as pressure for commercial organizations to contribute positively to society increases – this pressure will continue as businesses wrestle with the challenge of realizing real benefits from corporate social responsibility both for the firm and for society.

Nonetheless, the number of organizations partnering with or working with NGOs is rising, as is the diversity of causes, issues, and social needs supported by NGOs. The figure below provides an overview of the increasingly interconnected NGO landscape and the key players within it.

PLAYERS
CO-OPERATING WITH NGO'S

Transnational Institutions

Governments

Businesses

CAUSES

Social Media

Social Responsibility Investment
Gender Justice & Diversity
Environment
Agriculture & Food Security
Economic Development

Education
Technical Assistance
Conflict & Emergency Relief
Social Communication & Advocacy

Human Rights
Social Development
Social Enterprises
Health
Trade

Foundations / Funds

Consumers/ Private Donors

Investors/ Financial Services

ACCESS/REACH NETWORKS

Community-based

International

City Wide

National

NGOs

Giving Money

Giving Time

Individual

Crowd Driven

COMMUNITIES/ INVOLVEMENT

6. PREPARING NGOS FOR THE FUTURE

The complexity of this landscape is revealed when looking at the different types of corporate-NGO partnerships. Corporate-NGO partnerships take different forms, but can be grouped by their leading characteristic. "Social investment" partnerships appear to be the most favored approach, providing support via donations including cash, products, gifts in kind, and employee fundraising. The "business" type partnerships refer to the use of advisory services to improve business/organizational practices, social business development, and social product development. This type of partnership is increasing due to the growing appetite among many businesses to leverage their competencies and assets in helping to address social challenges.

Types of partnerships undertaken

As far as you are aware, which of these different types of partnerships does your organization currently undertake? Tick all that apply (companies and NGOs combined)

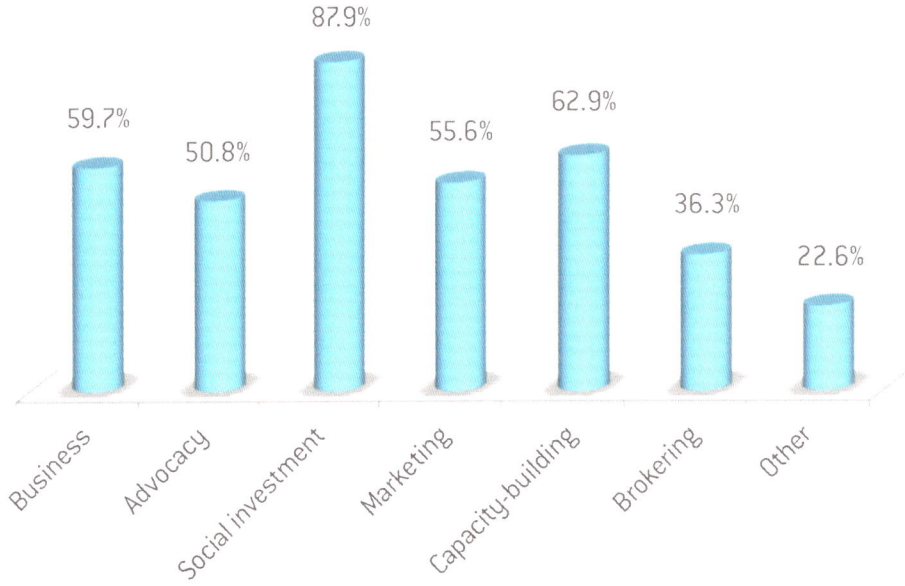

Source: The C&E Corporate-NGO Partnerships Barometer 2011

6. PREPARING NGOS FOR THE FUTURE

6.2 HOW ARE NGOS PREPARING FOR THE FUTURE? CASE STUDIES

Catalyzing change: a new model of philanthropy – Realdania

Realdania was established in 2000 when the association Foreningen Realdanmark sold its mortgage credit and banking activities to Danske Bank. Mortgage credit law prevented the association from returning its net capital of €1.4 billion to its members. The decision was therefore taken to establish Realdania with the purpose of supporting projects within the built environment for the common good, and to ensure that the funds would also benefit future generations.

Today the member-based philanthropic organization supports projects in three focus areas: cities, buildings, and built heritage. Within these Realdania targets five programme areas: room for all, the potentials of outlying rural areas and the open land, innovation in construction, living built heritage, and cities for people.

In the last 13 years Realdania has supported philanthropic initiatives with a total project value of approximately €3.7 billion. Of this amount, Realdania's grants account for €1.9 billion, while other project partners have financed the additional amounts. Since it was founded in 2000, the organization has funded or co-funded over 2,000 projects of which 700 are currently active. On average, the organization engages in philanthropic activities with a total budget of 5.9% of its investment capital per year. It mainly supports projects in Denmark but is also involved in a variety of international activities.

Implications of global trends for Realdania Global challenges such as climate change, health-related issues, food security, and water crises are rising. The challenges are so complex and interconnected that it is impossible for governments around the world to solve them alone. Therefore many are increasingly partnering with other stakeholders, from businesses to community groups, to develop solutions that will lead to sustainable future societies. Foundations worldwide, such as Realdania, recognize that they too have a role to play in such partnerships to create positive social change, leading to the blossoming of catalytic philanthropy.

Rethinking your playing field Realdania recognizes the power of working in a catalytic way to address its goal of improving the quality of life of the Danish people. Jesper Nygård, CEO of Realdania, told us, "As a Danish philanthropic organization we don't just want to hand out money. What we want to do is to share knowledge, transferring it from project to project, as well as contributing knowledge ourselves. A catalytic mindset is all about aligning actions and mindsets and this resonating throughout everything you do. It is not necessarily about bringing a lot of money, but more about bringing the right amount of money and knowledge to change a mindset or change the way you have done things in the past."

Catalytic philanthropy means taking a different approach than conventional or strategic philanthropy as the following table illustrates.

6. PREPARING NGOS FOR THE FUTURE

Characteristics of conventional, strategic, and catalytic philanthropy

	Conventional philanthropy	Strategic philanthropy	Catalytic philanthropy
What is the objective?	Donate money to common good/non-profit causes	Develop new solutions	Assume co-responsibility and engage others to create a better world
What is the key question?	Which charitable organizations should I support and how much money should I give them?	How can philanthropic donations create sustainable solutions?	How can a project achieve catalytic effect with measurable impact?
Who is responsible for success?	Beneficiaries	Contributors and beneficiaries	Contributors, beneficiaries, and partners
What is getting funded?	Individual projects and organizations	Individual projects and initiatives	Processes/actions across sectors
What kind of project is funded?	Charitable one-off projects	Strategic one-off projects	The long-term process of change
What tools are used?	Applications, donations	Partnerships, knowledge, donations	All possible tools, e.g. networks, partnerships, in-house-competences, knowledge, advocacy
How is information used?	To compare funding requests	To show good examples	To support and motivate changes
How is impact measured?	Donor evaluation	Project, donor, and internal evaluation	Overall impact versus tangible goals

Source: Translated from "Katalytisk filiantropi mere engagement – større effekt," MandagMorgen and Realdania.

Redefining your ambition Realdania, along with other leading catalytic philanthropic organizations worldwide, aims to actively engage multiple stakeholders and communities in realizing its ambition of driving sustainable positive changes environmentally, socially, and economically. This ambition can perhaps best be summarized as orchestrating "collective impact."

Jesper Nygård explained, "Part of our learning is that over generations Denmark has developed a society where the state plays a huge role compared to other countries. But even in a society like this, there is a growing realization that the public sector cannot solve every issue. If we are to succeed in the sustainability challenges we face, we cannot – as a business, an individual, or a community – just sit back and point to the government and expect them to create a solution. They will only be solved if we do it together."

The foundation therefore sees part of its role as working with its almost 170,000 members to try to solve some of these issues: "The more we cooperate, understand, and respect each other, the easier it is to address the environmental, social, and economic challenges on our common agenda and the result is much better than doing it alone."

Creating options Succeeding through partnerships and networks is paramount for Realdania. That means learning from others worldwide engaged in catalytic philanthropy through building relationships, for example with leading American foundations. Jesper Nygård noted, "A strong network is important to us and we are using our international experience in making efforts to build up a Danish foundation network that I believe, in the next couple years, will get stronger as domestic foundations start to share knowledge."

This learning creates new options for the foundation to pursue. Another critical way that it does so is by combining the different perspectives of its partners and networks, as Realdania's CEO explained: "You need to understand and respect that each party's perspectives, operating frames, and environments are different. For example, the business community is very often focused on tomorrow and the next quarterly results report, while the politicians have next year's finance bill and elections at the top of their minds. On the other hand we have the freedom to be a little more risk taking, visionary, and to think long term. Combining these three perspectives, the business communities' competence in making money, the politicians' governance frameworks, and our long-term freedom, offers wonderful opportunities but only if we are capable of cooperating."

Reshaping how you work Just as businesses are becoming more actively engaged in addressing social challenges and developing new business models to deliver on both purpose and profit, so too are leading non-profit organizations such as Realdania rethinking their role, operating models, and ways of working.

One approach Realdania is using to change ways of working in the built environment sector is by using model programs, bringing together private, public, and civil society organizations. Jesper Nygård explained how the foundation had taken this approach to hospices, "In 2004 the Danish government introduced a new plan for hospices. At that time there were only a few, so the bill outlined the need for thirteen more hospices in Denmark, which was a very rational and generous decision. The problem was that the government did not have the tools to ensure that these hospices became 'best practice' or rather 'next practice' institutions. This is where Realdania came in and offered to create a model program for developing a 'good hospice.'

"It was a complementary partnership. The government had both the desire and the money to build the new hospices to the best standards, while we had the desire and ability to contribute the knowledge that would optimize the investment. First, we gathered national and international knowledge, and then developed this into a model program. The next step was to offer around one million dollars to each of a small handful of hospices that would be initial test sites for implementing the model program. The critical thing was to test the model program so that we could learn what worked in practice – and what did not – which then meant that we could share and transfer the knowledge from one hospice to the next.

"Since then the model program has been revised two or three times and today we have very close cooperation with PAVI – The Danish Knowledge Centre for Rehabilitation and Palliative Care. All palliative wards and hospices built or rebuilt subsequently have been built around the concept and learning of this model program. In summary, we were able to combine knowledge with relatively small donations, making it possible to optimize the government's spending in this area. Today, our world-class hospices offer just one example of how working in such catalytic partnerships can mean that two plus two equals a great deal more than four."

Learn-act-learn-adjust As the model program demonstrates Realdania is constantly learning and adjusting its approaches to maximize impact. Looking forward, the current challenge for the organization is to become even better at working through networks and at partnering with private businesses, public institutions, and civil society to solve more of Denmark's sustainability issues.

Jesper Nygård told us, "It's really a craft; an art if you will. It is like being a good soccer player or a good shoemaker. You need to understand craftsmanship. It is extremely important to cooperate respectfully with others, but it is not enough simply to respect the other party, you also need to understand their perspective, the framework within which they think and operate. Our view is that the craft of building networks, sharing knowledge, and tackling important environmental, societal, and economic challenges through partnerships is the essence of working in a problem-driven, catalytic way."

Sources: "Catalyzing change: a new model of philanthropy, a conversation with Jesper Nygård," CEO of Realdania; www.realdania.dk; "Katalytisk filantropi mere engagement – større effekt," MandagMorgen and Realdania

6. PREPARING NGOS FOR THE FUTURE

World Wildlife Fund (WWF) for a sustainable planet

"We have only this generation to get sustainability and the environment right. We all need to work together as never before to get there," says James P. Leape, Director General, WWF International. WWF's mission is to stop the degradation of the planet's natural environment and to build a future in which humans live in harmony with nature, by: conserving the world's biological diversity; ensuring that the use of renewable natural resources is sustainable; and promoting the reduction of pollution and wasteful consumption.

Implications of global trends for steering the world towards sustainability As the world's population rises along with wealth and urbanization, particularly in rapidly developing economies, the demand for natural resources including water, food, minerals, metal, agricultural land, and energy is accelerating extremely fast. Today we are using close to 30% more natural resources than the Earth can replenish as well as releasing far more carbon dioxide than the atmosphere can absorb leading to a degradation of our ecosystem and likely causing climate changes. If the current consumption trends continue, the world's population could demand twice as many resources as the planet can supply by the 2030s – risking disasters and conflicts as people and nations compete for ever scarcer resources, whether water, fuel, or rare minerals. Tackling the pressing resources challenge will require an unprecedented level of international cooperation, not only amongst governments and societies but among business and their stakeholders.

Rethinking your playing field To respond to the vast environmental challenge to conserve the world's biodiversity and reduce humanity's global footprints WWF has developed a strategic plan containing some ambitious goals by 2020 and 2050.

By 2020:

- Biodiversity is protected and well managed in the world's most outstanding natural places
- Populations of the most ecologically, economically and culturally important species are restored and thriving in the wild
- Humanity's global footprint falls below its 2000 level and continues its downward trend, specifically in the areas of energy/carbon, commodities (crops, meat, fish, and wood), and water

By 2050:

- The integrity of the most outstanding natural places on Earth is conserved, contributing to a more secure and sustainable future for all
- Humanity's global footprint is within the Earth's capacity to sustain life and natural resources are shared equitably

To achieve these goals, the WWF is focusing its efforts on areas where it sees the potential to make the greatest impact:

35 priority places: e.g. Amazon, Yangtze, Great Barrier Reef, Namib-Karoo-Kaokoveld Deserts, Himalayas, Arctic, Southern Oceans, West Africa, Fiji, Vanuatu.

36 priority species: e.g. elephants, rhinos, reef-building corals, Asian big cats, gorillas, tunas, turtles, threatened hardwood timber species like mahogany and ramin.

6 priority footprint areas: carbon, cropland (for food, fiber, and biofuel crops), grazing land, fishing, forest (for timber, paper, pulp, and fuel wood), and water.

Examples of progress towards these goals include:

- A three-year campaign by WWF and partners saw the area of Australia's Great Barrier Reef Marine Park under strict protection increase from 4.6% to 33% – creating the world's largest network of marine highly protected areas
- Years of effort by WWF, the Ramsar Convention, and the Central African Regional Program for the Environment (CARPE, a USAID initiative), led to the creation of the world's largest freshwater protected area in 2008: the 6.5 million hectare Ngiri-Tumba-Maindombe wetland in the Democratic Republic of Congo

6. PREPARING NGOS FOR THE FUTURE

- One London housing development has halved the ecological footprint of an average Londoner – and the people living there didn't need to change a thing. The homes were built with reclaimed steel and timber from responsibly managed forests. They are also energy efficient, needing only 10% of the heating of regular houses. Rainwater is harvested and sewage water is recycled. Hot water and electricity are provided by solar panels and an onsite combined heat and power plant running on tree surgery waste. Residential, business, and tourist developments in Europe, North America, China, and South Africa – and even the London 2012 Olympics and a whole new city in Abu Dhabi – have similarly embraced WWFs One Planet Living concept for a more sustainable future

Redefining your ambition Often organizations focus on immediate symptoms of issues, which in the case of WWF could be trying to mitigate the impact of e.g. a large-scale tourism resort, illegal logging, or poaching. However, in defining its ambition and strategy, the organization is rather focusing on the root causes of such problems that may be more difficult to address but yield a far higher impact, for example working with local or national governments that allow unsustainable activities to develop more sustainable policies and practices.

This understanding of the multiple stakeholders involved and the root causes of issues has allowed WWF to identify five global priority drivers to tackle. The first two relate to financing, both public and private sector, working with institutions around the funding that each controls and directs in respect of environmental and development issues. A third driver is business practices: the standards, guidelines, and ethics of businesses working in sectors that affect the environment. Laws and regulations are the fourth driver, focusing on national and international laws, policies, and frameworks relating to, e.g., water, wildlife, forestry, fisheries, land use, poverty, development, agriculture, energy, and CO_2 emissions. The fifth driver relates to consumption choices and beliefs and attitudes towards nature. In each case, WWF seeks to influence the driver, and help stakeholders move towards more sustainable practices.

Creating options However, given the vast numbers of stakeholders involved – essentially every person and organization on the planet – WWF recognizes that it alone cannot change the habits of 7 billion people or even the habits of for example 1.5 billion producers. What it can do, though, is influence key players whose actions have the greatest potential to impact the organization's goals. Research from the WWF shows that by shifting 20% of demand, it can shift up to 50% of production. Therefore, WWF is calling on the world's major corporations to make conservation a core part of their corporate strategies, thereby pushing the commodity market towards a world where sustainability becomes the norm.

It is pursuing three paths to engage these corporations: *First*, through multi-stakeholder engagement, often in the form of round table discussions. These discussions bring together expertise and interests across the entire value chain within a sector, from production to marketing as well as other interested parties such as producer groups and NGOs, to debate issues, options, and solutions. *Second*, it engages directly with the most important companies to transform their operations, engage their supply chains, and reduce their footprint. Working hand in hand with these companies and using their existing platforms means that transformation at scale can be achieved faster. *Third*, it is tackling the area of commodity finance to influence the investment decisions of the financial institutions that support global trade.

Reshaping how you work The key driver of success, essential for change, is partnerships. WWF works with everyone and at all levels from politicians, policy makers, business and industry leaders, bankers, development and conservation workers, to local community members, indigenous peoples, farmers, fishers, landowners, consumers, activists, and donors. Its networks are extensive, reaching from the boardroom to farm gate and beyond.

In each case, partnership is focused on areas where the corporation can realize a significant impact on sustainability, by combining their understanding of the issues and expertise with that of WWF. Examples of successful partnerships include:

H&M & WWF In 2013 H&M entered a three-year partnership with WWF to develop a global water strategy that will be implemented across the fashion retailer's 48 national markets and 750 direct suppliers.

6.   PREPARING NGOS FOR THE FUTURE

IKEA & WWF A 10-year partnership has led to transformational changes – from timber to cotton, to carbon and now looking into their customer's home.

Coca-Cola & WWF Since 2007 they have worked together to conserve and protect priority river basins and catchments around the world; to improve water efficiency and reduce carbon emissions across Coke's manufacturing operations; and to promote sustainable agriculture throughout the company's supply chain.

CARE & WWF In 2008 they launched a strategic alliance to address the root causes of poverty and environmental degradation.

Learn-act-learn-adjust WWF is active in more than 100 countries worldwide, with a dedicated and passionate staff and more than 5 million supporters globally. To achieve sustained success it is important for WWF to catalyze and drive changes through long-term initiatives. Engagement, collaboration, and creative solution are the key, but driving the journey towards a sustainable planet is a huge task that cannot be realized without the support of donors, local communities, governments, NGO partners, businesses, scientists, aid agencies, fisheries and forestry organizations, consumer groups, and other essential partners. It therefore constantly seeks to expand its networks and to learn not only as an organization but to share this learning with all relevant stakeholders.

Sources: "A roadmap for a living planet," WWF; "Better production for a living planet," WWF; "Building a sustainable future," WWF, Environmental Leader

Synergos: building networks for collaboration

Founded by Peggy Dulany in 1986, the Synergos Institute is a non-profit organization dedicated to "helping create a world that is just, peaceful, and sustainable, where people everywhere are empowered, aware of their common humanity, and able to realize their full potential." Its mission is focused on building partnerships to address critical social and economic issues: "Synergos helps solve the complex problems of poverty and inequality by promoting and supporting collaborations among business, government, civil society, and marginalized communities. We create the conditions for these partnerships to be successful by building trust, designing and implementing change processes, enhancing the effectiveness of bridging leaders and institutions, and sharing our knowledge and experience."

Working with partners who come from very different spaces and contexts, Synergos' role is not to impose fixed ideas about how best to solve problems, but rather to help the key stakeholders to generate, test, and implement innovative solutions that lead to systemic and sustainable change. Examples of the institute's work include: supporting the empowerment of girls in urban slums in India; creating and delivering offerings to networks of philanthropists, civil society leaders, social entrepreneurs, and leaders in the children's sector; and improving the effectiveness of government agriculture, education, and health ministries. Through these partnerships, stakeholders have addressed critical challenges including food security, under-nutrition, education reform, and infant and maternal mortality.

Implications of global trends for Synergos Creating thriving partnerships around pressing global issues and acting as a bridge to finding viable and creative solutions presents its own challenges in an unequal, uncertain and multipolar world. In over 25 years, the organization has worked in over 30 countries and regions, including Brazil, Canada, Ecuador, India, Mexico - including the U.S.-Mexico border, the Middle East, Mozambique, Namibia, South Africa, and Zimbabwe.

This global context means that Synergos needs to find ways to work in countries where the culture, politics, and society are very different. To be locally responsive requires the organization to constantly adapt its approaches to address local realities. As Peggy Dulany said, "In some countries, like Mexico, in which collaborative initiatives and strategies are not common, our role may be to find existing bridging leaders and build their capacity so that they can act once the society is ready. In other countries, where there's already the climate for collaboration, the role may be to help build specific initiatives."

6. PREPARING NGOS FOR THE FUTURE

A further challenge for the non-profit sector, particularly since the economic crisis, has been funding. It has become increasingly difficult to raise charitable funds for what are often long-term initiatives, as, once involved, Synergos tends to stay involved over time because initiatives do not come to fruition immediately. Conversely, charitable funding is typically based on projects, versus this type of long-term commitment.

Rethinking your playing field To address the challenge of working in very different contexts, Synergos has constantly built on its strength in terms of local understanding, drawing on this in different situations, e.g. being able to introduce the Justice Initiative from South Africa to Colombia. A key part in developing both this understanding and identifying areas where its partnership approach can make a real difference is building networks. This is part planning and part "conscious" serendipity, as Peggy Dulany points out, "We need to have a broad enough network so that these serendipitous connections can happen on the one hand, so we're constantly broadening, broadening, broadening. But on the other hand, specific initiatives have to be driven by our partners, with some help from us to shape them, or conscious, very intensive involvement on our part, such as in our partnership with Unilever, Unicef, and Indian organizations in India to address child under-nutrition. This took a lot of time and energy over many years, and we're still connected, even though we don't have staff formally associated with the initiative. The organization created was totally Indian with Synergos only serving on its board."

Both in recognition of its own funding challenges and also of the importance of the private sector in addressing major social problems, in 2008 Synergos began offering consulting services. The value proposition is based around Synergos' expertise in stakeholder engagement, broad international networks, and staff experience both in international development and management consulting. Synergos Consulting helps companies advance both corporate and social interests and build sustainable business practices into their core business models. Offerings include stakeholder mapping, experiential learning, and assistance in the design and implementation of business initiatives with positive social impact. The revenues serve to finance other non-profit initiatives, where there are not apparent funding sources, either for regions of the world that are neglected by funders, or more importantly, new ideas that are hard to get funded in the beginning. In five to ten years Dulany sees this new consulting component as being a bigger part of what the organization does, as its services become more in demand.

Redefining your ambition The institute's vision has evolved over time. Originally its ambition focused around working with communities and building institutions. The latest strategy takes this work further, recognizing the need to help the leaders that will contribute to the success of the partnerships and initiatives the institute supports to transform personally into what Dulany calls "bridging leaders."

She said, "In my view, unless the leaders of today and tomorrow are self-aware individuals, and connected to their sense of higher purpose, they won't reach their potential – life is so stressful. There's so much more to do than any individual can possibly do, that they're probably at some point going to implode, or at least be less effective, as they move forward." Insights into how to approach assisting this type of personal development were developed through dialog at retreats initially involving the organization's Global Philanthropists Circle members, and later members of its Senior Fellows' network. These insights were developed further through the U-Process, an approach developed by Otto Scharmer, Peter Senge, Joseph Jaworski, Betty Sue Flowers, and others. The method helps leaders to develop the understanding of situations within the diverse group of people who will be working on the situation together, marrying this with their own sense of deeper purpose, and then using the resulting creative energy to develop solutions that can be worked on together in partnership. But it's about more than a method, Dulany explained: "In a complex society like India you need to align interests, purpose, issues, and commitment to make a difference."

Beyond working with communities, institutions, and leaders, Synergos has also expanded its ambition to bring business leadership into its work. Dulany explained: "Because my role has always been to broaden the net, anytime I find people from any sector or any group that we're working with feeling left out or not finding it interesting, it kind of sets off a little alarm bell in my mind, and leads me to think, well, how can we bring them in?

6. PREPARING NGOS FOR THE FUTURE

"An issue has always been how do you bring the business leadership into this? How do you bring businesses into socially responsible behaviors? An obvious answer is through its leadership. There's an emerging desire among business leaders to have businesses be more holistic. This immediately creates an opportunity, because for the non-profit sector, that's their purpose. Some of the most creative solutions have come out of business.

"To find ways that business leaders would understand and resonate with, ways in which we could bring them in, together with government and the non-profit sector, I had to really stretch my way of articulating things. And in a way, that stretching helped to push me to not only to articulate new ways of working together, but to conceptualize these in a different way."

With high ideals and ambitions, Synergos has articulated clear measures of success in terms of its impact. These include helping to develop strong bridging leaders across all their networks who are creating partnerships to deal with issues of poverty and justice around the world. It's not about the institute doing partnerships, but helping support people with the capacity to create
such partnerships themselves. As part of this, many of these bridging leaders will have gone through their own personal transformation, so that they are working from a holistic perspective, both in terms of life, leadership, and their analysis of the problems they want to solve. Through their work in partnerships they will be supporting other people in similar ways, engaging others in the vision and mission.

Reshaping how you work The organization's ambitions and ways of working are constantly evolving, Dulany explained. "Every time we get to a plateau, I see a next step. Then it's a matter of both understanding what that next step is that I see but don't necessarily know how to get to, and then bringing all the constituencies on board. There have been times when it's been frustrating for the staff. Just as they embraced what we are doing – such as earlier work promoting community foundations and institution building – then we started shifting towards bridging leadership and large-scale partnerships."

As a result of the shifts in ambition, not just towards bridging leadership, but also major partnerships, consulting services, and engaging more closely with business leaders, the organization has had to reshape itself. It has had to redefine its value proposition to partners and clients, so that it can work in these new areas. It has also had to develop the new skills and capabilities required, including changing staffing in some cases and the staffing model itself.

Dulany does not anticipate building a large in-house consulting pool. Rather, Synergos is leveraging its global networks to building a pool of people who can do this type of work, across the world, supported by a small in-house team to manage the work, help with marketing, quality control, and sharing new ideas across the networks. This model will allow the organization to be flexible, while at the same time training a whole cadre of people in managing partnerships and becoming bridging leaders that are willing to reach out across divides and bring people together.

Being able to work in a networked way outside the organization also means adopting the same systems-based thinking at Synergos. The organization has broken its own silos, bringing all network units together to drive as much cross fertilization as possible through regular meetings, cross-unit teams, and communications technology. Dulany's view is that creating the opportunity for people to connect will drive innovative thinking on the future as well as sharing knowledge on building and successfully implementing partnerships. However, it is now easy to get funding for meeting and "networking." This was another factor behind the organization's shift in its revenue model: membership fees for the Global Philanthropists Circle, and income from consulting services will enable it to finance these essential aspects of its work.

Learn-act-learn-adjust The shift in focus of Synergos has followed a logical progression from institution to partnership, and then the individual, Dulany explained. "It actually started with partnership, but we couldn't do it without strengthening institutions, then now wanting to strengthen the individuals."

As the institute moves forward, this process of learning and transformation will continue. Most important has been engaging the institute's staff, said Dulany, "Allowing them to experience what it was we were talking about in terms of personal

6. PREPARING NGOS FOR THE FUTURE

transformation to develop bridging leaders. Over two years, at a retreat in Montana, we took the entire staff through the same process. Since then we have regular efforts, whether it's a retreat or just a staff meeting, where we bring in the same methods and processes, so that people really have a chance to participate and experience what it is we're talking about. Now we are actually living a model that includes personal transformation, not just teaching it out there."

Sources: Interview with Peggy Dulaney, Founder and Chair, Synergos Institute by Thomas Malnight and Kees van der Graaf (2010), Synergos website

6.3 IN BRIEF EXAMPLES OF NGOS PREPARING FOR THE FUTURE

Stefan Crets, Executive Director of CSR Europe on Sustainability Corporate social responsibility (CSR) has increasingly become part of core business for companies; today the key to success is social innovation. It's about which products and services a company can offer that contribute to sustainability issues on local, regional, and even global levels. Europe's leading business network for corporate social responsibility, CSR Europe, launched their Enterprise 2020 initiative as an ideal model of what a company should be focusing on. It consists of two components which together help companies to meet sustainability challenges and growth: 1) Having in place and improving tools, instruments, and practices for impact management on the compliance and governance level; and 2) Social innovation as a core business strategy to deal with current sustainability challenges such as climate change, water and resource scarcity, ageing populations, and poverty. However, it is clear that CSR should be in the company's own interest. These components should be integrated into both strategy and operations in order to harvest the benefits of new business opportunities. Such genuine approaches have shown significant growth over the last 20 years. (Source: Global Trends interview with Stefan Crets, Executive Director of CSR Europe)

Waste Concern In the slums of Bangladesh, most garbage is left to rot on the streets. To tackle the problem, two enterprising local engineers launched the company Waste Concern – one part non-profit and one part for-profit. Lions Clubs International and the United Nations Development Programme made small initial contributions to cover the cost of buying some land and equipment, and the engineers set about hiring some of the unskilled and unemployed women who lived in the slums to collect garbage and bring it to the Waste Concern facility. In partnership with a major Dutch corporation, Waste Concern now has the capacity to serve 3.6 million people and to handle 700 tons of garbage per day. The company employs more than a thousand women, reduces health risks from festering garbage, recycles countless tons of rubbish, reduces greenhouse gases by 90,000 tons per year, and increases crop yields for small farmers through the sale of its fertilizer. Applying new and multiple perspectives to innovation around a clear need have driven the organization's success. (Source: Fast Company)

Causes – the one stop destination for your civic life Causes wants to be the one-stop destination for your civic life, just as Facebook is for your social life and LinkedIn is for your professional life. Until 2013 it was an online advocacy and fundraising application within Facebook but because its users wanted more freedom to connect with likeminded people through other platforms, it was reincarnated outside the walls of Facebook in spring 2013. Causes is the world's largest online platform for activism with about 186 million registered users and has raised over US$48M for charities, collected 34 million signatures for grassroots campaigns, and organized thousands of awareness campaigns. The platform enables users to create grassroots groups that take action on a social issue or to support a specific non-profit organization. It also runs a sponsorship program, which allows companies to support the causes and non-profits they care about, by providing matching grants. What makes it different from other social good sites is its business model. Its competitors often take a cut of the donations or sell details of contacts, or both. Causes instead uses native ad units meaning that when you sign a petition, your email address will never be sold to organizations soliciting donations. Causes also uses Network For Good to process credit card payments at cost so as much money as possible goes to the causes users support. Despite the success of Causes, the social good space it is crowded with many sites such as Jumo, HopeMob, Google's OneToday, and topic-specific sites competing for pledges and donations. (Sources: Techcrunch, Mashable)

6. PREPARING NGOS FOR THE FUTURE

iGive – easy donating online There is a growing expectation for everyone, businesses as well as individuals, to step up to a bigger role in society and to help those in need. In the early days of the internet e-philanthropist Robert N. Grosshandler saw its potential as a mechanism to facilitate giving as more and more people started living and shopping online. He wanted to enable the economic power of individuals to benefit their chosen communities, developing the company's vision as, "In the near future, all consumer transactions will contain a percentage that benefits causes close to home." How it works: one click when you shop and you have instantly supported a cause you care for. iGive is an unique shopping directory with a built-in charity donation function that allows users to support any charity by donating a percentage of their online shopping expenditure, and to submit own new causes if they cannot find one they like on the current list. 1403 online stores now participate in the program, with 59,252 charities and non-profit organizations listed. Since 1997, over 350,000 people have donated more than US$7 million to over 35,000 causes. (Source: iGive)

ThinkImpact – social change through relationships and ideas Shocked by the poverty of small rural villages when travelling at the age of 18 in South Africa, Saul Garlick was inspired to do social good. Coming back to America he raised US$10,000 to build a school in the village of Mpumalanga, South Africa. Returning a few years later he found the school in a devastating condition and realized that funding a cause was not enough – something more sustainable was needed. The understanding that social change comes from relationships and ideas – not bricks and mortar or money – led to ThinkImpact being born. ThinkImpact is an educational travel company, but it does not have volunteer, intern, or study abroad programs and it does not perform traditional international development work. Rather it seeks to bring together students and local community members to spark ideas and create businesses in rural Africa and Latin America by sending students around the world to explore different cultures, tackle tough challenges, and form relationships with people they would not otherwise meet. ThinkImpact started as a non-profit but in mid-2013, Saul Garlick decided to reincarnate the company as for-profit. The reason was that dependence on donations and grants restrained the company's operation and made it unsustainable. Today the company is B Corp certified and works with impact investors. ThinkImpact is just one of many businesses in the evolving social good field that shows that profit-making enterprises can be driven by social impact, not just the bottom line. (Source: New York Times)

Pencils of promise – a pencil is enough to change a life "It began with at question. A small boy begging on the streets of India. 'What do you want most in the world?' I asked. 'A pencil.' I reached into my backpack, handed him my pencil, and watched as a wave of possibility washed over him." So begins the story of the founder of Pencils of Promise, Adam Braun. Since government funding and private donations have slowed down, non-profits have had to find new ways to finance their projects. Braun believes that the non-profit sector can learn and get help from the for-profit sector, choosing to partner with businesses to run campaigns that provide mutual benefits. In an article from Forbes he states, "We don't just ask for money; we earn it. We are able to bring real value to companies through marketing efforts and expanded social media following." Since Pencils of Promise was founded in 2008, it has helped break ground on over 200 schools, but it does not just build the schools. The organization involves the local community, which needs to put in around 10-20% of the funding for the project. Most times the community contributes through providing labor and materials, which Braun says holds the community accountable for the project as it is a value exchange between two parties in a business transaction. Instead of referring to the organization as a non-profit organization Braun likes to say Pencils of Promise is a for-purpose organization, focused on the bottom line. However, instead of gross profit, its bottom line is gross efficacy. (Source: Forbes)

6.4   FOOD FOR THOUGHT ON THE FUTURE LANDSCAPE OF NGOS

The rise of philanthrocapitalism and impact investment

Philanthrocapitalism is a blend of for-profit and non-profit. With the global economy under pressure as it recovers from the recession it is crucial to mobilize all available capital as efficiently as possible to continue to make progress in creating a more sustainable and equitable world. Charitable donations no longer provide enough capital to solve pressing social and

6. PREPARING NGOS FOR THE FUTURE

environmental challenges at global scale and many thousands of people and institutions around the globe now believe our era needs a new type of investing. Using profit-seeking investment or impact investment to generate social and environmental good is now moving from the periphery of activist investors to the core of mainstream financial institutions.

Impact investors share the same vision of combining financial returns with positive social/environmental impact. Investors though can be categorized into two broad groups:

Financial first investors seek to optimize financial returns with a floor for social/environmental impact. This group tends to consist of commercial investors who search for investment vehicles that offer market-rate returns while yielding some social/ environmental good. Examples include: BlueOrchard, ProCredit Holding, BelAir SA Fund, Lyme Northern Forest Fund, JP Morgan Urban Renaissance Property Fund.

Impact first investors seek to optimize social or environmental returns with a financial floor. This group uses social/environmental good as a primary objective and may accept a range of returns, from return of principal to market rates. They are willing to accept a lower than market rate of return in investments that may be perceived as higher risk in order to help reach social/environmental goals that cannot be achieved in combination with market rates of financial return. Examples include: Charity Bank, Root Capital, Aavishkaar, Ignia, Pico Bonito. (Sources: The Monitor Institute - Investing for Social and Environmental Impact, 2009; The Parthenon Group – Investing for Impact, 2010) Let's take a look at what each type of investment looks like in practice.

Financial first investor BlueOrchard specializes in asset management and microfinance projects that target positive social impact and produce market returns of 2% over LIBOR.When founded in 2001 BlueOrchard saw itself as a pioneer with a mission to "bridge the gap between microfinance and private capital." To date BlueOrchard-managed funds have provided nearly US$2 billion in loans to more than 260 microfinance institutions (MFIs) that together reach 30 million clients in 50 countries. In 2013 the company created and strengthened academic ties with prestigious institutions in Switzerland and the U.S. to train a new generation of microfinance experts as well as bringing together world-class researchers with experienced practitioners to address critical development issues. (Sources: Blueorchard, Knowledge@Wharton)

JP Morgan Urban Renaissance Property Fund, another financial first investor, aims to earn market rate returns while supporting projects that propagate urban renewal and green development. The U.S. targeted fund invests in real estate projects, predominantly affordable and key-worker housing, retail, mixed-use development, or hospitality sectors as well as in projects with green specifications. It targets a financial return at market rate levels of 15%, net of fees. (Sources: Social Investments Funds; The Parthenon Group, "Investing for Impact", 2010; selected case studies)

Generation Investment Management was founded in 2004 with the intention of showing how integrating sustainability research into a long-term investment strategy could strengthen fundamental investment analysis. It is a London-based financial first investor with global operations. The investment style blends traditional equity research with a focus on sustainability factors, including social and environmental responsibility, and corporate governance. The company works together with a number of leading organizations, e.g. World Resources Institute, Natural Resource Defense Council, Global Impact Investing Network, towards a more sustainable future. (Source: Generation Investment Management)

Impact first investor, Bridges Ventures Social Entrepreneurs Fund, was the first UK based co-mingling fund established specifically to provide financing for social enterprises in the UK. It has raised £11.75M for investment in scalable social enterprises that deliver high social impacts while operating sustainable business models. It aims to provide capital to social enterprises seeking to scale up but unable to obtain commercial finance because they cannot deliver market-rate returns or offer the usual exit opportunities. Investment is via equity or quasi-equity instruments with flexible structures such as subordinated debt with royalty payments. It also provides operational support to the enterprises that it funds. The fund has so far committed a total of £7.2M, of which £3.5M has been invested in nine social enterprises. Across the portfolio to May 2013, the investees have supported 984 jobs and created 387 jobs, hired 284 formerly unemployed people, and trained a total of 1,850 individuals. (Sources: Social Investment Funds – selected case studies, Bridges Ventures)

6. PREPARING NGOS FOR THE FUTURE

Root Capital is an impact first, non-profit social investment fund that aims to improve rural prosperity in poor, environmentally vulnerable places in Africa and Latin America. It targets the "missing middle" between micro and commercial finance, bridging this gap by providing long-term or short-term loans against factoring agreements or signed purchase orders. It also provides financial education and strengthens market connections for small agricultural and food processing businesses. Root Capital has recently received the British government's DFID Award for Achievement in Impact Investing, which recognizes pioneering investment funds that have a clear strategy to make financially sustainable investments that benefit the poor. (Sources: Social Investment Funds – selected case studies, Root Capital)

Founded in 2002 the impact first, for-profit venture fund Aavishkaar is a pioneer in early stage investing in India. It is guided by the fundamental belief that investing in early stage entrepreneurial ventures can not only deliver commercial returns, but also bring about significant efficiencies and developmental impact to rural and underserved communities. Aavishkaar provides micro-equity funding in exchange for common equity in commercially viable companies. It also provides operational and strategic support for its target businesses, which are those that provide goods and services to rural or semi-urban communities, or organizations that increase income in those communities. (Sources: Social Investment Funds – selected case studies, Aavishkaar)

Social innovation through the Granny Cloud

Say education and most people associate it with physical classrooms, blackboards, and long-winded teachers or professors, but it doesn't have to be that way. Disruptive forces are changing traditional education from face-to-face learning towards virtual and interactive learning.

One excellent example is SOLEs & SOMEs (Self Organized Learning Environments & Self Organized Mediation Environments) or better known as the Granny Cloud. It's the brainchild of Professor Sugata Mita and the idea was born from the result of his learning experiment called the Hole-in-the-Wall. The aim of the project was to give very poor children from India and South America access to a computer through a "hole-in-the-wall" – and then see what happened (today in India, and other developing nations, there are now about 500 Hole-in-the-Wall computers, mainly in poor areas of cities). The project taught him that children could learn quickly from each other with only little adult involvement. Motivated alone by their curiosity and peer interest, they became their own teachers and motivators.

With these results in mind Professor Sugata Mita created the innovative Granny Cloud project in 2009. A UK based initiative, this is like a school in the cloud where grannies, grandpas, and others communicate via Skype with children in India and Columbia taking on the mentoring role that all grannies do so well, to tell stories, to stimulate fresh ideas, and new ways of looking at the same old things. Here, learning it is about attitude, about encouraging, nurturing, praising, and offering guidance rather than directing, instructing, and examining. It is not about *making* learning happen but about *letting* learning happen, based on the foundations of broadband access, collaboration, and encouragement.

Today more than 300 "grannies" are involved. In February Professor Sugata Mita was awarded the TED Prize for his work in education. His wish for the School in the Cloud is "...to help design the future of learning by supporting children all over the world to tap into their innate sense of wonder and work together. Help me build the School in the Cloud, a learning lab in India, where children can embark on intellectual adventures by engaging and connecting with information and mentoring online. I also invite you, wherever you are, to create your own miniature child-driven learning environments and share your discoveries." (Sources: BBC, TED)

6. PREPARING NGOS FOR THE FUTURE

Watsi: crowdfunded medical treatment for the developing world

The growth of crowdfunding sites like Kickstarter, Peerbackers and Quirky has been a trend for some time. Offering a simple, low-cost way to fund new business ideas versus using traditional financial service providers, the approach is gaining real traction with new businesses and investors alike. While there are countless examples of for-profit businesses getting crowdfunded, Watsi, founded by Chase Adam at the start of 2013, is currently the only crowdfunded non-profit as well as the first non-profit ever to be included in Y Combinator's[14] startup class. Y Combinator investors are typically looking for equity and profit, but in the case of Watsi the criteria for investment is Watsi's ability to help those in need of medical care than cash. Armed with the support and acceptance of Y Combinator, it has had success with getting donations from Khosla Ventures, Tencent, Ron Conway, and the Draper Richards Kaplan Foundation.

So what exactly is Watsi doing? The organization is simply utilizing crowdfunding to provide medical care in the developing world. It enables donations as small as US$5 to directly fund medical care and resources and unlike other non-profits donates 100% of their proceeds. Modelled after for-profit companies, the organization was able to raise US$1.2 million while spending only US$135,000 meaning that every dollar spent produced $9 for low cost, high impact, medical treatment in another country. The company's day-to-day running costs are funded separately through private donors, foundations, and corporations. To date, the organization has funded medical treatments for more than 1,110 patients in 16 countries. (Sources: Watsi, Huffington Post)

The big challenge for Watsi in the future will be to scale up its operations. By receiving seed funding from Y Combinator, Watsi is redefining the non-profit fundraising industry because the concept of running a non-profit organization alongside for-profit start-ups is new. However, it lacks precedent as few other organizations, such as Kiva, have done something similar. If Watsi succeeds in making this business model work, it is very likely we will see many more non-profits using this approach in the future. (Source: Fast Company)

[14]Y Combinator is an American seed accelerator (modern, for-profit type of start-up incubator), started in March 2005. Y Combinator provides seed money, advice, and connections at two three-month programs per year. In exchange, they take an average of about 6% of the company's equity.

6. PREPARING NGOS FOR THE FUTURE

6.5   SUMMARY: 8 PRINCIPLES OF PREPARING FOR THE FUTURE IN ACTION IN NGOS

The NGOs and similar organizations highlighted above offer some creative and innovative insights into what it takes to prepare an organization for the future. While it could be argued that they have the freedom to be more flexible in terms of innovations to meet their purposes goals than traditional businesses and government institutions, at the same time they have significant constraints in terms of funding and influence. In assessing how they are preparing for the future, this tension is clearly driving significant innovation, with the following insights standing out:

1. Embrace ambiguity: don't just think outside the box, throw away the boxes

The new model of NGOs for the 21st century is built on the premise that one organization cannot accomplish ambitious goals alone; multiple stakeholders need to be engaged and boxes are a hindrance, not a help. Thus many, if not all, the organizations highlighted in this chapter are actively **pursuing cross-sector relationships, breaking down boundaries** between governments, businesses, NGOs, and other stakeholders locally and globally. Foundations such as Realdania and Synergos, along with organizations such as Waste Concern and ThinkImpact are **embracing new funding and operational models** that are neither solely "business" nor solely "NGO" but take aspects of each. Philanthrocapitalists are **redefining what "return" means** in a much broader societal as well as financial sense, while the Granny Cloud is **taking a new perspective on under-utilized resources** such as retirees, pulling them out of their boxes and giving them new roles.

2. Think first from the outside-in, then inside-out

Many NGOs are born and driven by global and local issues, from environmental concerns to social inequality and hunger in a region. As such they tend to have a **broad and global perspective** on the challenges they are trying to address. In addition, NGOs have traditionally lacked resources, particularly in terms of funding, even as many have tried to address the resource scarcity of others. Scarcity breeds innovation and many of the organizations above have simply had to learn from the outside and take new perspectives on ways to operate, borrowing from the private and public sectors and other stakeholders. It is
also clear that their success is built on broad engagement of others to support their goals. As the CEO of Realdania notes, to do so it is critical to **recognize the different perspectives and environments of other stakeholders, and build mutually beneficial solutions**.

3. Identify and address root causes, not symptoms

The challenges that NGOs take on are important and ambitious. Even so, WWF demonstrates that it is critical to **focus on the areas where it can have greatest impact**, highlighting both its priorities for action and the drivers it wants to address in terms of changing mindsets and behaviors. Synergos also suggests that to address the root causes of issues is a **journey that takes time**, not only in terms of commitment to action, but in progressively building the different communities, institutions, and leaders to take on the work. It also means understanding that **one-off actions are not enough** as Pencils of Promise demonstrates. Rather the **engagement of the community** that will benefit from the NGOs' work is critical to sustaining positive change.

4. Practice two-directional thinking

Time is an important factor in NGOs' planning and strategies. Many have long-term goals, such as WWF; and Realdania notes that NGOs and foundations have the freedom to be more risk-taking and visionary than their private and public sector counterparts. However, **vision needs to be balanced with action on the ground today** to deliver the value expected by supporters, donors, and other stakeholders. A number of the organizations highlighted above have **clear targets and metrics for performance** in the short-term as well as long-term goals, bringing both together in a clear path towards their ambitions.

5. Manage in relationships/networks versus transactions

Networking, collaboration, partnership, and engagement are critical in looking at NGOs' approaches to preparing for the future because the power of NGOs is found in influence as well as action. Networks are constantly being broadened in the search to **pool and partner on resources and knowledge**, as well as to create public awareness of and support for each organization's purpose and aims. Collaborators range from individuals to institutions with Synergos highlighting the **importance of systems thinking** both inside and outside the organization. Such thinking allows organizations to move beyond simply providing resources or solutions to **act as catalysts for change**.

6. Focus on co-creation

Co-creation is the essence of many NGO initiatives and models. Being catalysts for change means that NGOs **engage others in the change process**, providing opportunities for supporters to contribute in ways that individual people or organizations may not have been able to do alone. Technology and communications advances have made a huge difference in this respect, with many of the next generation NGOs such as Causes, iGive, Watsi and the Granny Cloud **leveraging technology** for contributions of member time, resources, and funds – as well as for sharing information, ideas, and progress. **Tapping into the crowd** in this way is key to driving the innovation and creativity many of the NGOs say is critical, given the ongoing pressures on funding, need for resources, and requirements to be locally responsive.

7. Align purpose and profit

NGOs have always been about purpose. The non-profit status of most such organizations means that finance has traditionally focused on fundraising, donations, and other non-business activities. However, a new generation of hybrid organizations is emerging which **combine purpose with profit**, or at least some business activities to generate the more secure and predictable cash flows required to fund longer-term projects. Waste Concern is one example, while Synergos' consulting activities provide needed revenues, and ThinkImpact has switched from non-profit to B Corp status to drive social impact. The rise of B Corps and philanthrocapitalism highlight the increasing blurring of boundaries between non-profit and for-profit, with the focus being on **combining financial returns with positive social and environmental impact**. These **new business models** are starting to move towards the mainstream and again highlight the substantial organizational innovation that is happening in the NGO sector. Looking forward, the Watsi example of a **crowdfunded non-profit** could also gain traction.

8. Embed continual challenge, avoid complacent compliance

Many of the NGOs described in this chapter **test and learn** to improve the value they add over time, for example through Realdania's model programs and Synergos' approach to constant adaptation. It is also evident that they **share knowledge and progress broadly**, not only within the organization but outside the organization. This transparency is a critical aspect of maintaining engagement with supporters, who are welcomed as challengers. Several also note the opportunity to **build networks of similar organizations** domestically and internationally to share and learn from best practices and from feedback on their progress.

The NGO non-profit – or not completely for-profit – sector is large and influential. More importantly it is showing substantial innovation, not just to meet the pressing global challenges the planet faces, but in engaging support, generating funds, and driving real change over time. These insights are ones that all types of organizations can take away and build on. But there remain challenges ahead for NGOs and their hybrid cousins:

- Delivering impact today, while building a realistic path towards future ambitions

- Building the networks and capabilities to engage, influence, and partner with a broad range of local and global stakeholders for mutual benefit

- Generating stable funds flows and resources to sustain long-term initiatives

- Balancing the demands of profit and purpose over time, without losing legitimacy in the eyes of stakeholders

7. PREPARING SOCIETIES AND COMMUNTIES FOR THE FUTURE

7. PREPARING SOCIETIES AND COMMUNITIES FOR THE FUTURE

Chapter seven focuses on how societies and communities within them are preparing for the future. As in the previous and subsequent chapters, the first subsection provides some context, looking the key trends that are impacting the landscape within which each type of organization is operating.

The second subsection focuses on detailed case studies, offering insights into how different societies and communities are approaching the challenges of preparing for the future in a world of rising societal challenges. In a slight difference to earlier chapters, two of the case studies focus on broader phenomena, which are impacting multiple societies and communities, namely the increasing power of the crowd, and the emergence of the sharing economy. Each detailed case study explores the organization's thinking and actions using the lens of the 3Rs model below: what are the key trends and implications impacting the organization; how did these drive rethinking the playing field; how did the organization redefine their ambition (vision, purpose, targets, measures) as a result; what were the options they considered in building an agenda for action; how did they reshape how they worked; and what is the ongoing process of learn-act-learn-adjust.

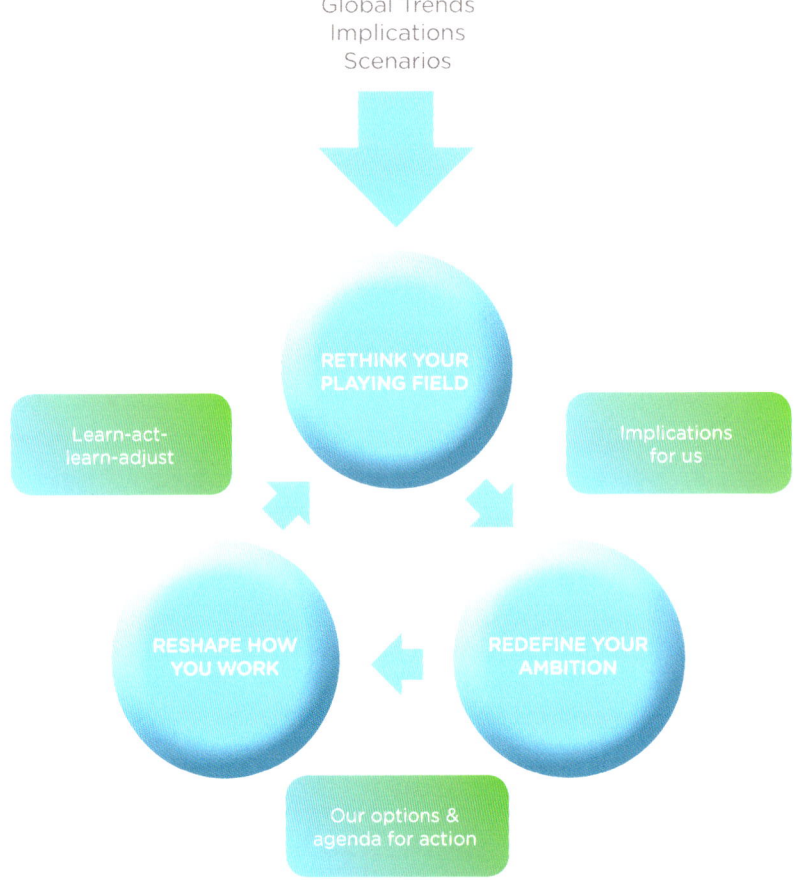

The third subsection provides some in brief examples of how other organizations are preparing for the future in specific areas, e.g. improving urban living and reinventing health care systems. The fourth highlights food for thought examples, which are designed to provoke thinking on some of the key challenges facing organizations in the future, which many societies and communities are grappling with, e.g. realizing the potential of the convergence of production and consumption in the maker movement, and addressing the issues around resource colonization.

Finally, in subsection five, we draw together some insights to take away from these examples using the 8 principles introduced in Chapter 3.

7. PREPARING SOCIETIES AND COMMUNITIES FOR THE FUTURE

7.1 THE SHIFTING BOUNDARIES OF SOCIETY

In 2000, leading management thinker Peter Drucker opined, "In a few hundred years, when the history of our time will be written from a long-term perspective, it is likely that the most important event historians will see is not technology, not the internet, not e-commerce. It is an unprecedented change in the human condition. For the first time – literally – substantial and rapidly growing numbers of people have choices. For the first time, they will have to manage themselves. And society is totally unprepared for it."

Societies and communities for centuries have been dictated by where we lived and how we were raised: from local village or religious communities, to national political parties, to educational peer groups. Now, many societies, particularly in rapidly developing economies, are becoming wealthier, more connected and more educated, as well as more knowledgeable about the world around them and their place in it. These changes reflect the economic power shifts from West to East and North to South as well as the growing penetration of digital technologies and ease of movement of goods, services, knowledge, and people globally. People worldwide have a growing number of choices in terms of how and where they live, work, and consume, in addition to with whom they associate and communicate despite high levels of government control in some of the fast growing regions.

This increase in choice is impacting traditional social structures, which are fragmenting, as families become more dispersed, populations become more diverse, single person households increase, and urbanization continues. While the gender divide has improved in terms of female participation in education, politics, and employment, significant inequalities remain.

Income inequality is also growing in some 80% of the world's countries despite the progress that had been made over the last two decades in reducing global poverty. However, the increase in commodity prices in recent years plus the financial and economic crashes mean up to 200 million people worldwide may have been plunged back below the poverty line according to estimates by the World Bank. Among those luckier people with higher incomes, the recession has taken its toll with a mindset of frugality becoming more widespread.

Previously isolated segments of society are demanding inclusion, highlighting divides and raising tensions. The number of international borders increased six fold from 104 in 1900 to 600 in 2000 according to the World Bank, as nations segment themselves to reflect the demands of different political, ethnic, or cultural groups. On July 9, 2011, South Sudan officially became an independent country, recognized by the UN. However, independence was only the start with significant challenges to be overcome including disputes with its northern neighbor over oil deposits on the border, currencies, and rebel activity in Sudan's Abyei, Blue Nile, and Southern Kordofan states. In 2012, domestic tensions in South Sudan came to the fore, with the country now in the throes of ethnic conflict in 2014, displacing hundreds of thousands of people and facing a humanitarian crisis. As the world continues to become more mobile, more such divisions may emerge along with associated political tensions. Global tensions continue over the crisis in Ukraine caused by Russia's annexation of Crimea, plus the dangers of potential conflict in Eastern Ukraine between Russian-speaking Ukrainians and those supporting the interim government. Voices are also being raised in secession calls from Scotland and Catalonia to India.

In a world where societies are fragmenting, communities are becoming increasingly important as a focus for identity and meaning. The difference is that the communities emerging are not dictated by proximity or tradition – although many still are – but rather by choice. An individual can choose to connect with like-minded people in multiple countries, virtually and physically, through few or many communities for different areas of interest. We define such communities of choice as social networks of people, groups, and organizations that have been selected by an individual as a peer or reference group. They connect people across borders and time zones based on shared interests, beliefs, cultures, location, characteristics, and/or experiences, and increasingly reflect a search for meaning, identity, and safety in a world of uncertainty and often overwhelming choice. Shared experiences seem to be becoming more important than physical possessions or characteristics, particularly as many communities are virtual, and in the more developed countries there is a growing question of "what's enough?" in a world of scarce resources.

7. PREPARING SOCIETIES AND COMMUNITIES FOR THE FUTURE

As communities of choice emerge and evolve, there remains much to be understood. However, what is clear is that the increasing power of communities – within and across borders – will be a catalyst in driving changes in broader societies, which are already facing their own challenges in a multipolar and mobile world, where trust in traditional institutions is falling.

These shifts in social organizations have significant implications for businesses and other stakeholders, which will have to adapt their offerings and methods of communication to connect effectively with the new social structures and communities of choice that are emerging. The table below summarizes some of the key characteristics of the emerging landscape of societies and communities.

	Individuals	Communities	Societies
Role	Adapting to life in new, multipolar worlds: • Virtual/physical • Generational shifts • Global mindset	Bringing together collections of individuals to promote shared needs, goals, interests Provide safety, identity, and meaning	Providing the "context" (e.g. economic, institutional, legal, social, educational, behavioral, media) within which individuals and communities can succeed
Interests	Searching for meaning amidst contradictions, volatility, and uncertainty Finding trusted "guides" for life, behaviors, relationships, and contributions to society	Expanding across societal boundaries/geographies, virtually and physically Offering flexibility of choice Developing interdependence to advance the collective good of communities	Reconciling competing models of governance, economic models, mindsets, and rights Developing a balance between the role of government and other stakeholders in society Addressing global challenges Maintaining power/ regaining trust
Power base	Increasing personal voice and transparency Ability to promote and advance self and/or collective good through personal choices	Increasing community voice and power through multiple communication channels – ability to challenge "context" Falling trust in institutions, growing trust in communities	Traditional governance institutions – being updated to reflect societal shifts Regulatory, military, media, and economic controls Increasing reflection of societal opinion and choice
Opportunities & challenges looking forward	Increasing potential power, uncertainty over responsibility: victim or part of collective movement of change Balancing self-interest and the collective good	Innovating new models of living, working and participating in society Promoting new behaviors Serving new needs	Building on the growing interdependence between societies and communities for collective advancement Tensions of globalization and fragmentation Tensions over global issues

One critical source of both opportunity and challenge looking ahead is how individuals, communities, and societies balance the collective view where they focus more on the greater good, and the more individualistic view where they focus more on "for my good." How these perspectives interact and build on each other will be important in defining the ambitions of societies and communities, and how these should be preparing for the future – as we explore in the case studies and examples below.

7. PREPARING SOCIETIES AND COMMUNITIES FOR THE FUTURE

7.2 PREPARING SOCIETIES AND COMMUNITIES FOR THE FUTURE: CASE STUDIES

Medellín, Columbia: reinventing cities

Throughout the 1970s and 1980s the city of Medellín in Columbia was notorious for being the most dangerous and murderous city on Earth. The city was the domain of drug lord Pablo Escobar and his empire the Medellín Cartel. Yet in 2012, just two decades after Pablo Escobar was killed, the city has reinvented itself and received the title "Innovative City of the Year" from the readers of the Wall Street Journal Magazine. It was chosen because of its progress, potential, and "rich culture and impressive strides in urban development" despite its past history of violence.

Implications of global trends for Medellín The reality is that despite its progress, Medellín is still struggling with its past. Although violent incidents have decreased, descendants of the Medellín cartel still haunt the streets of the city along with other gangs making many communities unsafe. Drugs and drug production along with its concomitant problems still are, and will be for years to come, a major challenge for the city although the administration in Medellín is playing a crucial part in solving these issues. However, the current Mayor Gaviria talking to The Guardian in the article "Medellín: Columbia; reinventing the world's most dangerous city" agrees, "that the wider context – the global setting, of which everything being done in Medellín is part – is crucial: 'We also need the consuming countries – the U.S. and Europe – to accept co-responsibility for that cycle. The rich, consuming countries have built a dam across a flowing river. And the waters rise, and we in the poorer, producing nations are drowning. We do not demean our own responsibility, and we are trying to stop drowning here in Medellín. But until the rich world breaks away the dam, we will drown.'"

Rethinking your playing field In Columbia urban development traditionally focuses on specific solutions to physical problems. In the case of Medellín, architecture and urbanism are rather used as tools for social development. This has led to positive physical, functional, and social changes in the city as well as a changing attitude and pride among the city's inhabitants. While these changes are often credited to the city's visionary mayor from 2004 to 2007, Sergio Fajardo, the transformation of the city's urban development began with thoughtful planning guidelines, amnesties and antiterrorism programs, and community-based initiatives led by Germany, the UN, and a Colombian national policy mandating architectural interventions as a means to attack poverty and crime.

Redefining your ambition One thing is to dream big and to use architecture to intervene in a decades-long problem of poverty and crime. The ambition of breaking this cycle and improving social and economic development was clear, but the bigger question was how this ambition could be achieved. The Council of Medellín tackled this challenge by outlining in its City Plan five guidelines for identifying and prioritizing projects to move the city towards its goals:

* The indicators of human development and quality of life will guide the public investment, focusing on first serving the people in greatest need.

* Public space and infrastructure must become the framework where education and culture are cultivated in places of encounter and co-existence.

* Urban projects must simultaneously integrate physical, cultural, and social components; improving not only places but also the life and interactions of people in the communities.

* The Integrated Metropolitan Transport System must be used as the organizing axis of mobility and projects in the city. All projects have to be directly linked to the main transport system.

* Medellín must become an educated city. Education and culture are priorities that guide programs and projects.

7. PREPARING SOCIETIES AND COMMUNITIES FOR THE FUTURE

Creating options Social urbanism was one of the fundamental pillars in the plan for change with the objective of promoting peace and social equity through urban policies. Priority was given to the areas of the city where bigger social and economic issues were found. The fundamental strategy in the project was that the planning and development of the urban projects could transform the physical environment while promoting profound social and cultural shifts in the communities where they were implemented. Aside from the usual investments in public infrastructure and as a result of this approach to city development, four specific targeted projects were established based on the guidelines proposed in the Medellín City Plan by the Council of Medellín.

Library, parks, and educational infrastructure – five striking new libraries with attached parks were built to serve underprivileged neighborhoods aiming to create central gathering spaces inside the targeted areas to help consolidate and give a clearer identity to the communities.

Comprehensive urban projects – to fight inequity and exclusion. The neighborhoods with the biggest inequities and violence issues were identified and important investments made in these specified neigborhoods.

Public housing for populations in risk zones – investment in housing was oriented to supply the needs of the population in critical economic and social conditions that are usually linked to inappropriate housing in risk areas.

Connecting the city – different areas of the city would be connected through the improvement of streets and pathways, the creation of Lineal Parks and an efficient and innovative public transport system.

Within these umbrella strategic areas of focus, some of the most important projects included: Línea K Metro Cable en la Comuna Nor-oriental, spans 2,0 km (2004); Orquideorama del Jardín Botánico, (Architect, Plan B Arquitectos + JPRCR Arquitectos, 2006); La Biblioteca España (Architect, Giancarlo Mazzanti, 2007); El Colegio en Santo Domingo Savio (Architect, Obranegra arquitectos, 2009); El Parque Explora (Architect, Alejandro Echeverri, 2007); Linea J Metro Cable Comuna Occidental, spans 2,9 km (2008); Los reacondicionamientos de los Coliseos para los juegos Sur Americanos (Architect, Giancarlo Mazzanti, 2010); Las piscinas de la Unidad Deportiva Atanasio Girardot (Architect, Paisajes Emergentes, 2010); Parque Biblioteca Pública León de Greiff (Architect, Giancarlo Mazzanti, 2011).

Reshaping how you work Medellín is one of a few cities in the world that benefits from a participatory budgeting system, a system that originated in Porto Alegre, Brazil in 1989, and allows its citizens to define priorities and allocate a part of the municipal budget in their community. In Medellín's case it is 5% of the municipal budget. The city is divided into small neighborhoods where its residents allocate money to, for example, health centers, college scholarships, and youth music groups. Though it might not be enough to make deep structural changes in a city, it can be a very valuable tool to empower its citizens, engaging them in understanding how they can help solve the problems in their own communities, and providing them with the resources to do so.

The city has also benefitted from a strong public-private partnership to fight violence and banish the ghosts of the past. Local government, businesses, community organizations, and universities have worked together, e.g. transportation projects have been financed through public-private partnerships; engineering firms have designed public buildings for free; and in 2006, nine of the city's largest firms funded a science museum.

The city has also managed to move away from the more traditional thinking pattern of "municipal decision-making and public-only financing" to a system that allows involvement, engagement, and taking ownership of your own community/city by the people and organizations within it.

Learn-act-learn-adjust The journey that the city of Medellín has been on is one that is not yet over and there are no promises that it will succeed in its ambitions in the end. This will only happen if every new administration that takes over in the city is committed to continue what has been started. Progress is still fragile and some of the forces that once made Medellín the most dangerous and murderous city in the world still haunt its darker corners. But there is hope; Mayor Gaviria told The Guardian that he hopes that within another five years, "Medellín will have reached a point of no return," depending on it being able to "face this particular phase in the violence, along with the rest of the country," while "taking advantage of this moment, in which young people are coming out of our public institutions with better education."

(Sources: Architecture In Development, The New York Times, WSJ, The Guardian, Wikipedia, npr)

It's getting crowded: the rise of crowdfunding, crowdsourcing – and pretty much every other type of crowd'ing you can think of

The crowd is in everything, almost. And if it's not there now, it soon will be.

The vast connectivity of the internet along with social and mobile networks, inside and outside the firm, has created a smorgasbord of opportunities for the crowd. Sometimes through need, sometimes through seeking creativity, crowds are coming together to address opportunities and challenges big and small, global and local. In this case study we look at the whole philosophy and practice that is growing around the crowd. How can your organization benefit and get involved?

Implications of global trends for the crowd "Lunch is for wimps." Famously uttered by Gordon Gecko in the movie Wall Street which celebrated the highs (and lows) of individualistic, investment banking hubris and greed, it summarized the philosophy of an era when everyone was concerned with themselves. This was an age before global connectivity of the type we know now. The mobile phone was not a fixture; neither were social networks, nor were text messages. The "discover" option on Twitter was not even on the horizon. Phones were clunky, laptops even clunkier, and connecting was expensive and limited to the people you knew or worked with. It was an era where young people were taught and encouraged to go out and make it for themselves, which they did in droves. The individual was king.

Fast forward a couple of decades or so. Ubiquitous connectivity, smart and mobile devices, and the growth of social media mean that younger generations today are realizing how quick, easy, and beneficial it is to pool resources and ideas. Research has shown for years that high-performing teams can do better than an individual. Now the opportunity is to go beyond teams to vast numbers of people, not just locally but worldwide, and tap into their knowledge, ideas, and resources: the crowd. Called by many names, the crowd can in some incarnations be the "global brain," in others "peer financing."

Why has the crowd become so important? Connectivity is the over-arching driver. It is possible not only to find experts or at least willing helpers on a given topic or problem, but also to connect with them in real-time, or certainly close to. With about 2.7 billion people – or almost 40% of the world's population online, and mobile phone penetration rates of nearly 96% globally (128% in developed countries and 89% in developing countries; source: ITU, 2013) much of the world can now talk to each other 24/7 if desired. Platforms including search engines and social networks are facilitating these interactions, allowing new businesses and business models to be built around the crowd.

Next, there has been a mindset change in business. No longer is it seen as advantageous to keep everything in-house, operating in closed systems. The world is moving too fast and becoming too networked for one organization to be able to do everything itself. Breaching the walls of the firm is not only necessary but beneficial, for example through outsourcing idea search, open innovation, and partnering with a broad range of stakeholders. In fact, the crowd probably knows much better than a firm what its customers want because the crowd includes the customer base.

Another driver of the use of crowds has been recession: many tasks can be done faster and cheaper by crowds than organizations and individuals. As managing costs became a critical issue, more organizations made the shift towards the crowd, sometimes reluctantly but finding in the process that the results exceeded expectations. They became converts. While there are many more drivers, a final one to take note of is the increasing search for meaning in people's lives in a confusing and uncertain world. Being part of a crowd brings a sense of community and accomplishment. In addition, as more and more people are aware of pressing global issues, if not experiencing them directly in the form of poverty, resource scarcity, or extreme weather events, there is a growing sense of shared responsibility and a desire to come together to tackle the challenges. Now, unlike in the past, people can do it globally and virtually as well as locally.

Rethinking your playing field Many innovative companies and communities are using crowds not only to rethink markets, but to invent new business models and approaches to work, life, and just about everything else.

Let's start with crowdfunding, which is reshaping the financial services industry in fundamental ways. It was initially conceived as a simple, low-cost way to fund new business ideas as an alternative to using traditional financial service providers and is gaining real traction with new businesses and investors alike. Leading companies in this area include: Kickstarter, Indiegogo, Crowdfunder, RocketHub, Crowdrise, Quirky, Appbackr, and Invested.in.but. The concept is spreading to non-profit and public good projects, for example My ideal city Bogotá, which is using crowdsourcing and crowdfunding solutions to solve the problems of Bogotá in Columbia: one effort involves 3200 investors (ordinary people) who decided to put together their money to build the first skyscraper in Colombia. (See more below. Source: PSFK) An even more innovative way of crowdfunding focuses on an individual's lifetime value in terms of earnings. One start up thinks this could be a new market: Upstart finds wealthy investors willing to give people hard cash in return for a stake in their future earnings.

Some financial services players are waking up to the threat and trying to engage the crowd themselves. Are you ready for a crowdsourced credit card? Barclaycard is making a bold step into uncharted territory with the Barclaycard Ring MasterCard, announced in March 2012. The Ring will actually be a social network moderated by Barclaycard in which card members will get full disclosure of the card's profits and losses; they will vote on changes in terms such as interest rates, annual fees, and late payment penalties; and most importantly they will participate in a rudimentary profit-sharing program called Giveback. (Source: Iconoculture via GT Briefing May 2012) Other well-established companies are also tapping into the crowdfunding arena, for example Chrysler's experiment in co-funding, helping people to crowdfund a Dodge through a "car registry."(Source: Slideshare)

Turning to crowdsourcing, it is redefining playing fields, tapping into the knowledge and ideas of a diverse group of people with an interest in a topic, issue, or brand to drive innovation and potentially new markets and business models. Innocentive is an often-cited example of one of the best open-innovation platforms, used by many companies to solicit ideas and proposals on how to tackle challenging problems. The advantages: it's fast, global, and has a well-qualified crowd. Other companies are using their crowds of customers (and suppliers) to provide feedback on everything from design to distribution, in some cases co-creating products and services with the people who will be using them.

It is not just the private sector using crowdsourcing. Block by Block gives people, especially youth, an opportunity to show planners and decision makers how they would like to see their cities in the future, while Neighborland allows people to share their ideas for improvement and gather support from people in the community.

Redefining your ambition The power of the crowd is changing how organizations think about their ambitions e.g. in terms of engaging others and the speed of change. P&G's Connect + Develop approach to open innovation works both ways — inbound and outbound — and encompasses everything from trademarks to packaging, marketing models to engineering, business services, and design. With a central team plus a huge range of external partners this approach is integral to the company's growth strategy and ambitions, targeted at delivering breakthrough innovations such as Swiffer that meet consumer needs and create new markets.

Redefining ambitions through crowdsourcing can impact many industries, even ones with high capital requirements and long development cycles such as pharmaceuticals. The International Laboratory for the Identification of New Drugs, otherwise known as "The ILIAD Project," aims to tap into citizen scientists around the world to find new antibiotics and other drugs, faster, more cheaply, and more efficiently than can be done by large drug companies. A key benefit would be that drugs that may not be cost effective for the big pharmaceutical players could see the light of day.

Reshaping how you work Crowds are not just about finding new markets or rethinking existing playing fields. They are also being used to reshape how organizations work, including existing business models. Take Walmart which is looking to jump on to the crowdsourcing bandwagon with an interesting delivery service concept for their online sales. Instead of having employees or a third-party delivery company deliver items that were purchased online, Walmart is thinking of tapping into their customers to bring these items to the online buyers. (Source: PSFK)

RelayRides is going social, enabling users to rent a car through Facebook by harnessing their social network. Just one of the many crowd enabled services reshaping transportation, it will impact how existing businesses – and stakeholders, such as regulators – work to address the increasing choices in the transport market, potentially shifting business models, processes, and portfolios. Already the major car hire companies, along with automotive players such as BMW (see Chapter 4) are starting to embrace the new world of crowdsourced transport, building new business models in the process.

Learn-act-learn-adjust By its very definition, the world of crowd-everything is one of constant knowledge sharing and learning. Look for the crowd to have an impact on an increasing number of aspects of life, society, and business in future.

Understanding the power of access and not ownership – the emergence of the sharing economy

Why pay full price for something when you can rent it cheaper from a stranger online? That is what an increasingly number of people are thinking today. Some share for fun, others of economic reasons but the fact is that we are sharing as never before, challenging established notions of how individuals, businesses, and governments interact, as well as elements of the legal system. As with the previous case study, the focus here is not just one organization, but the whole philosophy and practice which is growing around the sharing economy and how it is disrupting one industry after the other. Will your organization engage with the opportunities of the sharing economy or be disrupted by this emerging trend?

Implications of global trends for the crowd Collaborative consumption, the sharing economy or the ownerless economy is exploding and creating new industries. Many people are increasingly questioning the value of having possessions such as cars, bikes, books, music, and even dogs. Today, technologies are available to let them share, rent, or barter for these items easily, almost anywhere: growing urbanization means that there is a critical mass of people to participate, so ownership is simply not necessary. Nor is it desirable for many as concerns over the environment and global issues prompt a rethink of consumption itself. The question is not just do we need to own it? It is do we need it at all?

The sharing economy has actually existed for decades: libraries have lent books, stores have rented music and movies – although physical renting is a dying market, and people have joined the gym instead of buying a treadmill or a rowing machine. What's new is that the digital age has made the potential for sharing goods and services much easier and more transparent, allowing the sharing economy to take root in an increasing number of communities and industries.

The term "the sharing economy" began to appear in the mid-2000s but as the financial crisis hit the world's economy in 2008 and unemployment rose sharply, sharing became a way for many people to "survive" in a restrained economy. New business structures were inspired by social technologies and today the growth of sharing platforms can be found in almost all categories from digital and physical media, transportation (cars, bikes, boats, air planes), to physical spaces such as garages, storage, parking, spare rooms, and infrequent-use items such as household items, event equipment, and sporting goods.

Who is driving the sharing economy? Some commentators suggest it is the debt-loaded millennials, while others believe the sharing user base is much broader and based on a renewed interest in all things green, as well as a new brand of thriftiness that started during the recession. (Source: The Line) According to a study by Latitude in collaboration with Sharable Magazine, "...participants aged 40+ were more likely to feel comfortable sharing with anyone at all who joins a sharing community (with varying levels of community protections in place) and to perceive 'making new friends' as a benefit of sharing, whereas millennials tended to feel comfortable sharing only within smaller networks. Attitudinally, however, millennials were more likely to feel positive about the idea of sharing, more open to trying it, and more optimistic about its promise for the future. It's worth acknowledging that millennials may simply consider a wider network of people to be 'friends' or to have more granular understandings of digital privacy controls, thanks to the rise of social networking – so the relative sizes of these two generations' trusted networks may not differ greatly, even if their labels do."

Rethinking your playing field Today, thousands of new businesses are renting or selling access, rather than selling products and services. Entrepreneurs have tapped into the possibilities of sharing business models, while individuals have gained from an exploding number of choices to meet their needs. However, in the sharing world trust is critical, because sharing means allowing strangers to share our personal space.

Today the sharing economy has grown into every industry and category and is reshaping many industries, e.g. car rental, accommodation, lending, and taxi services. Among some of the leading sharing economy platforms you will find: Airbnb (accommodation), Lyft (ridesharing), Park at my house (people renting out parking spaces), TaskRabbit (outsourcing of errands and tasks), Spinlister (equipment rental including bikes, skis, and snowboards), Car2Go (car rental for 38 cents per minute, drop off at any destination), DogVacay (board your dog in a real home), EatWith (authentic dining experiences in which people pay to dine in private homes), Rent the Runway (rents high-end designer apparel and accessories), Uber (connects passengers with drivers of vehicles for hire), Chegg (specializes in online textbook rentals in both physical and digital formats, homework help, and scholarships through Zinch), and Lending Club (peer-to-peer money lending platforms).

As the collaborative consumption movement starts to impact every industry, it is becoming big business. Rachel Botsman, author of "What's mine is yours," says the consumer peer-to-peer rental market alone is worth US$26 billion. Since Airbnb was launched in 2008 more than 4 million people have used it, 3 million in 2012 alone – reports in March 2014 of its latest capital raising suggest that it could be valued at an eye-popping US$10 billion, more that hotel stalwarts such as Hyatt. In November 2012, Lending Club, one of the leading peer-to-peer money lending platforms in the U.S., exceeded more than US$2 billion in loans, and is doubling in size every 12 months. In Europe, the market for car sharing services is estimated to grow from 0.7 million subscribers in 2011 to 15 million by 2020. By 2014 more than 1.5 million people had used the TaskRabbit online service to hire strangers to do odd jobs, and in October 2013 Chegg filed a public version of its documentation to go public, seeking to raise US$158 million by selling 14.4 million shares at between US$9.50 and US$11.50. (Sources: Boston Magazine, npr, Airbnb, VentureBeat)

Redefining your ambition Companies that believe sharing is only a reaction to the recession and a niche trend that soon will disappear could well be in for shocks ahead. The economy of sharing is changing the way we behave, consume, seek new options, and commit to decisions. Sharing has become a new cultural phenomenon for people to fulfill their needs.

Those firms that buy in to the concept increasingly want to participate, so much so that there's now a venture capital firm, Collaborative Fund, dedicated to investing in sharing-based start-ups. In other internet-related markets the influx of venture funding has been a core force in accelerating growth of the sharing economy. According to Altimeter, which surveyed 200 sharing start-ups, there has been an influx of more than US$2 billion, with the average of funding per start-up at US$29 million. Such venture capital interests could be the key to rise in the sharing economy.

Today the sharing economy concept is slowly finding its way into the corporate world. Some companies have joined the movement by setting up a sharing business unit, e.g. BMW rents cars from San Francisco dealerships and Toyota rents out from dealership lots. Others are entering partnerships to become a part of the sharing world, e.g. Patagonia partners with eBay in a campaign that urges its customers to "buy used and sell what you don't need" and NBC has partnered with Yerdle, a startup founded by former Walmart executives, to foster peer-to-peer sharing. Some firms are also experimenting with a sponsorship approach, e.g. Barclays sponsors London's public bike-sharing program while Citibank sponsors the one in New York.

There is still a long way to go before the corporate world fully embraces this emerging trend but there are many opportunities to be explored. It is time for your company to redefine your sharing ambitions and how these will transform your value propositions in the future.

7. PREPARING SOCIETIES AND COMMUNITIES FOR THE FUTURE

Reshaping how you work Sharing, as noted above, is not really new. Neither does it come from a place where the laws of capitalism don't apply. However, somehow it makes capitalism more efficient. In a Washington Post article, Dominic Basulto offers his insights about the sharing economy and capitalism: "...these sharing economy companies are going places where Adam Smith's 'invisible hand' cannot. They are re-calibrating supply and demand, giving consumers access to otherwise unused capacity or idle assets. Instead of representing an entirely new underground economy, the companies of the sharing economy represent more of a supplement, adding capacity while driving down prices in ways that help consumers."

Not everyone feels so positively about the sharing economy. Some incumbent players are looking for ways to slow down, or even stop, something they are having a hard time keeping up with. One weapon of choice is the law, another is taxation. Capitalism is catching up with the sharing economy and some companies are suffering setbacks due to legal and tax challenges. The issue is not that the sharing economy is illegal or avoiding tax but that the current systems are not geared to handle these new business models. Airbnb announced in a blog post on October 6, 2013 that they are fighting an "unreasonably broad" demand from the Attorney General in New York: Airbnb recently made commitments to clarify short-term rental laws, work with city leaders to ensure that the Airbnb hosts pay applicable taxes, and weed out the few "bad actors" among their community. The ride-sharing services Lyft, Uber, and Sidecar have also been fighting several lawsuits, e.g. allegedly ripping off drivers, unfair competition, and labor violations. As for copyright on 3D printing, the sharing economy legal boundaries are not straightforward, so it is likely that lawsuits will define what is and is not possible. These lawsuits may well be game changers for the sharing economy companies.

As with tapping into the crowd, there will be a long learning curve for the sharing economy.

7. PREPARING SOCIETIES AND COMMUNITIES FOR THE FUTURE

7.3 IN BRIEF EXAMPLES OF SOCIETIES AND COMMUNITIES PREPARING FOR THE FUTURE

My ideal city – crowdfunding Bogotá, Columbia Just like many other cities around the world Bogotá in Columbia has experienced rapid population growth over the past years. It has triggered infrastructure issues such as problems with transportation, security and housing, and widespread corruption and lack of political consensus is delaying any progress in the city. To redevelop Bogotá a team of partners has launched the global conversation site My Ideal City. The site is open for everyone and discusses trends in urban living across the world. Its ultimate goal is to prepare Bogotá for the future by presenting an urban redevelopment plan to city planners. Bogotá is also home to the world's first ever crowdfunded skyscraper. The world's largest crowdfunding initiative has generated over US$200 million from more than 3,500 supporters to build the highest skyscraper in Colombia, not to mention the first new one in 40 years. The 66-storey tower called BD Bagata will be built in Bogotá Downtown, and accommodate offices, a three-floor shopping mall, 396 apartments, and a 364-room hotel. The developers and founders of the skyscraper hope it will be up and running by 2015, attracting 12,000 visitors a day. (Sources: PSFK, Prodigynetwork, Phaidon)

Reinventing health systems Innovation has traditionally been driven by developed countries with the infrastructure of innovation; the great universities, the Nobel Prize winners, the advanced capital markets, and well-developed management systems. Not anymore! At the Narayana Hrudayalaya Hospital open-heart surgery is performed at much lower cost than in the U.S. Labor costs cannot explain the difference. It is pure and simple innovation. The Indian hospital has applied a model from the manufacturing sector to healthcare using standardization, specialization of labor, economies of scale, and assembly-line production. They use the same world-class equipment you will see in the Mayo Clinic (one of the best hospitals in the U.S.) but they use it 20 times more frequently, driving the costs down. In the Cayman Islands, a short 60 minute flight from Miami in the U.S., the Narayana Hrudayalaya Hospital is now building a 2,000-bed hospital to serve American patients – potentially the first step in radically shaking up the U.S. healthcare industry. (Source: An interview with Professor Vijay Govindarajan via DNA) Such affordable healthcare innovations have the potential to reshape societies around the globe.

Bioenergy villages in Germany Demand for energy is rising worldwide, along with concerns over the environmental and climate impact of continued use of fossil fuels. A substantial amount of energy consumed goes towards heating, raising the question of how heating can be addressed in the quest for a more energy-efficient and low-carbon future, free from the continued volatility of energy prices. One small village in Germany, St. Peter, is showing the way – and demonstrating the power of communities in taking on major global challenges. A bioenergy village, the district heating network is run by a co-operative, BürgerEnergie St. Peter, set up after citizens came together in 2008 to tackle the energy and heating issues described above. Typically, bioenergy villages produce more renewable electricity than is consumed by its residents, source over 50% of heat consumption from renewable sources, and have renewable generation facilities that are mostly citizen-owned.

With 167 buildings connected to the local grid and another 40 due to be, St. Peter's renewable energy sources include windmills, co-owned with a private developer, and solar panels on many buildings. However, it took the challenge a step further with the 2008 proposals to develop a biogas plant to meet the district's entire heating needs. Now in operation, with €1.4 million funding from local investment, the biogas plant sources its inputs from the co-operative's members including local land-owners and farmers, households, hotels, the local swimming pool, town hall, school, church (St. Peter), tourist information centre, and the village's small businesses. The benefits have included a 25% drop in the annual cost of heating, as well as total community savings of 850,000 litres of oil and 3,700 tonnes of CO2 per year. The co-operative now has an annual turnover of €1 million, 55% of which is from supplying heat and 45% from selling electricity. As other countries and governments around the world seek new ways to deal with energy and environmental challenges, the clear lesson from the success of St. Peter, is that there are potentially huge benefits from involving local communities both in the planning and operation of innovative programs. (Source: Respublica)

The villagers of St. Peter are not alone. The number of energy cooperatives in Germany has been growing enormously in the last decade, offering substantial support for the country's renewable energy goals.

7. PREPARING SOCIETIES AND COMMUNITIES FOR THE FUTURE

Number of German energy companies

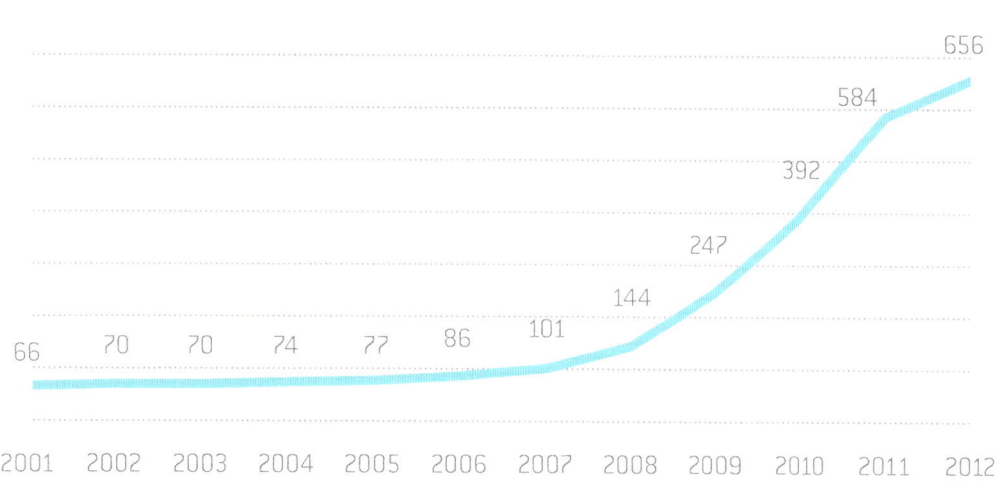

656
584
392
247
144
101
86
77
74
70
70
66

2001 2002 2003 2004 2005 2006 2007 2008 2009 2010 2011 2012

Sources: Klaus Novy Institut, DGRV, Stand: 7/2013, via www.unendlich-viel-energie.de

Social good Non-profit DoSomething.org was founded in 1993 with the aim of mobilizing young people (13 to 25 years old) to drive social change. What makes it different from many other non-profits is what the organization wants: it doesn't want the young people's money but their passion, time, and creativity. It strives to inspire a culture of volunteerism and activism to empower young people to take action on causes they care about. A few years ago a new membership model was launched looking to create a movement of 5 million active users and in December 2013, 2,250,224 members were helping to improve their communities and the world. Between 2011 and 2012 campaign participants increased by 590%. The organization is working with a zero dollar, creative marketing budget, so instead of paying for marketing it links up with brands like Aeropostale, JetBlue, JCPenny, VH1 and others to get across its message of youth volunteerism and advocacy. The benefit to partners is valuable content instead of money, e.g. exclusive access to celebrities or member surveys. Numerous campaigns have been realized, covering everything from animal safety, bullying, sex and relationships, to human rights and education. Among those in 2012 and 2013 are the Teens for Jeans campaign where members collected 1,020,041 pairs of jeans for homeless youth and 93,871 members stood up to bullying through the Bully Text campaign.

Creative Currency A fascinating new business model and approach to distributed innovation is being forged in San Francisco by Creative Currency, whose team includes a non-profit digital culture firm, a social enterprise community, an innovative city government, and a major financial services provider. The aim: harness technology and the power of many ideas to improve people's lives in underprivileged parts of the city. The innovation model is founded first in understanding the community's needs deeply, followed by rapid prototyping through tapping into hundreds of designers, developers, and leaders of the digital economy. Project development and acceleration involves testing and integrating community feedback, followed by seed funding of top projects and mentoring. One project involved a weekend-long "hackathon" to figure out how technology could help people who don't have roofs over their heads, much less web browsers. The result: a mobile wash station for people to take showers and launder their clothes. The project, RefreshSF, will be funded through small donations made via text message to pay both for the wash stations and to employ attendants to keep them clean.

7.4 FOOD FOR THOUGHT ON THE FUTURE LANDSCAPE OF SOCIETIES AND COMMUNITIES

The maker movement

Manufacturing of goods is one of the biggest sectors of the global economy and with the size of the global middle class expected to increase to 4.9 billion by 2030 demand for goods is unlikely to slow down. Historically, manufacturing has been driven by companies with the means to operate at large scale. However, in the 21st century the internet and technology advancements are shifting the advantage in production away from scale – and therefore away from the owners of large scale facilities – towards flexibility and agility. DIY (do-it-yourself) has always existed but is today rapidly transforming from the traditional "how to mend a sock or change a tire" towards the ability to make or design something for yourself or others. As more and more people get involved, it is not only start-ups but also larger companies that are taking advantages of this growing "maker" culture.

In 2005, Dale Dougherty of O'Reilly Media launched the Make Magazine, a quarterly journal about DIY projects. The year after he launched a nationwide series of Maker Faire that became the first showcases for an emerging movement, the "maker movement," developing around a growing DIY culture. This movement has led to an increasing number of regular events and participants around the world, e.g. in 2012, a crowd of 120,000 people visited such an event in San Mateo, California.

DIY doesn't only have to be "made-by-you-for-you." With the widespread use of the internet and modern technology it is easier than ever for a single individual to create and distribute items that are customizable and unique without having middlemen like manufacturers. With the slogan "We make invention accessible," a member community of 180,000 people and an online collaborative crowdsourcing platform Quirky helps aspiring inventors and its community to bring products to life. Products chosen by the crowd get designed, manufactured, and marketed by Quirky. The inventor and any other contributors receive up to 30% of any resulting revenue. Since its launch in 2009, Quirky has collaboratively developed over 200 new products. Its national retail partnerships include Apple, Bed, Bath & Beyond, Target, Barnes & Noble, OfficeMax and many others.

In case you don't own a 3D printer, help is at hand. 3D Hubs, a manufacturing network started in Europe, now works with communities around the world. It is like Facebook except for products. The idea of the company is to network 3D printers together through a web interface and get users to register their printer availability on a map so users can find the nearest one. Customers can select a hub near where they want to send an object and ask a local Hubber to 3D print and deliver it. Does it have the potential to transform the global manufacturing economy? That is to be seen, but certainly what the Dutch founders Bram de Zwart and Brian Garret are aiming for.

The maker movement is not only for individuals. Some large corporations have jumped on the bandwagon, starting to tap into the potential of the maker movement. One example is GE Garages which offers high-tech, hands-on lab spaces where makers can come and learn modern ways of prototyping and manufacturing new products using devices like laser cutters, 3D printers, CNC mills, and injection molders. It aims to spark interest and engagement for modern making, from prototyping inventions to modern manufacturing-based technologies through hands-on experiences. It is developed in partnership with Skillshare, Quirky and Make Magazine. Elsewhere, U.S. firm RadioShack has found its way into the excitement of the maker movement. In cooperation with Make Magazine, RadioShack has launched the cobranded product line Arduino, a popular open-source electronics platform that lets makers easily create interactive objects. It includes LEDs, robotics kits for kids, microcontrollers with Wi-Fi, a line of mini-PCs, and tools. All of these items will be sold exclusively through RadioShack stores and by Make online. (Sources: Wired, GE Garages, On 3D Printing, 3D Focus)

7. PREPARING SOCIETIES AND COMMUNITIES FOR THE FUTURE

Resource colonization in Africa impacting communities

The sharp rise in food prices in 2007-08, followed by a period of higher and more volatile prices, was a wakeup call for many countries about their vulnerability to food insecurity. Some responded by seeking opportunities to secure food supplies overseas through "land grabbing." Governments in the Gulf States such as Bahrain, Qatar, Kuwait, and Saudi Arabia and in Asian countries such as China, India, South Korea, and Japan have all been investing, particularly in Africa, to secure agricultural land. However, it is not just governments. Private equity funds, university endowments, pension funds, and hedge funds are also capitalizing on a potential future lack of natural resources by investing in foreign land and agriculture businesses.

Africa is home to one in four of the world's hungry people but with the right sustainable solutions it could not only feed itself, but also provide significant surplus for export as the continent has half of the world's unused land suitable for farming. However, millions of hectares of land have been acquired across Africa in recent years and, in most cases, this land is earmarked for industrial agriculture for export purposes. Such intensive agricultural production demands tremendous amounts of water and therefore the acquisition of land to produce export crops could just as well be framed as "water grabbing" in the already water scarce continent.

In June 2013, the aid agency Oxfam urged G8 to fight land grabbing (and water grabbing) in Africa, as this practice is neither fair nor sustainable long-term for the African people. Part of the problem is that about 90% of land in sub-Saharan Africa is untitled. As a result communities or single farmers that may have lived and farmed the land for many generations have no enforceable legal claim to it. This calls for solutions such as giving local populations the protection of legally enforceable land rights, which is both more fair to indigent farmers and may induce those with a commercial interest to invest in a more responsible way. Countries such as Botswana and Ghana have already improved their laws so traditionally held lands have the force of private property. However, many other African countries still sell the land and evict current farmers leaving them no choice except to give up the land that may have fed their families for generations. (Sources: The Oakland Institute, Voice of Africa, CNN, Proceedings of the National Academy of Sciences (PNAS), Zukunftsstiftung Entwicklungshilfe)

Diasporas – the untapped potential?

3.2% of the world's population is migrants; putting them all together in one country would create the world's fifth most populous country with 232 million people. Europe and Asia combined host nearly two-thirds of all international migrants worldwide. Europe is the most popular region with 72 million migrants in 2013, compared to 71 million in Asia. Since 1990, Northern America has recorded the biggest gain in the absolute number of migrants, adding 25 million and has experienced the fastest growth in migrant stock by an average of 2.8% year. (Source: UN) According to Gallup these migrants are not alone. Around 13% of the world's adults – or about 630 million people – say they would like to leave their country and move somewhere else permanently, with the U.S. being the most desirable destination.

Diasporas have always been a strong economic force with global remittances from migrants tripling over the past decade and now outstripping official aid. As travel becomes cheaper and easier, these networks are getting larger and more connected, helping to spread knowledge, wealth, and product demand, as well as opening doors by connecting people and businesses globally. Yet many countries and companies do not recognize the potential of the diaspora network and how it can contribute to economic progress and business growth. Clearly, disaporas are important in terms of spending power. But this is just once facet of the potential benefits for organizations and governments.

Diaspora networks can speed up information flows, e.g. a cousin living in Bangladesh knows about a great production site and alerts his cousin in Germany who is looking for place to outsource. In addition, many diasporas include people educated at Western universities who may return to their home country but keep exchanging ideas with their friends still living and working in other countries, promoting knowledge flows globally. Another important "gift" is cultural awareness and language skills, which are critical factors for success when companies want access to, e.g. foreign markets, production sites, and manpower. A study from Harvard Business School suggests that U.S. companies that employ lots of ethnic Chinese people find it much easier to set up in China without a joint venture involving a local firm. (Source: The Economist)

The U.S. has 32 million Mexican-Americans; Germany has 4 million residents of Turkish descent; and the UK has 3 million South Asians. The growth of these global migrant communities has led some companies to develop strategies to tap into new growth opportunities. One example is Bangladesh's largest food company PRAN RFL that started targeting the Bangladeshi diaspora, expanding to serve immigrants from India, Sri Lanka, Nepal, and Pakistan, then concentrating on Muslims from the Subcontinent and finally launching as a brand in the UK, where it is now growing overseas. Another example is the Indian consumer goods company Dabur that is growing outside India by serving the needs of an expansive Indian diaspora community. It has created a customer segment that spans South Asia and the Middle East by using Bollywood star-based advertising as well as building on similarities in personal care product preferences. It has also made its way into developed markets like the UK and the U.S., replacing the Bollywood strategy, which would not resonate in the West, with an all-natural products strategy. (Source: HBR)

7. PREPARING SOCIETIES AND COMMUNITIES FOR THE FUTURE

7.5 SUMMARY: 8 PRINCIPLES OF PREPARING FOR THE FUTURE IN ACTION IN SOCIETIES

Societies and the communities that make them up are changing rapidly, driven by factors including digital technologies, urbanization, and the increased mobility of people and information around the world. Ubiquitous connectivity is creating interdependence between communities locally and worldwide. Choice on an unprecedented scale is giving individuals and communities influence over their lives, even as they search for meaning and identity and inclusion. A hotbed of innovation offers the potential to disrupt today's supply and demand paradigms and the notion of value itself. Against this backdrop the following insights are worth noting:

1. Embrace ambiguity: don't just think outside the box, throw away the boxes

Boxes are well and truly being thrown away as societies and particularly communities within them **use their increasing choices to take new roles** whether becoming part of the crowd, part of the sharing economy, or a young volunteer with DoSomething to tackle social issues. **Supply and demand paradigms are being challenged** as the maker movement gets rid of the middleman and empowers new producers, sharers rent, or share rather than buy, and the power of tapping into the crowd offers access to unused capacity and idle assets, as well as knowledge. **New business models are being built** to harness the power of connectivity and choice, from P&G's Connect + Develop to The ILIAD project and crowdfunding skyscrapers.

2. Think first from the outside-in, then inside-out

Communities and societies have more information than ever before and **access to vast global networks of people and organizations**, including friends, advisors, experts, designers, suppliers, diasporas, and more. Outside ideas and knowledge are actively being used to broaden horizons and **drive innovation** and creativity. However, global information access and choice can be overwhelming and there are **tensions between globalization and fragmentation**. People need help making choices and want inclusion, **seeking to find identity and meaning** often through the communities to which they choose to belong. Yet, **many businesses and societal institutions are slow in adapting** to the societal and behavioral changes highlighted in this chapter, and the opportunities of the outside thinking that these can provide.

3. Identify and address root causes, not symptoms

The **speed of social change is accelerating**. Many communities have grasped the chance to get involved in tackling their social issues, like the bioenergy village of St. Peter in Germany and the citizens of Bogotá and Medellín. These initiatives often **contribute to addressing broader global challenges**, challenging institutions to provide the context within which such "bottom-up" action can be coordinated to achieve maximum impact. In doing so, it is important to understand the root causes of challenges, as the mayor of Medellín notes when discussing the need for developed countries to **accept some co-responsibility for the social impact** of drug and violence issues in the city, a theme that is also relevant to resource colonization in Africa. Shared social responsibility is a theme that is highlighted by the shift towards a sharing economy, which **fundamentally challenges traditional concepts of value**: material possessions, status, and power are giving way to convenience, shared experiences, "giving back," creating, belonging, and the accomplishment of being part of the crowd as sources of value.

7. PREPARING SOCIETIES AND COMMUNITIES FOR THE FUTURE

4. Practice two-directional thinking

In practice, many community-driven initiatives are related to short-term needs, but even without conscious definition of long-term ambitions, the adoption of new roles by individuals and communities and **changes in behavior can collectively drive disruptive change**, for example in financing through crowdfunding or production through 3D printing. The potential for such disruptive changes need to be taken into account by the organizations and institutions that will be impacted by them. Larger social projects such as the reinvention of Medellín have long-term ambitions and recognize the **importance of focus and prioritization**. A key insight from this project is that for social development to succeed, administrations need to put in **place a path forward that subsequent administrations can commit to continue. Showing tangible results in the short term** is important to generate this long-term commitment, as is **engaging the people and organizations** that will benefit from progress.

5. Manage in relationships/networks versus transactions

The power of communities to share knowledge and pool resources depends on the ability to **create and manage networks over time**. Digital technologies are critical in doing so, but many of the examples above also note the **importance of education and culture** in creating the shared cohesion required for networks to be productive. Preparing societies and communities for the future also relies heavily on building partnerships between diverse stakeholders in the public and private sectors, as well as the communities themselves, as seen in My Ideal City Bogotá, Creative Currency, the UK's Big Society, and Germany's bioenergy villages. **Trust is the currency of the connected world**, and the organizations and communities that build such trust focus deeply on engagement as a continuous process.

6. Focus on co-creation

Co-creation is at the heart of the crowd and of the sharing economy. **Innovation is being accelerated** in many markets and industries by the knowledge sharing, new business models and partnerships that organizations such as Quirky, Innocentive, and GE Garages are orchestrating. **Tapping into the needs, input, and characteristics of specific communities** such as diasporas or travellers on a budget is allowing companies to develop more valuable offerings for and with these communities. However, a significant challenge amidst all this innovation is that the **regulatory and institutional context is not keeping pace with the speed of change**, for example leading to legal challenges to sharing services such as Airbnb and Uber and confusion over 3D printing intellectual property rules. As with the notion of value, the **notion of ownership is shifting** as many stakeholders create together and new frameworks will be needed.

7. Align purpose and profit

A key question in the development of communities and societies is how the **balance of self-interest including profit and contribution to the greater good (purpose)** will evolve over time. Many social development initiatives are purpose-led, without a profit motive, although many still incorporate operational discipline in how they measure results, e.g. in Medellín and the Creative Currency initiatives. However, many community-led initiatives do have tangible financial results, as well as positive social benefits demonstrating that **profit and purpose are not mutually exclusive**, e.g. cost savings in bioenergy villages and the returns from a crowdfunded skyscraper. There are also an increasing number of **hybrid and innovative organizations emerging** in the crowd and sharing sectors where individuals, communities, and organizations are combining financial returns with social progress, e.g. the for-profit Narayana Hrudayalaya Hospital's contributions to affordable healthcare and car-sharing services' contribution to reducing environmental impact.

8. Embed continual challenge, avoid complacent compliance

One of the most exciting aspects of the new roles available to communities, the crowd and sharers, is that these **connections and collaborations offer almost unlimited potential to test and learn**. Networks and partnerships can reconfigure fast, information sharing is a core behavior, and feedback is rapid. With so many potential connections and ideas, **innovation is essential and ongoing**. The challenge for most organizations is to keep up, because if they do not innovate, someone else will.

The changes in societies and communities, both in roles and configuration are some of the most profound with implications for all the other types of organizations covered in this report: consumption patterns impact business, crowd-driven social projects impact governments and NGOs, and combining purpose and profit impacts all types of organization. It is therefore critical that the increase in partnerships between different types of organizations continues, as no one organization can deliver on consumers', customers' and societies' demands alone. However, there are challenges in harnessing the power and influence of communities and societies:

- Building trust with and engaging multiple, diverse networks with different experiences, needs, and interests to achieve common goals and mutual benefits

- Establishing the required coordination and leadership of efforts to develop a common ambition and path towards it, including measuring results

- Maintaining leadership of efforts over time, recognizing that political and institutional contexts may shift

- Creating the context to support fundamental social and behavioral changes, including addressing regulation and funding

- Balancing the demands of profit and purpose over time, to create mutual benefits for individuals, communities, societies, and organizations

8. SPECIAL FOCUS: RESHAPING EDUCATION

8. SPECIAL FOCUS: RESHAPING EDUCATION

Education has been a focus in preparing all the different types of organizations we investigated in this report. In this special focus section, we explore how education is being reshaped to prepare future generations – and how more change is needed.

The war for talent is well and truly alive and kicking. An estimated 600 million new jobs need to be created worldwide in the next 15 years, in particular in Asia and Sub-Saharan Africa, to keep up with the massive need for employment globally. (Source: 2013 World Development Report)

Education is a critical enabler of economic and social development. Yet, there is increasing criticism of many education systems and institutions across the globe, as youth unemployment reaches critical levels in many countries, and businesses protest that the next generations entering the workforce do not have the right skills. In fact, some leaders suggest that whole swathes of young people are unemployable.

8.1 THE CHALLENGES FOR EDUCATION

It's nothing as simple as poor education, at least in the traditional sense, as each new generation is entering the workforce better qualified than the one before it. The problem is an emerging split between unemployable workers – those who do not have the specific knowledge or skills needed in the future – and the in-demand workers, who have these things in abundance. "Skill development is amongst the single biggest issues that will impact India's growth in the future," according to Sanjeev Asthana, Founder and Managing Partner of I-Farm Venture Advisors Private Ltd in India. "We have almost 14 million youths coming into the job market every year, and they are largely unskilled. While they can find some form of employment at the most basic level, the difference between them earning US$100 a month and US$300 a month is simple skill sets.

"It's a huge disconnect that in a country like India with a huge pool of labor, the big issue for any industry or services sector is that they don't have enough employable people to work, whether it is in agriculture, textiles, hotels, transport, logistics, you name it. There's a mass of people and a mass of jobs out there but the two are simply not getting matched. There's a difference between unemployment and unemployability. Yes, you're available for employment, but you're not employable because you don't possess the skills required." [15]

This mismatch is not just an issue for India or other high-growth countries, but one that is confronting societies and businesses around the world. The only way to close the gap is to make sure that workers are prepared to fill the jobs of the future, which means that governments, educators, and businesses need to rethink education and training, including who delivers it. Some facts from the OECD highlight the importance of education:

- Unemployment rates are nearly three times higher among people who do not have an upper secondary education (13% on average across OECD countries) than among those who have a tertiary education (5%)

- Across OECD countries, people with a tertiary education are more likely to have a job, and to be working full time, than those without

- People with at least an upper secondary education are more likely to have a job than those without this level of education

- People with higher (tertiary) education in OECD countries can expect to earn 1.5 times as much as a person with only an upper secondary or post-secondary non-tertiary education

So what will it take to reshape the education "industry" and prepare our educational systems and institutions for the future – and in fact who should the educators be?

In the following framework we look at different levels of skills and the types of institutions that are traditionally charged with developing them, plus key questions around developing these skills.

[15] *"Ready? The 3Rs of preparing your organization for the future"* by Thomas W. Malnight, Tracey S. Keys, and Kees van der Graaf, 2013

8.   SPECIAL FOCUS: RESHAPING EDUCATION

Type of skills	Educational institutions	Key questions
Future leadership	Tertiary educational institutions; business schools; company training and development programs; policy makers	What are the skills required for future leaders? Who should be responsible for developing them?
Future skilled	Primary and secondary schools; tertiary educational institutions; trade schools; business schools; apprenticeships; company training and development programs; policy makers	Are business schools and similar institutions relevant? Are they teaching the skills of the future – or of today? What's the role of the state versus private sector, versus others?
Skilled	Primary and secondary schools; tertiary educational institutions; trade schools; business schools; apprenticeships; company training and development programs; policy makers	Are countries/companies developing enough of the "right" skills for today? Is educational spending delivering the desired benefits? Which models/systems are best? What's the role of the state versus private sector, versus others?
Employable (basic skills)	Primary and secondary schools; further education institutions; trade schools; apprenticeships; company training; NGOs; policy makers	What are the basic skills required for employment today and in future? How can provision of basic skills be improved? How can equitable and comprehensive coverage of educational opportunities be ensured? Why are some systems/institutions failing – how can this be overcome?
Unemployable	Primary and secondary schools; NGOs; policy makers	How to raise the unemployable to at least the level of basic skills? What's the role of the state versus private sector, versus others?

The youth unemployment challenge In all regions of the world, the young people (aged 15-24 years) who will drive the future workforce are struggling to gain traction in the labor market. Estimates from the ILO reveal global youth unemployment of 73.4 million or a rate of 12.6% in 2013, up 3.5 million since 2007, and estimated to increase to 12.8% by 2018. In some countries such as Spain, Greece, and South Africa the rates of youth unemployment are alarmingly high – at 50% or more. In all G20 countries, except Germany and Japan, the youth unemployment rate is more than twice as high as that for adults. The ILO emphasizes that the crisis has trapped many young people, in particular in developed economies, in low productivity, temporary, part time, or other types of work that will not pave the way for a better job in future.

Another unfortunate trend is the rapid increase in young people in developed economies that are neither in employment nor in education. (Source: ILO) Not having access to the means to gain necessary skills early on will have tremendous implications for these young people and our future workforce. If no urgent action is taken by businesses and governments to address this challenge, the current generation of young workers risks keeping the label "the lost generation."

The ageing population challenge Demographics are changing too, adding a different set of challenges, with some countries seeing their workforces diminishing as populations age, while others with large youth cohorts are promised "the demographic dividend" – if skills can be matched to jobs.

As the planet's population grows rapidly, many countries will see a decline in the working-age population. For the first time in 2010, the European labor market saw more people retiring from the labor force than entering it. Currently the gap is "only" 200,000 but it is expected to reach 8.3 million by 2030. In Japan, more people are already leaving the labor force than there are people prepared to take over. A similar challenge will hit the Russian, Canadian, South Korean, and Chinese labor markets by the end of this decade. Other emerging countries, e.g. India, Brazil, Mexico, and Indonesia, could see benefits from the relocation of jobs as these countries have a much younger population. However, a positive effect will only be seen if these countries provide their youth with educational and economic opportunities to develop their skills. (Source: Ernst & Young)

Worrying about an ageing workforce may sound strange in a world struggling with high unemployment rates. However, the world is not only getting older but also healthier allowing people to stay in the workforce longer. Projections suggest that life expectancy will surpass 100 years in some industrialized countries by the second half of this century. Why is this important? As labor markets tighten, in particular in Europe and Japan, companies will mostly likely need the contribution of older workers. Often older employees are seen as a burden compared to the younger employee so attitudes and training opportunities, as well as their physical roles, e.g. allowing them more flexible roles and schedules in the workplace, need to be redefined in order to retain and make the most of an older workforce. (Source: Harvard Business Review) Looking forward, the Global Talent 2021 report suggests that many countries, particularly developed ones such as Japan, the U.S., Germany, France, and the UK, will suffer from a talent deficit.

The future skills challenge Building knowledge for today's jobs is not likely to be enough to keep up with the rapidly changing nature of work in the future. Globalization and ease of mobility as well technological advancements are changing the characteristics of the global labor market, the nature of jobs themselves, and how work will be done.

We are living in a world only few could imagine some 50 years ago. Even fewer have the ability to image how the workplace could look like just 50 years from now. Powered by technology, fuelled by information and knowledge, we are moving rapidly (if we haven't already made the shift) from an industrial to a knowledge economy. Consequently the nature of work is changing, with shifts from jobs such as typists and switchboard operators to computer engineers and data analysts – jobs that require a higher skill level. The skills required of the children starting school now may not yet be fully determined, but it is clear that these skill shifts will continue – and that younger generations need to be better prepared.

The skills that make workers and leaders successful today will most likely not stay the same forever. The future will increasingly demand skills including:

- **Social intelligence/collaboration** This is a skill that has always been important to navigate many aspects of work and life. However, collaboration and teamwork as well as an office full of technological distractions and demands are increasing the need for this skill among workers as well as managers. In addition, companies are becoming less hierarchical, more networked, and increasingly virtual making the ability to collaborate, build relationships, and trust even more important. The challenge is to change our educational system from one that promotes one-to-one competition towards a system that requires more teamwork and collaboration.

- **Agile thinking** Emerging market companies are growing at a faster speed than developed-market companies even when operating in a neutral environment where none of them are based. The management mindset of developed market companies is often not as willing to adapt as that of emerging market companies, which are built for agility and speed. Today, uncertainty rules the market, changes can be abrupt, and yesterday's market conditions are different to today's. Creative thinking, the ability to innovate, deal with complexity, ambiguity and paradoxes, and prepare for more than one scenario is critical for future success. (Sources: McKinsey & Company, "Winning the $30 trillion decathlon"; Towers Watson, "Global Talent 2021")

- **Human-machine collaboration and co-dependence** Technology is penetrating every aspect of our lives and if you want to be at the top of the game in the labor market, digital and technology skills are not only nice to have, they are a necessity. For decades smart machines and technology advances have underpinned most, if not all, major transformations in many industries, replacing but also augmenting the skills and jobs of human workers. Today, it is no longer a question about whether we want to be a part of workplace automation and human-machine dependence but more a question of how the human worker can work best alongside the machine and what skill level is needed. To do so may require rethinking the content of work, and preparing our future generations for a workplace where human-machine collaboration and co-dependence is the norm. (Inspiration: Future Work Skills 2020)

- **Cross-cultural understanding** As companies cross borders into new geographic markets it will become increasingly important to learn to navigate in a diverse environment. Cross-cultural understanding and communication will play a critical role in successfully carrying out business in a globalized world. According to the report Global Talent 2021, global operating skills such as the ability to manage diverse employees (49.1% of respondents indicating important), understanding international markets (45.7%), the ability to work in multiple overseas locations (37.5%), foreign language skills (36.1%), and cultural sensitivity (31.5%) will be increasingly in demand over the next five to ten years.

8.2 THE NEED TO RETHINK EDUCATIONAL INSTITUTIONS

In 2010 a man with a college degree would earn 67% more than a man without, up from 58% in 2008. For women the number is 59% in 2010, up from 54% in 2008. But not everyone can afford a higher education and during the last decade fees have increased – often substantially – in many surveyed countries, e.g. Germany, Australia, Austria, Japan, the Netherlands, New Zealand, Portugal, and the U.S. (Source: OECD)

The good news is that disruptive forces are changing the landscape of education as traditional face-to-face learning moves towards virtual and interactive learning that can reach every corner of the Earth. These trends are breaking down the barriers to expensive, rigid, and bureaucratic academic institutions. MOOCs (Massive Open Online Classes) are reinventing education as we know it, making education accessible to anyone who wants to learn, anywhere, anytime, opening up elite tertiary educational systems, e.g. edX (Harvard University and MIT) and Coursera (Stanford, Princeton, Michigan, and Penn). High quality education is now much cheaper – if not free – and open to all.

However, recent reports are casting doubt on whether MOOCs are really paying off. Sebastian Thrun, a pioneer in the field and founder of Udacity is moving away from the concept, which he believes has not delivered, as completion and graduation rates from online courses have fallen well below expectations. But MOOCs are simply one tool to tackle cost and accessibility issues, and will likely have an evolving role. Positive signs of progress include MOOCs generating increasing revenues from paid certifications that students have passed an online college course, the arrival of digital course materials and apps, and moves towards the acceptance of online course credits towards degrees which could generate a global market in higher-education credits. (Source: The Economist)

Looking forward, all these developments are driving a fundamental rethink of what educational institutions do, why they do it, and how they deliver it.

Inside educational institutions – the world is our classroom Education is a basic need. Economic and social development depends on it; the ability for individuals to reach their full potential depends on it; business success depends on it. While governments, businesses, non-governmental, and other private institutions play a tremendous role in educating our current and future workforce, educational institutions remain the cornerstone of knowledge and innovation.

However, these institutions – whether primary, secondary, or tertiary – need to step out of their comfort zones to reflect an increasingly complex world. Constantly developing technology, the mindsets of the new digital natives and the future skills challenges demand radical shifts both in educational content and delivery.

The good news is that disruptive forces are already starting to change the landscape of education, with traditional face-to-face learning moving more towards virtual and interactive learning. These trends are not only changing how we learn but are making education accessible to anyone who wants to learn, anywhere, anytime. New approaches to learning, most enabled by technology, include:

8. SPECIAL FOCUS: RESHAPING EDUCATION

Personalized learning Learning is tailored to individual needs, taking a holistic view of the individual's skill levels, interests, strengths, challenges, and prior knowledge. The learner owns their learning and may choose to learn anything from short, bounded subjects (microlearning) to broader topics and skills. In each case the learning is adaptive to the individual's needs.

- **Hybrid or blended learning** Typically integrates learning partly in a brick-and-mortar location away from home and partly online, with the student having some control over the time, place, path, and/or pace of study. The approach is often more of facilitation than traditional teaching, with the student often having the opportunity to partly personalize the learning and to bring their own device (BYOD).

- **Interactive digital learning/eLearning** Taking advantage of online educational resources, social media, and tools such as interactive whiteboards and smartboards, interactive digital learning or eLearning can be done on-demand, anywhere and anytime, across multiple devices and platforms, including mobile. Such learning often includes virtual teaching modules, videos, collaborative learning, and game-based learning. It can be self-paced with moderation done online, and provides some opportunities for students to adapt and personalize learning. MOOCs take this a step further, globalizing the opportunity for sometimes thousands of students to take a course, using open courseware to allow access to education across digital platforms.

- **Learning spaces** For those students who value face-to-face learning and learning from peers, but do not want to attend traditional educational institutions, new types of physical learning spaces are also springing up around the world. From "meetups" and "techshops" to community labs and hackathons, these spaces are incredibly diverse, offering the chance to learn from practitioners as well as academics and to combine learning with action.

All of these emerging approaches to learning are underpinned by an increasing array of learning resources in the digital world, from the internet and Wikipedia to a growing volume of free digital academic research and new learning tools such as apps and wearable learning devices, e.g. Google Glass.

Importantly, these shifts in educational delivery are becoming widely accepted. In November 2013 a panel of expert thinkers debating the future of business education at the Thinkers50 event, agreed that "Blended education is the future." Santiago Iñiguez, the dean of Madrid's IE Business School, said: "It's high-quality online learning combined with face-to-face sessions. Technology won't replace professors, but we need to bring the professors into this new world." He added that the infinite amount of knowledge available online needed editors to make sense of it. (Source: HR magazine) Looking at the enormous amount of literature on the efficiency of digital technology and online learning environment, educators and students still have a long way to go to realize its full potential but progress is being made.

It needs to be. Just as digital technologies have transformed publishing, media, retail, and many other industries, they are now catching up with the educational system. It is just a matter of time before education, as we know it, changes from its traditional form to better connect, engage, enrich, and motivate all generations of learners from kindergarten, to high school, to higher education, and workplaces. eLearning is already gaining significant traction within both educational institutions and companies.

8. SPECIAL FOCUS: RESHAPING EDUCATION

Selected facts about eLearning
In 2011, it was estimated that about US$35.6 billion was spent on self-paced eLearning across the globe. In 2013, eLearning was a US$56.2 billion industry, and is set to double by 2015.
More than 7.1 million students were taking at least one online course during the fall 2012 term, an increase of 411,000 students over the previous year.
33% of higher education students now take at least one course online. 90% of academic leaders believe that it is likely or very likely that a majority of all higher education students will be taking at least one online course in five years' time.
The percentage of academic leaders rating the learning outcomes in online education as the same as or superior to those in face-to-face learning grew from 57% in 2003 to 77% in 2012, but fell back to 74% in 2013.
Only 5% of higher education institutions currently offer a MOOC (Massive Open Online Course), another 9.3% report MOOCs are in the planning stages.
Over 41.7% of global Fortune 500 companies now use some form of educational technology to instruct employees during formal learning hours, and that figure is only going to steadily increase in future years.
e-Learning is the second most valuable training method for corporations that they use. It saves businesses at least 50% when they replace traditional instructor-based training with eLearning and cuts down instruction time by up to 60%.
Companies who utilize eLearning tools and strategies have the potential to boost productivity by up to 50%. For every US$1 that company spends, it is estimated that they can receive US$30 worth of productivity.
eLearning has the power to increase information retention rates by up to 60%. That means that, not only is eLearning more cost efficient, but also it is also more effective in terms of how much knowledge is truly acquired during the learning process.
It has been estimated that nearly 25% of all employees leave their job because there simply are not enough training or learning opportunities. On the other hand, companies who do offer eLearning and on-the-job training generate about 26% more revenue per employee.
72% of companies who were included in a recent survey stated that eLearning helps them to keep up-to-date with changes in their industry, which helps them to remain competitive within their niche.

Sources: Adapted from eLearning Industry, and Babson Survey Research Group, Pearson and the Sloan Consortium, 2013

8.   SPECIAL FOCUS: RESHAPING EDUCATION

Learning environments will be increasingly intelligent, connected, personalized, and available in real-time. Content will be found in abundance, as the internet becomes our external brain. The need for traditional memorizing of information declines while creativity and agile thinking as well as social and collaboration skills become increasingly important. However, practical experiences to test learning may become more scarce.

Before we get too excited, it should be noted that even though the technology is here, change is far from everywhere and not always happening at the pace that some might wish. The mammoth cost of digitizing every traditional primary, secondary, and tertiary educational institution is one barrier, another is shifting the mindsets and skills of millions of teachers, professors, and human resource professionals.

The fundamental challenge is that today's adults have been educated in a 1.0 education model, today's teachers are teaching in a 2.0 model but their students are living in a 3.0 model. These three models chronicle the major paradigm shifts that education has witnessed over the last century. They also represent the huge abyss between the actual needs of our students and what is actually being delivered to them in schools, as outlined in the table below.

	Web 1.0	Web 2.0	Web 3.0
Meaning is...	Dictated	Socially constructed	Socially constructed and contextually reinvented
Technology is...	Confiscated at the classroom door (digital refugees)	Cautiously adopted (digital immigrants)	Everywhere (ambient, digital universe)
Teaching is done...	Teacher-to-student	Teacher-to-student and student-to-student	Teacher-to-student and student-to-student, and student-to-teacher
Schools are located...	In a building	In a building or online	Everywhere and thoroughly infused into society
Parents view schools as...	Daycare	Daycare	A place for them to learn, too
Teachers are...	Licensed professionals	Licensed professionals	Everybody, everywhere
Hardware & software in schools...	Are purchased at great cost and ignored	Are open source and available at lower cost	Are available at low cost and are used purposively
Industry views graduates as...	Assembly line workers	As ill-prepared assembly line workers in a knowledge economy	As co-workers or entrepreneurs

Source: Educational technology and Mobile learning , www.educatorstechnology.com

As the use of technology evolves and mindsets shift, there are likely to be several steps between models 2.0 and 3.0. With this in mind it is reassuring to see that some educational institutions are making substantial progress:

- At the San Francisco Flex Academy, a hybrid high school, the learning environment resembles a large office space rather than a traditional classroom. Students arrive in the morning and go to work at cubicles while an "academic coach" circulates throughout the room to offer assistance with specific questions from students. For additional help, students can meet with teachers individually. (Source: Great Schools)

- At the 230-student Carpe Diem Collegiate High School and Middle School, Arizona, students spend 60% of their time on computers during the day and 40% on face-to-face instruction. Each student is assigned a PC in a cubicle as his or her own

8. SPECIAL FOCUS: RESHAPING EDUCATION

workspace and follows a daily schedule that can be adjusted based on the student's need for more individualized attention from on-site teachers, either one-to-one or in small workshops. (Source: Education Week)

- A partnership between Knewton and Cambridge University Press is developing a new generation of digital products by integrating the Knewton API with the innovative Cambridge LMS platform, which currently serves over 250,000 students and teachers globally. This will enable Cambridge to incorporate recommendations and analytics into both self-paced and instructor-led blended learning materials to help educators monitor student performance in real-time. (Source: Knewton)

- The Wharton School of the University of Pennsylvania and Cisco are developing the learning experience of the future – one that blends life-size visual communication via telepresence with collaboration technologies that significantly enhance the way faculty, students and alumni interact and learn, no matter how distant they may be from physical classrooms. (Source: Wharton News)

8.3 WHOSE ROLE IS IT TO EDUCATE FOR THE SKILLS OF THE FUTURE?

Educating our future workforce as well as reeducating our current workforce is an enormous task and one that requires more than changes in educational institutions. The question is who should be responsible for doing so. As in many sectors and markets, one organization is unlikely to be able to deliver the full solution alone. This means that in addition to academia and educational institutions themselves, there are a range of other organizations that need to rethink their roles in developing the skills of the future, including governments, NGOs, businesses, and other private institutions. Increasingly they are doing so, often in partnership and with a range of business models, as the examples below show:

- HacKIDemia is bolstering local education efforts across the five continents. At the crossroads between the maker movement, education, technology, and social good, this little-known Berlin-based organization sets up and conducts STEAM (for science, technology, engineering, arts, and maths) workshops specifically designed for children. (Source: VentureBeat)

- ScriptEd is a non-profit that teaches young students computer programming and places them in technology-based internships. ScriptEd has helped 100 students in New York City learn how to code in 2013. Ashoka and American Express honored Maurya Couvares, founder of ScriptEd in May as an Emerging Innovator in May 2013. Her tech education non-profit will include students from two new schools in 2014 and hopefully expand to a new city. (Source: Huffington Post)

- Unmanned Vehicles University is the only institution in the U.S. to offer post-graduate engineering degrees, both masters and doctorate, in unmanned aerial vehicle systems. Otherwise known as drones. The program, which is the first of its kind, is the brainchild of retired U.S. Air Force colonel and F-4 pilot Jerry LeMieux, "We look at the jobs first and then we designed the courses and curriculums around getting a job," LeMieux told abcNews' Nightline news program. (Source: ABC News)

- Chinese computer maker Lenovo is partnering with top-ranked Chinese universities to identify top talent that may have gone abroad to study, but might be interested in returning to work in their home land. The company is building this talent pipeline three to four years down the road. (Source: ChinaDaily Asia)

- Despite much scepticism among some in the academic environment, Wal-Mart Stores Inc. has partnered with American Public University to provide online college degree programs to Wal-Mart's U.S. workforce. (Source: Phys org)

- The IMF, responsible for promoting financial stability in the world, is joining the online university network platform edX (set up by Harvard and MIT) in 2014 to run finance courses free of charge. It aims to give the public a better understanding of the big picture behind problems such as unemployment and to empower people to understand financial issues facing their country. (Source: BBC)

8.   SPECIAL FOCUS: RESHAPING EDUCATION

- Education and training, when linked to the specific skill needs of employers, can meet students' needs for good jobs and employers' needs for a skilled workforce. Skills for America's Future, an initiative of the Aspen Institute, in partnership with the Pritzker Traubert Family Foundation, is aiming to improve the skills of America's workers by challenging community colleges and employers to make these links, creating important opportunities for workers to get the skills they need to succeed. (Source: PRNewswire)

- Since 2008, financial services provider Barclays has been working with UNICEF to help improve youth unemployment by equipping disadvantaged young people across the world with the skills they need to set up their own business or to find employment through the Building Young Futures programme. For example, as a part of the programme staff from Barclays in Brazil volunteer to share some of their skills and expertise with young people through training and mentoring. (Source: The Guardian)

- Recognizing that it has lost its competitive edge in the world, in 2011 the UK government put in place a Plan for Growth to provide the infrastructure and skills base that mid-cap businesses need. They pledged to expand the University Technical Colleges programme, to establish at least 24 new colleges by 2014, and to create 50,000 additional apprenticeship places from 2011-2015. (Source: Gov.uk)

- With a tremendous need to educate its youth, in 2009 the Indian government launched the National Skill Development Corporation to fund training centres and liaise with industry. The National Skill Development Corporation works with 84 approved partners across India. As of April 2013, its partners had trained 620,000 people in 28 states and territories. More than 78% of graduates found jobs. By 2022 it has the target of training 150 million people. (Source: National Skill Development Corporation)

- MIIWIN:NET wants to get more young people into work by job sharing among young and older employees. It proposes an intergenerational professional network conceived to facilitate contact between people in order to share a job post and knowledge. The platform proposes that older workers share a job with younger people, allowing those approaching retirement to share knowledge with those being incorporated into the job market, easing both entry and exit from the job market and addressing youth unemployment.

- In India, Tata Power has launched a "Village Education Excellence Program" to cover villages surrounding the company's proposed project site. The education program designed by Tata Power focuses on conducting Math, Science, and English classes twice a week for 450 students. (Source: The Hindu Business Line)

- Brazilian giant Odebrecht, a global organization serving many industries, is strengthening relationships with community educational projects, e.g. "Building up talents through the history of professions" in Angola where 250 young people participate in courses including accountancy and management, plumbing, carpentry and masonry, computer services, machines and motors services, low tension electricity, electricity services, and electronics. (Source: Odebrecht)

- In England, Google provides funds to support Teach First, a charity that puts "exceptional" graduates on a six-week training program before deploying them to schools where they teach classes over a two-year period. (Source: BBC)

How will your organization take on the challenge of education?

ABOUT THE AUTHORS

Tracey S. Keys

is Director of Strategy Dynamics Global SA. She has many years of experience as a consultant and executive, focused on complex strategy and organizational issues, and has worked with leading companies globally. Prior to founding Strategy Dynamics Global SA, Tracey worked with senior executives at IMD, and has held senior roles at the BBC, Booz &Co., Deloitte & Touche, and Braxton Associates, as well as being an active advisor to a number of start-ups. Tracey is a Fulbright Scholar and holds an MBA from The Wharton School, University of Pennsylvania where she was distinguished as a Palmer Scholar. She is also a co-author of *Must-Win Battles: How to Win Them Again and Again, Ready? The 3Rs of preparing your organization for the future, The Global Trends Report,* and co-editor of *Mastering Executive Education: How to Combine Content With Context and Emotion.*

Thomas W. Malnight

is Professor of Strategy at the International Institute for Management Development (IMD) in Lausanne, Switzerland, where he has led a major research initiative on "Leading in the Connected Future" involving face-to-face interviews with more than 150 CEOs and other top leaders from businesses and organizations around the world. Among other work, Tom is the co-author of *Must Win Battles: How to Win Them Again and Again, Ready? The 3Rs of preparing your organization for the future,* and *The Global Trends Report.* Previously, Tom was on the Faculty of the Wharton School of the University of Pennsylvania and has a DBA from the Harvard Business School and an MBA from the Wharton School.He works extensively with top leadership teams in challenging how they view their changing competitive landscape; how they shape their future and strategies for moving forward; how they engage and align priorities and actions across their organizations; and how they work together as a focused high performing leadership team.

ACKNOWLEDGEMENTS

The authors would particularly like to thank Head of Research, Christel K. Stoklund, and Researcher Lene M. Toubro for their invaluable contributions in developing this fieldbook and supporting materials. We would also like to thank Wendy Stephens of Dark Iris Design (www.darkirisdesign.co.uk) for her skill and patience in ensuring the best possible design for the report, and the team at ActivateMedia (www.activatemedia.co.uk) for translating all the Global Trends reports and materials so effectively on to the website. Many thanks too to all our clients, friends, and colleagues who have offered advice and suggestions as we compiled this fieldbook.

COPYRIGHT

ISBN 978-2-9700847-5-4

9 782970 084754 >

CPSIA information can be obtained at www.ICGtesting.com
Printed in the USA
LVIW01n1549160715
446500LV00006B/34